Syllabus B

AQA/NEAB MODERN WORLD History

Photographic acknowledgements

The authors and publisher would like to thank the following for permission to reproduce photographs:

Cover photograph: Berlin Olympics 1936 © Telegraph Colour Library

AKG: 46M, 118A, 199B, 122C, 125F, 126A, 130G, 131H, 132I, 142D, 144F, 149C; Camera Press: 236I; Center for the Study of Cartoon and Caricature: 243D, 244E; Corbis: 168C, 198E, 179B, 257C, 261F, 281F; Corbis/Michael Nicholson: 261D; Daily Mirror: 209A; Daily Mirror/Centre for the Study of Cartoon and Caricature: 9C, 210D; David King: 91I, 93K, 94A, 96D, 99H, 104E, 111I, 112K, 114A; e.t.archive: 59D, 61H; Gateshead Central Library: 207J; Hulton Getty: 12F, 41D, 50B, 62I, 64N, 74D, 88C, 90G, 97F, 100A, 106A, 172C, 182A, 183B, 184C, 185E, 201B, 211F, 213H, 216C, 220B, 249B, 254E, 264A, 276C; HMSO: 196G; Imperial War Museum/Bridgman: 19E; Imperial War Museum: 25O, 59C; Low/Solo Syndication: 136C; Mary Evans: 188; National Air & Space Museum, Smithsonian Institution: 57J; P. Jones Griffiths/Magnum: 260E; PA News: 193C; Peter Newark: 43I, 55G, 152A, 158C, 159E, 160F, 164A, 170A, 176F, 242A; Popperfoto: 86A, 92J, 93K, 103B, 139A, 166B, 180C, 195F, 212G, 221C, 225D, 229G, 232A, 233B, 239L, 246G, 247H, 252D, 266B, 267C, 269H, 270J, 271K, 273A, 275B, 282D; Public Record Office: 60F, 61G, 64O, 81D; Punch: 70H; Scholastic: 194D, 203E; School of Slavonic Studies: 71I; Solo Syndication: 51C; Solo Syndication/Centre for the Study of Cartoon and Caricature: 71J, 79I, 83J; Topham: 52D, 162I, 163L, 205H, 222D, 226E, 230H, 235E, 238K, 241M, 245F; TUC: 197H.

With thanks to John and Andrew Frost at John Frost Historical Newspaper Service for the loan of the newspapers used in 189H, 196G and 197H.

Heinemann Educational Publishers
Halley Court, Jordan Hill, Oxford, OX2 8EJ
a division of Reed Educational & Professional Publishing Ltd
Heinemann is a registered trademark of Reed Educational & Professional Publishing Ltd

OXFORD MELBOURNE AUCKLAND
JOHANNESBURG BLANTYRE GABARONE
IBADAN PORTSMOUTH NH (USA) CHICAGO

© Tony Hewitt, Jim McCabe and Alan Mendum 1999

First published 1999

ISBN 0 435 31194 8

02 01 00
10 9 8 7 6 5 4 3

Designed and typeset by Pentacor plc, High Wycombe, Bucks

Illustrated by Pentacor plc, High Wycombe, Bucks

Cover design by Carla Turchini

Printed and bound in Spain by Edelvive

Contents

Chapter 5

Governments in Action: USA, 1919–41

Chapter 6

Governments in Action: Britain 1905–51

Coursework or Paper 3 Topics:

Chapter 7

Vietnam Post-1939

Chapter 8

Arab-Israeli Conflict

Chapter 1

Conflict in the Modern World, 1900–18

At the beginning of the 20th century there was great tension between the major powers of Europe. France sought revenge for the loss of the provinces of Alsace and Lorraine to Germany after its defeat in war in 1870-71, whereas Germany had begun to build a navy in order to set up an overseas empire. This was a challenge to Britain which responded by increasing the size of its own navy. Germany's actions in Morocco and support for Austria-Hungary in Bosnia convinced other countries that Germany wanted to dominate the world and led to the formation of the Triple Entente between Britain, France and Russia. This alliance rivalled the Triple Alliance of Germany, Austria-Hungary and Italy.

The assassination of an Austrian Archduke at Sarajevo in 1914 was the spark which brought the alliances to war. Germany's attack on France through neutral Belgium brought Britain into the war. The Germans expected to defeat France quickly but they failed to do so and trench warfare resulted in battles such as the Somme in 1916. Germany's use of the submarine against neutral ships brought the USA into the war in 1917 and the Germans were forced to seek peace in 1918.

The First World War had a lasting effect on life in Britain. The government had to take greater control over the lives of its citizens during the war. Men were forced to join the armed forces, women had to take their place in industry to ensure that the supply of munitions did not run out and censorship was used to keep up morale. Food shortages caused by the action of German submarines eventually resulted in rationing. Air and sea attacks by the Germans made the people of Britain realise that modern warfare was no longer restricted to the soldiers on the battlefield.

This is a Paper 1 topic and you will be required to answer a number of structured questions on it. These will test your knowledge of change in the nature of conflict throughout Units 1 to 8.

Origins of Conflict

Events leading up to the First World War c.1900–14

In 1914, the Great Powers of Europe went to war. The major cause of that war was a series of rivalries between the Great Powers that can be traced back to the previous century. In the early years of the 20th century those rivalries became stronger until war became almost inevitable.

1.1 Why did tension increase in Europe between 1900 and 1914?

The Great Powers in 1900

Germany

In 1871, the German state, Prussia, had defeated France in war. This victory led to Prussia joining all the German states together to form the German Empire with the Prussian leader becoming Kaiser (Emperor) of Germany. France was forced to accept a humiliating peace settlement at the Treaty of Frankfurt in 1871. By this treaty, the Germans took the two French provinces of Alsace and Lorraine and the French were forced to pay 200 million francs in war damages to the Germans.

By 1900, Germany was rapidly overtaking Britain as the most important industrial country in Europe. The Germans' modern steel works produced enough steel for the munitions factories to make enough weapons for their army. They needed a strong army to prevent the French from trying to win back Alsace and Lorraine.

The Kaiser of Germany in 1900 was Wilhelm II, the grandson of Queen Victoria of Britain. Like many other Germans he wanted his country to have an overseas empire to match that of Britain. He talked of Germany having its 'place in the sun'. To achieve this Germany needed a strong navy and the Kaiser announced his intention to build one.

France

The French could not forgive the Germans for the loss of Alsace and Lorraine in 1871 and were looking for an

Source A

Germany has gone beyond her rights as a civilised nation in forcing defeated France to give up Alsace and Lorraine which contains one and a half million of her people. It was with a knife at her throat that France, bleeding and exhausted, signed us away. Give us our freedom. Give us justice.

A deputy from Alsace-Lorraine speaking to the German Parliament in 1874.

Things to do

1 If you were a politician living in one of the following countries in 1900, which country would you say was your main rival? Explain why.
   (a) France;
   (b) Austria-Hungary;
   (c) Great Britain.

2 How does Source A help you understand why there was rivalry between France and Germany?

opportunity to take revenge. They had built up their industry and their army and had been trying to make alliances with other Great Powers since 1871. France had a large overseas empire and felt threatened by the ambitions of Kaiser Wilhelm.

Britain

Britain was a trading nation whose wealth depended on its overseas empire. To protect this wealth Britain needed a strong navy to keep the trade routes open. As an island, Britain felt safe from invasion as its navy was greater than that of any other state. It had no need of help from other powers, so it chose to be isolated, a policy known as 'splendid isolation'. At the beginning of the 20th century, however, Britain felt threatened by the growing power of Germany.

Austria-Hungary

This was a large empire made up of many different nationalities, including Germans, Hungarians, Czechs, Poles and Serbs. It faced problems trying to keep all these different peoples, who each had their own language and customs, together as one country. Its leaders were particularly worried about the growth of Serbia as they feared that the Serbs of Austria-Hungary would want to join Serbia.

Russia

This was the largest but by far the most backward of the Great Powers. Its people were poor and there was little modern industry. The Russians believed that they should have influence over the Slav people, who included the Serbs, so they supported them against Austria-Hungary. This meant that there was great rivalry between Russia and Austria-Hungary in the area known as the Balkans. Russia also wanted to extend its influence in this area to gain access to the rich trade in the Mediterranean.

Italy

This was a relatively new country, formed in 1861. Before then the country had been a collection of small states. By 1900, Italy was allied with Austria-Hungary and Germany in the Triple Alliance, but was also in dispute with Austria-Hungary over land on the borders of the two countries. This meant there was a conflict of interests within the alliance.

Source B

Kaiser Wilhelm II drawn by a French artist. Note that the Kaiser is shown as the centre of attention with his place in the sun. The Kaiser had a withered left arm and this is clearly shown in the picture.

Things to do

1 What message do you think the French artist was trying to portray in Source B? Use the detail in the picture to support your answer.

2 What problems do you think a historian would have using Sources A and B as evidence of relations between France and Germany at the beginning of the twentieth century?

The Alliance System, 1900–14

The Alliance System, which involved the Great Powers of Europe, is often seen as a major cause of the First World War. This was because of the build up of tension between the Great Powers. As relations between rival countries worsened their allies would often support them, and so the tension would increase. In 1900 Germany was allied to Austria-Hungary and to Italy in what is known as the Triple Alliance. Under this alliance these countries agreed to help one another if they were attacked by any other power. France was allied to Russia by a treaty made in 1894, under which both countries agreed to help each other if Germany attacked them. In 1904 Britain signed the *Entente Cordiale* (Friendly Agreement) with France. The two countries agreed to be on good terms and not to quarrel over ownership of colonies. Britain also reached a friendly agreement with Russia,

in 1907, and so the Entente Cordiale became the Triple Entente. The Great Powers of Europe were now divided into two opposing alliances.

But the treaties were defensive. Countries agreed to help one another only if they were attacked. So how could they cause a war? One reason is that they were secret treaties, so the rival powers did not know that the alliances were defensive and feared that they were directed against them. This led to each alliance trying to get the better of the other in a series of disputes between 1900 and 1914. This had the effect of increasing the tension between the powers, strengthening the alliances and creating a situation in which one incident could lead to war. This is exactly what happened when Archduke Franz Ferdinand of Austria-Hungary was assassinated in 1914.

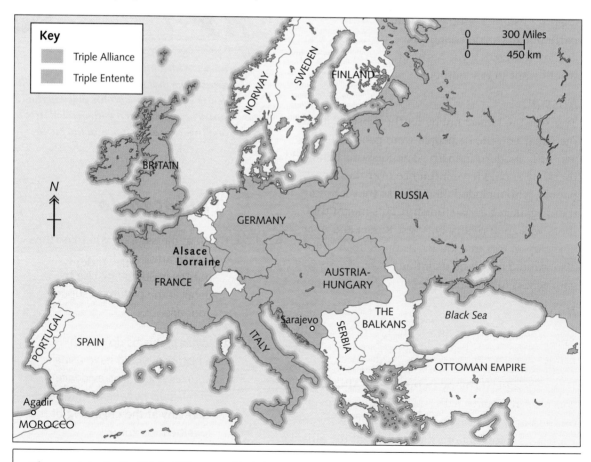

The countries in the Triple Alliance and Triple Entente.

Rivalry increases

Between 1905 and 1914 the Great Powers were involved in a series of crises in Morocco (in North Africa) and the Balkans (Eastern Europe) and they were involved in a race to build up their arms and navies. The effect was that the rival alliances grew stronger and more aggressive and this eventually led to war in 1914.

Events in Morocco, 1905-6

In 1905 when on a visit to Morocco Kaiser Wilhelm II promised to support Morocco's independence. This upset the French, who were interested in occupying Morocco as a colony. Wilhelm was also testing the strength of the new friendship between Britain and France. In a conference held at Algeciras in 1906 Britain and Russia stood by France and it was agreed that Germany should have no say in Morocco. This strengthened France's alliance with Britain who shortly afterwards made a colonial agreement with Russia, in 1907, so forming the Triple Entente with France. The Germans sensed they were being surrounded and the Kaiser became even more resentful.

A British cartoon of 1905 of the Entente Cordiale.

The Bosnian crisis, 1908-9

Bosnia was a Slav state in the Balkans. In 1908 it was annexed by Austria-Hungary and became part of the Austrian Empire. This was opposed by Serbia, which was also a Slav state and had ambitions to include the Slavs of Bosnia within it. But Serbia was too small to do anything about it on its own, so it looked to Russia for support. Russia supported Serbia but in 1909 backed off going to war to help Serbia gain Bosnia when Germany made it clear that if Russia declared war on Austria, Germany would declare war on Russia.

The crisis was important because Austria-Hungary now felt confident that it could rely on German support. This helps explain why Austria-Hungary acted as it did in 1914 (see pages 12–13). Russia had backed down in 1909, but by 1914 had built up its armies and was determined not to back down again when the next crisis came. Serbia had to accept that Bosnia was part of Austria-Hungary, but now looked for an opportunity to get its own back on Austria-Hungary. Italy had been concerned by Austria-Hungary's action in the Balkans and feared that it could get drawn into a war, so became less enthusiastic towards the Triple Alliance.

Things to do

1 Explain how Europe had become divided into two different groups by 1907.

2 Why were events in Morocco (1905–6) and Bosnia (1908–9) so important in the period leading up to the First World War?

Origins of Conflict

Morocco again – the Agadir crisis 1911

In 1911 there was a rebellion against the Sultan of Morocco which was put down with French help. This was an opportunity for the French to take Morocco. They were prepared to grant compensation to countries such as Germany and Spain who were concerned by the French action. But the Germans sent a gunboat, the *Panther*, to Agadir, a port on the Atlantic coast of Morocco, to challenge the French. The Kaiser hoped to force the French into giving Germany a share of Morocco. The British were alarmed that Germany was going to set up a naval base in Agadir to challenge Britain's naval supremacy.

Germany's aggressive action in Morocco confirmed Britain's worst fears: Germany was aiming to dominate Europe. Britain's response was to support France over Morocco. The British and French also made a naval agreement by which Britain promised to defend the north coast of France if it was attacked from the sea. The French took over Morocco as a protectorate, that is they governed the country without it becoming part of the French Republic. Germany was given 100,000 square miles of the French Congo in compensation, but the land was mostly swamp and jungle. The Agadir crisis was a clear victory for France and the Entente. The Kaiser was determined not to be the loser in the next crisis.

> While great naval power in the hands of Britain cannot constitute a menace, in the hands of Germany it will be a great peril to the world. This is even more so as the recent history of German policy of daring aggression and the lack of space at home compels Germany to conquer the colonies of others or perish.

A comment from a British newspaper, the Daily Mail, *February 1903.*

A Dreadnought *battleship.*

The naval race, 1906–14

As an island with a large overseas empire, Britain needed to have a powerful navy, particularly since the British army was very small. In 1900 Britain had the largest navy in the world. When the Germans began to build their navy in 1898, the British thought that it was an attempt to challenge Britain and its colonies. These British fears were partly responsible for Britain entering into agreements with France and Russia.

The German navy only became a real threat to Britain after 1906, when both sides began building *Dreadnoughts*, a new battleship that could easily destroy any of the older type battleships. Britain's naval supremacy was in the older ships, so the race was on to build the most *Dreadnoughts*.

The naval race reached its peak in 1909. The Germans refused to agree on the number of *Dreadnoughts* they would build. The Liberal government in Britain only planned to build four *Dreadnoughts* in 1909–10. Many in Britain believed that the German fleet build-up was aimed at challenging British naval superiority. Public pressure demanded the government spend more money building *Dreadnoughts*, under the slogan 'we want eight and won't wait'. The government gave way and increased spending on the fleet to maintain Britain's naval superiority over Germany.

The naval race did much to make the British resent the Germans and lead Britain into better relations with France. However, this was not a main cause of Britain going to war in 1914, as by then Britain had far more *Dreadnoughts* than the Germans.

The build up of armies, 1900–14

The existence of large armies in Europe was another threat to peace. Military leaders argued that the only way to ensure peace was to have a strong enough army to prevent an invasion from another country. This view was supported by the manufacturers of arms who made vast profits from the arms race.

Apart from Britain all the Great Powers increased the size of their armies during this period (see diagram below). Britain was the only power that had not introduced conscription (compulsory military service) before 1914. In 1913 the French raised the period of compulsory military service from two years to three and the Russians raised theirs from three to three-and-a-half years. This meant that both countries would have more trained men. By 1913 the German army was very powerful and only Russia had more men in arms.

Though the Russian army was the largest it was badly equipped and much inferior to that of Germany. The Germans took pride in their armed forces and this was encouraged by the Kaiser who enjoyed being photographed in military uniform (see Source B on page 7).

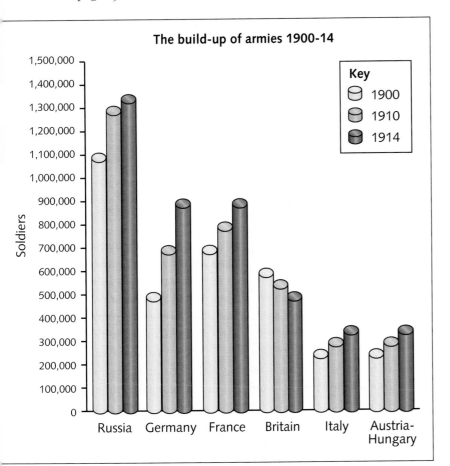

The build-up of armies 1900-14

Key
1900
1910
1914

Things to do

1 Why do you think Source D opposes Germany having a powerful navy?

2 How did **(a)** the Agadir crisis and **(b)** the naval race affect relations between the Great Powers in the period 1905–14?

3 Which was the greater threat to the peace of Europe, Morocco or Bosnia? Explain how you made your choice. (You will need to look back at pages 8 and 9.)

4 Does the fact that the Great Powers increased the size of their armies in the period 1900–14 mean that they thought war was inevitable? Explain your answer.

Summary

Relations between the Great Powers

1904	Entente Cordiale.
1905	First Moroccan crisis.
1906	Launch of the Dreadnought – the naval race begins.
1907	Triple Entente.
1908	Bosnian crisis.
1911	Agadir crisis.

Origins of Conflict

1.2 Why did the assassination at Sarajevo lead to the outbreak of war in 1914?

Assassination at Sarajevo

On 28 June 1914, the heir to the throne of Austria-Hungary, the Archduke Franz Ferdinand, visited the Bosnian capital of Sarajevo. A group of Serbian terrorists planned to kill him to publicise their opposition to Bosnia being part of Austria-Hungary. There were two attempts. In the first a bomb was thrown at the Archduke but he deflected it so that it fell behind the car, exploded and injured several people in the following car. The Archduke continued the visit but insisted on visiting the injured in hospital. On leaving the hospital the driver of the car took a wrong turning. As he stopped to reverse, one of the waiting assassins, Gavrilo Princip, fired two shots: the first one hit the Archduke, the second hit his wife. The Archduke's wife died immediately and he died on the way to hospital.

Source F

An artist's impression of the assassination of the Archduke Franz Ferdinand. This was drawn in 1914.

Things to do

1 How accurate a picture of the assassination do you think is given in Source F? Explain your answer.

2 Do you agree with what the Kaiser says in Source G? Look back at pages 6–11 to help you answer the question.

3 Do you think the person who drew Source H approved of the German invasion of Belgium? Explain your answer.

4 Why did the assassination of the Archduke Franz Ferdinand lead to war?

Such a murder would normally have been a matter for the two countries involved alone. But relations between the alliances of Great Powers were so strained in 1914 that it led to the outbreak of the First World War. Some politicians in Austria-Hungary saw the assassination as an excuse for attacking Serbia and solving the problem of the Serbs within the Austrian Empire (see page 7). The Austrians issued an ultimatum to Serbia to comply with ten conditions, even though they had no proof that the Serbian government had anything to do with the assassination. Serbia replied very favourably to the ultimatum, accepting nine of the ten points. But the Austrians were not satisfied and declared war on Serbia on 28 July 1914.

From assassination to war

The Austrian declaration of war on Serbia was the first step towards general war in 1914. After the Bosnian crisis of 1908 Russia felt that it had let down its Slav allies in the Balkans, so it was determined not to back down again. On 30 July the Russians mobilised their army and prepared for war. They did this without consulting Britain or France. Germany supported its ally Austria-Hungary by declaring war on Russia on 1 August and two days later went to war with France. At this stage the British were not keen to join the war and the British Foreign Secretary, Sir Edward Grey, said that Britain would remain neutral unless Germany attacked France. If Germany did, then Britain would offer assistance to the French.

On 3 August 1914 the Germans launched the Schlieffen Plan. This was an attack on France from the north through Belgium. To the surprise of the Germans, their invasion of Belgium brought the British into the war. Britain and most other European countries had guaranteed Belgium's neutrality by the Treaty of London in 1839. Britain now stood by that agreement and the Kaiser was astonished that the British had joined the war over 'a scrap of paper' which seemed to have so little relevance to Europe in 1914.

In August 1914 all members of the rival alliance systems, except Italy, declared war on each other. The outbreak of war was the result of a series of crises and mistakes. Events before 1914 had pushed the Great Powers towards war, events after Sarajevo sparked off the war.

Source G

I no longer have any doubt that Britain, Russia and France have agreed among themselves to wage war to destroy us. The encirclement of Germany has already been achieved.

Kaiser Wilhelm II speaking in 1914 before the outbreak of the war

BRAVO, BELGIUM!

This British cartoon, published in August 1914, shows Belgium being bullied by Germany.

Summary

Events leading to war

28 June	Assassination of Franz Ferdinand.
23 July	Austrian ultimatum to Serbia.
28 July	Austria-Hungary declares war on Serbia.
1 August	Germany declares war on Russia.
3 August	Germany declares war on France.
	German troops enter Belgium.
4 August	Britain declares war on Germany.
5 August	Austria-Hungary declares war on Russia.

Origins of Conflict

The Changing Nature of Warfare

The Western Front

In 1914, most people expected a speedy finish to the war. The Franco-Prussian War of 1870-71 had been a short war won by a quick knock-out blow. It was expected to be the same in 1914. The failure of the Schlieffen Plan, the impact of new weapons and the use of trenches led to the war lasting until 1918.

2.1 Why was the First World War not over by Christmas?

The theory of the Schlieffen Plan

Germany had the problem of what to do if there was a war with both France and Russia, who had been allies since the Franco-Russian Treaty of 1894 (see page 8). The German answer to this war on two fronts was to attack France first before Russia was ready. The German Head of General Staff was Count Alfred von Schlieffen, and he devised a plan to defeat France within six weeks by attacking through Belgium. Once the French were defeated the Germans could then turn to the east and defeat Russia. Von Schlieffen believed that it would take the Russians at least six weeks to be ready for war because of the size of the country and its poor transport.

The plan depended on the right wing of the German forces attacking France through Belgium and Holland, leaving only a few troops to hold the French attack on Germany in Alsace and Lorraine. The plan was changed

Source A

A British howitzer used in the Battle of the Somme and during the war.

in 1914 by General Moltke: he only attacked through Belgium and strengthened the forces in Alsace and Lorraine at the expense of the right wing. The plan involved moving large armies quickly over great distances, which would be difficult. The Germans also failed to foresee the effect that the invasion of Belgium would have on Britain, or perhaps they felt that the British army was too weak to cause them any problems.

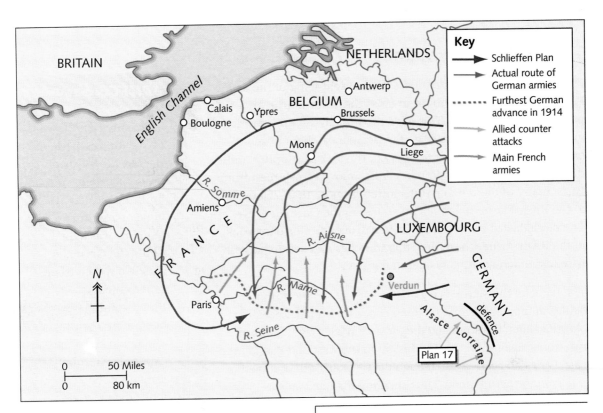

The Schlieffen Plan.

Failure of the Schlieffen Plan

At first the German attack was successful. They were held up by the Belgian fortresses, particularly at Liege, but eventually these fell to the German heavy artillery. The last Belgian fort fell on 16 August. But the heroic resistance of the Belgians delayed the Germans sufficiently to give the British time to mobilise their army. The British Expeditionary Force (BEF), over 100,000 strong, arrived in France on 21 August and was in action the following day. Belgian resistance had also given the French army, under General Joffre, time to re-organise. The French abandoned their own plan to attack Germany through Lorraine (Plan 17), which was being defended by the German army, and decided to concentrate on the defence of Paris. In spite of this, the Germans appeared to be winning through the sheer size of their attacking force of over 1 million men.

The Schlieffen Plan, however, was beginning to run into trouble. The BEF delayed the German advance for a full day when they attacked at Mons on 23 August. The Germans suffered heavy casualties but the BEF was forced to

retreat because of the lack of support. The area of attack had been narrowed and instead of attacking the coast and capturing the Channel Ports, the advancing German army began heading for Paris. On 25 August, General Moltke made a critical mistake. He was worried about the speed of Russian mobilisation on the Eastern Front, so he withdrew 100,000 men from the Western Front and sent them to defend Germany's eastern border against the expected Russian attack. Instead of taking the troops from Lorraine, where they could have been spared, Moltke took them from Belgium, so weakening further the crucial right wing of the Schlieffen Plan. Moltke appeared to think that victory in the west had been won. This was far from the truth. The Germans were having difficulty keeping their armies supplied because they were advancing so quickly, and Moltke's headquarters remained in the rear in Luxembourg, which meant that he lost contact with the commanders of the front-line armies. This loss of contact with front-line commanders led to the collapse of the Schlieffen Plan at the Battle of the Marne.

The Changing Nature of Warfare

The Battle of the Marne

One of the German commanders on the right wing of the army, Von Kluck, ordered his troops to cross the River Marne and pass to the east of Paris. This gave the French the opportunity to counter-attack. By this stage the German soldiers were exhausted by the speed of the march, the lack of supplies and the hot weather. On 6 September Joffre moved fresh men from Paris, many of them being transported in more than 250 taxis, to the River Marne to launch an attack on the German army. The battle lasted a week. The French drove the Germans back to the River Aisne where they dug trenches and set up barbed wire and machine guns to defend them.

The Battle of the Marne is regarded as one of the most important battles in modern history. German hopes for a quick knock-out blow had been thwarted and they were forced to fight a war on two fronts: against France and Britain in the west and Russia in the east. Paris had been saved, though the Germans still occupied much of northern France. The Schlieffen Plan had failed.

There followed one final battle in the war of movement, the battle for the Channel Ports. The first battle of Ypres took place between 12 October and 11 November 1914. The BEF resisted the German attack at a cost of 50,000 men, though the Germans lost at least twice as many. The BEF saved the Channel Ports for the Allies, which meant that British troops and supplies could be readily transported to France.

The long slog

The war of movement was over and all hopes of a short war were ended. The Germans had lost many of their best men, the French had suffered over a million casualties and most of the BEF had been killed at Ypres. Both sides now concentrated on defence and dug trenches. The war now developed into a long slog. The stalemate had begun: the Western Front did not move more than ten miles either way for the next four years.

The Western Front, 1914–18.

Conflict in the Modern World, 1900–18

> ## Source B
>
> The Schlieffen Plan died with the Battle of the Marne. It was of profound importance, for it meant that all hope of a swift knock-out blow was over. Could the Germans have won? The troops sent to the Eastern Front would have been more than enough to close the gap in the German army that the French took advantage of.

A modern historian's view of the Schlieffen Plan.

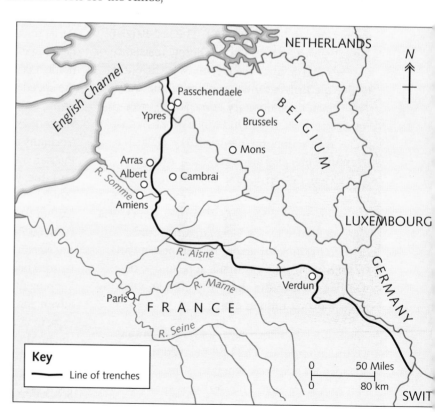

Trenches, weapons and strategy

Up until the First World War most military leaders believed that battles and wars were won mainly by cavalry charges, with the infantry (foot soldiers) following behind the cavalry. The use of trenches and new weapons soon made them realise that this was no longer possible. Horses were easy targets for the rapid fire of machine guns, especially when trying to gallop across the mud of a battlefield.

Technology had made it possible to produce heavy artillery more powerful than anything seen before. Large guns, such as the howitzer, could fire shells at enemy targets hundreds of yards away. Smaller versions of field guns were also used in artillery attacks and hand-held trench mortars were used by the men in the trenches.

The machine gun was the main weapon used on the Western Front. But it was underestimated by the British generals who believed that a battalion only needed two machine guns. The Germans were much quicker to recognise its value and set up machine gun posts, enclosed in concrete, to protect their trenches. The rapid fire of the guns made it very difficult to capture trenches. The only defence against them was to 'dig in' by building trenches. These new weapons and the trenches led to a stalemate, with neither side being able to make any significant advances. Both sides were forced to make greater efforts to develop new weapons to break the stalemate. Until they did there seemed little prospect of either side winning the war.

Source C

German troops 'digging in' at the end of 1914.

Things to do

1 What was the contribution of each of the following to the failure of the Schlieffen Plan:
   (a) Moltke's mistakes;
   (b) Russian mobilisation;
   (c) Belgian resistance?
   Which were the most important reasons?

2 Do you think that the Schlieffen Plan could have succeeded? Explain your answer.

3 Why was the Battle of the Marne so important in the First World War? Give reasons for your answer.

4 Why did both sides dig trenches at the end of 1914?

The Changing Nature of Warfare

2.2 What were the effects of the military deadlock on the Western Front?

The nature of trench warfare

The generals believed that the only way to win the war on the Western Front was to take over the enemy's trenches and drive their forces back until they surrendered. For four years the army generals followed the same tactics in their attempts to create a break-through. Each attack would begin with a heavy artillery bombardment from behind the front line which was intended to break up the barbed wire defences, destroy the machine-gun posts and many of the front trenches. This bombardment would often continue for days before the next stage in the attack.

When the bombardment finished, the men in the trenches were ordered to go 'over the top'. This meant that they climbed out of the trenches and advanced across 'No Man's Land' towards the enemy trenches. On their backs the men carried their personal kit, including clothing, and weapons which weighed at least 28 kilograms. They advanced over ground which had been churned up by previous attacks and artillery bombardment.

When they reached the enemy trenches, they had to weave their way through the barbed wire and capture them.

As early as March 1915, a British attack at Neuve Chapelle broke through the German front line, but poor communications and lack of ammunition led to a delay which gave the Germans time to recover and build a second line of defence using bicycle-mounted sharp-shooters. But this success convinced the British generals that with better support a breakthrough could be achieved by these methods.

The use of gas, 1915

When the Germans broke through the Allies' front line at Ypres in April 1915 their success was due to a new weapon – poison gas (chlorine). The gas attack took the Allies by surprise and caused panic in the trenches. The Germans were then able to make the initial advance, but the wind changed direction and blew the gas towards the German lines, causing more German casualties than Allies. Soon both sides were using gas.

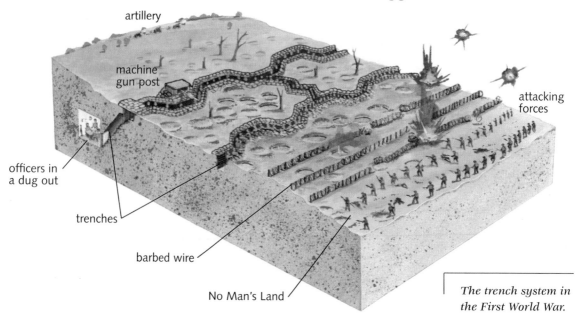

artillery

machine
gun post

attacking
forces

officers in
a dug out

trenches

barbed wire

No Man's Land

The trench system in the First World War.

'Hell', a contemporary painting by a French artist showing a First World War battlefield.

Source D

We have heaps of gassed cases. I wish those who call this a holy war could see the poor things burnt and blistered all over with great mustard-coloured blisters, with blind eyes all sticky and glued together; always fighting for breath with voices a mere whisper saying their throats are closing and they will choke.

An eyewitness account of the effects of gas on the Western Front.

The chlorine gas irritated the lungs and many of those affected died of suffocation. The Germans later used phosgene which was more powerful and in 1917 used mustard gas which had no smell. This gas temporarily blinded its victims, burned their skin and poisoned their lungs. In the worst cases death was slow and painful, taking up to four weeks. Others who survived the war died later of lung disease.

But gas became largely ineffective when gas masks were introduced to protect soldiers against it. The main effect was psychological: soldiers lived in fear of the next gas attack.

Verdun, 1916

The military leaders decided that the only way to win the war was to wear down the enemy by attrition. This involved shelling the enemy's defences and launching attacks that used up the enemy's supplies of men and equipment.

The British and French strategy for 1916 was to launch a joint offensive on the German line at the River Somme in the summer. However, the Germans made the first move and launched an attack on the French fortress of Verdun in February. Falkenhayn, the successor to Moltke, felt that he could defeat the whole of the French army at Verdun because they would defend it to the last man. The Germans succeeded in taking some of the outer forts, but the main fortress held firm under the leadership of General Petain, who announced *Ils ne passeront pas* (They shall not pass). The French suffered greatly at Verdun and urged the British to launch their offensive on the Somme as early as possible in order to lift the siege of Verdun.

Things to do

1 Why was it difficult to take enemy trenches in the First World War?
2 How effective was gas as a weapon?
3 How could you decide if Source E is accurate?

The Changing Nature of Warfare

The Somme 1916: a battle of attrition

Verdun changed the offensive on the Somme. Instead of being a joint offensive it became largely a British attack – the French were only able to contribute half the men they had promised at the beginning of the year. The offensive was rushed forward to the end of June and the main aim of the Somme now became to relieve Verdun, or as Rawlinson, one of the commanders of the 4th army, put it, 'to kill as many Germans as possible'. The British commander in chief, General Haig, was still intent on achieving a breakthrough, but this was not now the main priority.

The battle began with a five-day bombardment of the enemy trenches. On 1 July Haig ordered the advance to begin. He told his troops that they should walk across 'No Man's Land' because there would not be 'even a rat' alive in the German trenches. While the bombardment was taking place, the Germans had withdrawn into especially prepared deep dug-outs. Once it had stopped, they prepared for the advancing British soldiers.

The Germans only had one order to give, 'Fire!' The British suffered 60,000 casualties, including 20,000 deaths, on the first day of the attack alone. But not even this scale of loss convinced the generals to change their minds about the methods of warfare they employed.

Source G

Haig realised that a major breakthrough was unlikely and settled for a long drawn-out war of attrition. His aim was 'to maintain a steady pressure on the Somme battle.'

The last chance of a breakthrough came on 15 September when the British used tanks for the first time. They were intended to lead the infantry, protecting them against German gun fire and crushing their barbed wire and trench system. The German troops were taken by surprise and retreated. But again the British were too slow to take advantage and the Germans were given time to build up their defences. By the end of the day all of the tanks had broken down, were stuck or had been eliminated by the Germans. Haig has been criticised for using tanks before the design was fully developed. But the failure in 1916 does not appear to have affected the surprise value of tanks which were used to great effect at Cambrai in 1917.

Source H

When the German troops crept out of their dug-outs in the mist of the morning and stretched their necks to look for the English, their blood chilled. Mysterious monsters were crawling towards them over the craters. Nothing stopped them. Someone in the trenches said, 'The devil is coming', and word was passed along the line. Tongues of flame leapt from the sides of the iron caterpillars. The English infantry came in behind.

A German war correspondent describing the effect the sight of British tanks had on German soldiers at the Somme.

Tanks could get up to speeds of 6 kilometres an hour on solid ground, but were much slower in the mud of battle.

They were armed with two high-powered naval guns and three machine guns, protected with armoured steel. Eight men were needed to crew a tank. Inside, the tank was noisy and extremely hot, with temperatures rising to 38°C. A crew could die if they stayed in the tank for more than three hours.

A major effect of the tank in battle was psychological. They frightened the enemy and the morale of those at home watching newsreels, and those on the battlefield watching from the trenches was raised by the sight of these 'metal monsters' lumbering towards the enemy. As technology improved they came to play a greater part in trench warfare.

Source I

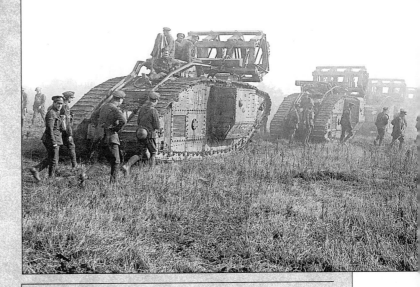

British tanks and infantry advancing at Cambrai in 1917. The tanks carried fascines which they dropped into trenches to allow them to pass over.

Effects of the Somme

At the end of September the rain fell and the Somme battlefield turned to mud. No side could advance in these conditions. The battle of the Somme ended in November 1916. Very little ground was won or lost. But the loss of life was massive. The British lost 420,000 men, the French 200,000 and the Germans 500,000.

The Somme offensive failed to achieve the breakthrough Haig had hoped for. Advances had been slow and when the enemy front line was broken the support was too slow in reaching the advancing soldiers. Artillery bombardments failed to destroy the enemy's defences, and they warned the Germans that a major attack was about to be launched, which gave them time to prepare for it.

However, for the Allies there were some positive results. Verdun had been saved partly by the attack on the Somme, though a Russian attack in the east, launched on 4 June 1916, probably had a greater effect as the Germans had to withdraw men from Verdun to resist the Russians. The French and British had co-operated and tanks and aerial photography had been used for the first time to support an advancing army. The British army had shown it could maintain a lengthy attack and German losses had a long-term effect on their military strength.

Conflict in the Modern World, 1900–18

Source J

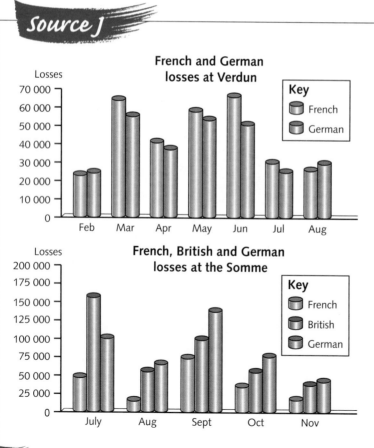

French and German losses at Verdun

French, British and German losses at the Somme

Source K

As a result of the Somme fighting we were completely exhausted on the Western Front. If the war lasted like this our defeat seemed inevitable. I cannot see as I look back how Germany could have mastered the situation if the Allies had continued their blows as they did in 1916.

An extract from the memoirs of General Ludendorff.

Things to do

1 Why did the British launch an attack along the River Somme?

2 Does Ludendorff's statement (Source K) justify Haig's tactics at the Somme?

3 Would you say that the introduction of tanks on the Western Front was a success? Explain your answer.

4 How far can paintings and photographs of the Western Front help us to understand what it was like?

Losses in the major battles of 1916.

The Battle of Passchendaele, 1917 – attrition continues

In 1917 the British launched a further offensive at Ypres. The attack began with a two-week bombardment on 31 July and made steady progress at first. Heavy rain then affected the battlefield and when the fighting centred on the village of Passchendaele the rain had turned the ground into a 'porridge of mud' and the attack ground to a halt in November.

The Battle of Passchendaele won very little land for the Allies. But it did weaken German morale because of the loss of life. However, it also affected British morale for the same reason. The British lost 250,000 and the Germans 200,000. Following the Somme no one wanted a repeat of this destruction of human life for such little gain. In 1917, both sides had hopes for the future: the Germans because the Russian Revolution led to Russia leaving the war, the Allies because the USA had entered the war on their side because of action by the German U-boats in the Atlantic. Germany was desperate to move its troops (around 400,000) from the Eastern Front to the Western Front to make a breakthrough before thousands of fresh American troops arrived.

Source L

The town of Ypres after the Passchendaele campaign.

The defeat of Germany, 1918

In 1918, the German General, Ludendorff, realised that Germany must win the war before the Amercan forces entered Europe. He had to force a victory in the West. Ludendorff launched the first part of his last offensive (code-named Operation Michael) in March 1918 at St Quentin. Early breakthroughs were aided by fog, but the attack ran out of steam. The Germans won 1,200 square miles of land but had gained an extra 50 miles of front which had to be defended. Ludendorff tried two further attacks, the first in the north, code-named Georgette, in April, and the second (Blücher) in May in the Champagne region of France. Both had early successes, but were eventually stopped with the help of the newly arrived American soldiers, and the Allies began a counter-offensive.

Under the new commander-in-chief of the Allied army, General Foch, the Allies began to advance. The lessons of Passchendaele appear to have been learned as the attacks were carried out on methodical lines: as soon as an attack lost its initial impetus, it was broken off and another one launched close enough to profit from the success. German morale appeared to have finally broken, with cases of whole companies surrendering to single tanks.

The attacks continued until Germany was forced to accept defeat. The Armistice (ceasefire) was signed on 11 November 1918.

The Changing Nature of Warfare

23

Life in the trenches and its effects

Men spent long spells in the trenches during the war. During battle they might have spent several weeks in the front trench, though normally it was only about four days at a time in the front trench and a similar time in the supporting trenches. During lulls in the fighting life was boring. Sleeping was difficult.

Sentries on daytime duty feared being shot by enemy snipers if they moved about too much. Despite the dangers trenches had to be repaired and food had to be distributed. At night the barbed wire had to be repaired and No Man's Land was patrolled to spot enemy activity and to recover the wounded.

There was a shortage of food and the menu was usually the same every day – beef, a biscuit and jam. There were few washing facilities and many men were infested with body lice. The crude sewage systems and rotting dead bodies created a foul stench, particularly in summer. Rats fed on the dead bodies. There was little protection from the cold and wet of winter. Men had to stand in pools of water, their toes swelling into the condition known as trench foot. Over 75,000 British soldiers suffered trench foot during the war. Washing and drying feet daily was one attempt to prevent it, but often toes had to be amputated. Disease and illness were common under these conditions.

And there was worse. There was the fear of death. Men lived in constant fear of attack from shells, gas and snipers. They knew that if they went 'over the top', the chance of returning was slim. Living in such constant fear caused some men to suffer shell shock, in which their whole body would shake uncontrollably and they would often stammer. Another fear was of falling into a shell hole of mud and drowning.

Things to do

1 List the discomforts, the fears and the diseases of the men in the trenches.

2 Why were newspapers not allowed to tell the story of the war?

3 How accurate do you think Source O is? Explain your answer.

4 What attitude towards the generals is shown in Source P? Why did the soldiers feel like this?

Source M

British soldiers in a trench during the Battle of the Somme, 1916.

Views of the Front

Having to live in these conditions and suffering the loss of comrades in attacks and the absence from loved ones at home changed the soldiers' attitudes to the war. Soldiers wrote home, but their letters were censored, so their families had no idea what conditions were like. Officials fed them stories of Allied victories. Newspapers were also censored and official photographers and war artists appointed by the government were the only ones allowed to depict scenes in the trenches. And they were only allowed to photograph or represent certain parts of the trenches – artists, for example, were not allowed to include dead bodies in their paintings.

Source P

Forward Joe Soap's Army, marching without fear

With our own commander, safely in the rear.

He boasts and strikes from morn till night and thinks he's very brave,

But the men who really did the job are dead and in their grave.

An extract from a popular song sung by soldiers in the trenches.

Source N

The battlefield is fearful. One is overcome by a peculiar sour, heavy and penetrating smell of corpses. Men that were killed last October lie half in swamp and half in beet-fields. The legs of an Englishman stick out into the trench, the corpse being built into the parapet: a soldier hangs his rifle on them.

Extract from a letter written by a German soldier, 27 April 1915.

Source O

The Harvest of Battle, *a painting by a war artist of the aftermath of battle on the Western Front, completed in 1921. The artist will have made sketches of the battle and used his sketches to complete the painting later.*

The Changing Nature of Warfare

Civilian Experience of War

The Home Front in Britain, 1914–18

When the war began no one expected there to be much change at home. The need for more men, arms and munitions, together with the shortages experienced at home because of the German blockade, led to the government taking more control over the lives of the people in Britain.

3.1 How did the First World War change life in Britain in 1914–18?

Recruitment

People in all countries greeted the war with enthusiasm in 1914. Lord Kitchener was placed in charge of the war effort in Britain and, as Britain only had a small force of trained soldiers, he realised the need to recruit men quickly. Kitchener launched an appeal for volunteers. Posters were displayed in all main towns. They appealed to people's patriotism, their family responsibilities and their fear and disgust of the Germans. Any able-bodied men who did not volunteer to fight were branded cowards. The feeling towards these men was publicly expressed by those women who handed out white feathers, the mark of cowardice, to any such man they saw in the street. At first there was a huge response to the appeal: half a million men signed up in one month. Many rushed to volunteer afraid that the war would be over before they could take part, some believing it would be over by Christmas. They reported to their local recruitment office, took the oath to fight 'For King and country' and signed on 'for the king's shilling'.

Source A

We said we would serve. We offered ourselves. Call it patriotism.

I was quite empty-headed and bored to tears with shop life. The chaps round about started to go, so I said 'I'm going'.

Well it was gonna be a change. Most volunteers went to get away from their environment.

The views of some recruits on why they joined up to fight in the war in 1914.

Source B

WOMEN OF BRITAIN SAY— "GO!"

Recruitment poster using women to persuade men to enlist for the war.

FOR HONOUR

"A SCRAP OF PAPER"

Source C

Propaganda postcard showing the British attitude to Germany invading Belgium.

By 1916 over two million men had been recruited to the armed forces.

As the war continued volunteers became fewer: in December 1915 only 55,000 volunteered compared to 436,000 in September 1914. People at home became weary of the war, sickened by news of casualties on the Front, suffering shortages at home and worried by attacks on Britain by air and sea. The enormous casualties on the Western Front meant that Britain needed more fighting men. So in January 1916 the government introduced conscription. All able-bodied men between the age of 18 and 41 could be enlisted to fight in the forces. Some saw conscription as limiting their freedom, particularly those who refused to join up because they were against war. They were known as conscientious objectors. Some were brought to trial and imprisoned or sent to the Front to act as stretcher-bearers.

Before conscription many of those who volunteered were skilled workers in essential industries, such as mining, which left those industries short of skilled workers. Many of these workers had to be sent back home.

So when conscription was introduced skilled workers in industries such as mining and farming were exempt; and up until March 1916 all able-bodied married men were also exempt.

Propaganda

Throughout the war the government used propaganda to encourage the people to continue making sacrifices and help the war effort. From the beginning posters and postcards were published stressing the justice of the war and the evil action of the Germans.

This was necessary to convince British people to make the sacrifices necessary to win the war.

Things to do

1   Why did people volunteer for the armed forces in 1914?

2   Why was conscription introduced in 1916?

3   Explain the techniques used in Source C to turn the British people against the Germans.

Civilian Experience of War

DORA

The Defence of the Realm Act (DORA) was introduced by the British government in August 1914. This law gave the government far more power than it previously had so that it could protect the country from invasion and do everything possible to win the war. Censorship was introduced, not only on news and letters coming from the Western Front, but on all matters concerned with the war. Newspapers were censored and it was forbidden to even discuss the war in a public place in an attempt to stop the spread of rumours. The only news of the Western Front that the public was allowed to hear through the media were stories of British heroism and German brutality. Official photographers took pictures of mock raids to give people at home an idea of the war. Even films had a patriotic theme.

DORA gave the government the power to take over factories and land for war production. Production of weapons and ammunition was increased by allowing women to work in the munitions industry, lengthening the hours of work and gaining more control over the use of skilled labour. British summer-time was introduced to allow more daylight for working, while beer was watered down and pubs were only allowed to open at certain times to reduce drunkenness which caused absence from work.

Shortage of food caused by the German U-boat blockade (see p 33) was also addressed by additional laws through DORA. Public parks

(see p 33)

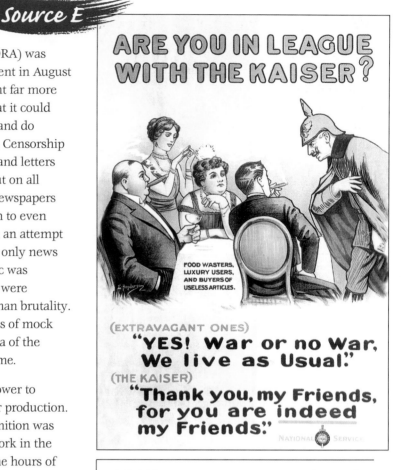

ARE YOU IN LEAGUE WITH THE KAISER?

FOOD WASTERS, LUXURY USERS, AND BUYERS OF USELESS ARTICLES.

(EXTRAVAGANT ONES)
"YES! War or no War, We live as Usual."
(THE KAISER)
"Thank you, my Friends, for you are indeed my Friends."

NATIONAL SERVICE

A British government poster encouraging people not to waste food.

were taken over for the growing of vegetables, the Women's Land Army was set up and posters were produced to encourage people to support the country by reducing the amount of food they had at meal times (Source E). Even feeding bread to pigeons was forbidden by law to prevent waste.

Despite these restrictions the government, in 1918, was forced to introduce rationing of foods such as sugar, butter and beef. People received ration books with coupons in them. The coupons had to be given in, along with the money, when food was bought, so this limited the amount of certain goods that people could buy each week and ensured that everyone was entitled to the same. But there wasn't enough time to extend rationing to everything during the war. Even so, the fact it was introduced showed how much more the government was involved in the lives of its citizens.

I am not allowed to tell you where I am, because the General is afraid you might tell someone at school, and he might tell the German master, and the German master might telegraph the Kaiser and tell him. And then of course the Kaiser would send an aeroplane to drop bombs on us.

A soldier's letter written to his family in 1914.

Women and the war

Before the First World War, women were often not treated as equals by men. The suffragettes had been campaigning for women to get the vote, but called off their campaign when war started. Women were to play a vital role in the war.

At the beginning of the war women were used to encourage men to join the forces, but later they began to take on the jobs left by men. This meant that women began to do jobs which they had never done before. They delivered the post, drove buses, worked as mechanics, window cleaners, firefighters and did much heavier work in shipbuilding and steelmaking. They proved that they could do the jobs as well as, and in some cases better than, men but they still received lower pay.

Over 100,000 women also responded to the government's appeal to work on the land by joining the 'Women's Land Army'. These 'Land Girls' replaced the farm labourers who had joined the forces and kept the country supplied with food. Other women wanted to play a more direct role in the war. Many of these volunteered for Voluntary Aid Detachments (VADs) run partly by the Red Cross. They served behind the lines tending to the casualties on the Western Front. The Women's Army Auxiliary Corps (WAACs) was formed in 1917 to take over the office jobs in the army, freeing the men to fight.

Edith Cavell

Edith Cavell was an English nurse in charge of a nursing school in Belgium when that country was occupied by the German army. The school was converted into a Red Cross hospital, with Edith as matron, to nurse the thousands of wounded Allied soldiers who had been captured by the Germans.

But Edith Cavell did more than nurse the soldiers, she also helped hundreds of them to escape. In 1915 she was arrested as a spy by the Germans and sentenced to death. Countries around the world pleaded for her to be spared. But the Germans executed her by firing squad.

Edith became a national heroine in Britain. Her death was used in the propaganda war against Germany and in recruitment campaigns to show how evil the Germans were. It also raised the image of women in Britain, showing them to be capable of great courage.

Civilian Experience of War

Women and munitions work

During the war many women began to work making shells in munitions factories. The work of these 'munitionettes' was vital for the war effort. The working day was lengthened because of the needs of the war and some women worked 12-hour shifts. Much of the work was dangerous as the women worked with toxic chemicals and explosions and fires were common. In 1917 a fire in the Silvertown munitions works in East London caused an explosion which killed 69 people and injured 400. Those who worked regularly with TNT found that their skin became yellow and they became known as 'canary girls'. This was a condition known as 'toxic jaundice' and could be fatal. By the end of the war over 900,000 women worked in the munitions industries, representing 60 per cent of the workforce.

Women welcomed the independence they gained during the war, when they could do the work of men and earn their own wages. They were proud to have played their part in the victory and men had recognised their ability and willingness to contribute to the war effort. It was partly because of the role they played in the war that women over the age of 30 were given the vote in 1918. In other ways the war changed little: when men came back from the war they replaced the women in the heavy jobs and women's employment returned largely to the pattern that it was before the war. Women had, however, gained a more positive image of themselves and attitudes were changing slowly.

Source F

Mabel Lethbridge volunteered for service in the danger zone where high explosives were poured and packed into shells. She worked a machine that forced amatol and TNT down into the eighteen pounder shell case. Four girls hauled on a rope to raise a massive weight then at a signal let it drop on the mixture until it was packed tight.

Description of a woman's job in a munitions factory.

Source G

Women in a munitions factory in 1916.

3.2 How effective were the measures taken to combat the new dangers and difficulties?

Danger of invasion

People on the east coast of Britain received a shock in December 1914 when German ships shelled Hartlepool, Scarborough and Whitby. There were over 500 civilian casualties in these raids, which created the fear of a German invasion. But the raids also helped to unite the British people and build up hatred towards the Germans. The government made full use of this in its recruiting campaign.

The danger of invasion also came from the air. The Germans had developed Zeppelin airships. The first attack by air on Britain was in January 1915 when two Zeppelins bombed Great Yarmouth and King's Lynn, killing two people and damaging houses. Further Zeppelin attacks in 1915 and 1916 concentrated on London, but they stopped in 1917 because of the British defences. The British used barrage balloons to defend themselves against the Zeppelins and sent fighter planes to intercept them. They also illuminated the sky with searchlights so the Zeppelins could be easily spotted and fired at. If a Zeppelin was hit it burst into flames, because it was filled with hydrogen. The crew had little chance of surviving.

Things to do

1 Give examples of how DORA changed life in Britain.

2 What do Sources D and E tell us about people's fears in 1914? Do you think they were realistic?

3 What new jobs did women do in the First World War? Why were they needed? What new dangers did they face?

4 How did the war affect the position of women in society?

Source H

A Zeppelin.

Civilian Experience of War

Aeroplane warfare

This was not the end of the air attacks. Aeroplanes had been used for reconnaissance since 1914 to photograph the enemy positions and aid an offensive. This led to dogfights between aircraft in the sky. The early planes were crude machines made of wood and canvas held together by piano wire. The pilots sat in the open cockpits with only goggles, leather helmets and thick coats to protect them from the cold. They had no radio, no parachutes and few navigational instruments. Even the engines were unreliable and it needed a lot of courage to fly them let alone fight in them. In 1917 the average fighting life of a front line pilot was two weeks.

Each side had their own 'air aces' such as Britain's Albert Ball and Mick Mannock, whose daring exploits were told at home raising the morale of the people. The German hero was the 'Red Baron', Baron Manfred von Richthofen, who destroyed 80 Allied aircraft before he was shot down in 1918.

The first weapons used were handguns, though these were soon replaced by machine guns. But the machine guns were mounted on the cockpit and a pilot couldn't fire straight ahead without shooting off his propellor. When the synchronised propellor was invented the problem was solved. The machine gun was now mounted on the propellor and bullets were fired between the propellor blades as they spun round.

Towards the end of the war faster and more manoeuvrable aeroplanes, such as the German Albatross and the British Sopwith Camel, were developed. Then planes, such as the German Gotha IV and the British Vickers Vimy, were developed to carry bombs. German bombers began raiding towns on the south coast from 1917 onwards.

Air raid damage in London during the First World War.

Conflict in the Modern World, 1900–18

Source I

The whole street seemed to explode. There was smoke and flames all over, but the worst of all were the screams of the wounded and dying and mothers looking frantically for their kids.

Description of an air raid on Folkestone in May 1917.

Over 1,000 people were killed in these attacks and many houses and shops were damaged.

The effect of these attacks on the war effort was not great. More important was the psychological effect they had on people. Britain was an island and had always been safe from invasion. This was no longer the case. For the first time British civilians realised that they were vulnerable. The government had to take measures to defend its citizens from future attacks. The British fleet guarded the east coast against further attacks and defences were introduced against air attacks. Improvements were made to British aircraft so they could launch attacks on German towns, and in 1918 the Royal Air Force was formed.

Source J

Submarine warfare

The British navy placed a blockade on Germany at the beginning of the war. The aim was to cut off the supply of food and raw materials from other countries that Germany needed to carry on the war. This was a long process and was partly responsible for the final collapse of Germany in 1918. The Germans launched their own blockade of Britain using the U-boat (German name for a submarine) to try to stop supplies coming to Britain from abroad.

In February 1915 the Germans declared the seas around the British Isles a 'war zone' and reserved the right to sink all ships, including neutrals, in these waters. This policy was called 'unrestricted submarine warfare'. The problem for the Germans was that U-boats had never been used before in a war and there were no rules governing their use. It was normal to warn a ship before it was fired upon so that the people on board could be rescued. This was not possible with a submarine because of the surprise nature of the attack. This policy resulted in the sinking of the British liner the *Lusitania* in 1915.

The sinking of the giant English steamship is a success. With joyful pride we contemplate this latest deed of our Navy. It will not be the last.

A report of the sinking of the Lusitania *in a German newspaper.*

A German submarine fired a single torpedo at the liner without warning and it sank in 18 minutes, killing over 1,000 passengers, including 128 Americans. The Germans, who believed the liner was carrying weapons, saw it as a great victory, but it offended many neutral countries, especially the Americans who protested against the German action. Britain made the most of the event in the propaganda war, portraying the Germans as murderers of innocent people. Although the British propaganda failed to bring the USA into the war, it managed to cover up other awkward questions being asked, such as whether the *Lusitania* was carrying explosives.

An artist's impression of the sinking of the Lusitania, 1915.

Renewal of unrestricted submarine warfare, 1917

The Germans called off unrestricted submarine warfare in 1915 because of protests from neutral countries. On 31 May 1916 the only major sea battle of the war took place off Jutland in the North Sea. The German Admiral Scheer tried to split the British fleet in an attempt to weaken it but he was drawn into a trap. In the battle the Germans lost 11 ships, the British 14. The Germans proved to have better armoured ships and more reliable weapons, but they were forced to return to harbour. The British claimed a victory because the German navy remained in port for the remainder of the war and mutinied when they were ordered out to sea in 1918. The failure of their fleet to break the blockade at Jutland led to the Germans resuming unrestricted submarine warfare on 1 February 1917.

The Germans now had far more U-boats available and they were certain that they could starve Britain into defeat. They were nearly successful. In April 1917, Admiral Jellicoe claimed that there was only six weeks food supply left in Britain. In January 1917, Allied losses at sea amounted to 386,000 tons. After the German decision to resume unrestricted submarine warfare, this rose to 881,000 tons in April. If losses had continued at this rate, it would have brought the Germans victory. Measures had to be taken to maintain essential food supplies that Britain needed to avoid starvation.

Source M

A German cartoon showing Britain in its 'Splendid Isolation'.

Things to do

1 How were people living in Britain affected directly by the fighting in the First World War?

2 How successful was the German U-boat campaign against Britain?

3 List the methods used by Britain against the U-boat.

4 'The German U-boat campaign was very successful and nearly won the war.' 'The German U-boat campaign was a mistake which helped lose the war.' Explain which of these two interpretations you think is more accurate.

Defeat of the U-boats

The most effective action taken by the British government against the U-boats was the introduction of armed convoys in April 1917. This meant that merchant ships travelled in groups across the Atlantic and were guarded by warships which had depth charges. This made it far more difficult for the U-boats to attack and put the U-boats in greater danger. Other ships, called Q ships, were camouflaged and disguised to confuse the U-boats. The mining and placing of submarine nets and floodlights in the Dover Straits prevented the U-boats from using the Channel and forced them to waste fuel by going around the coast of Scotland. There were also attempts to mine other waters around Britain to make things more difficult for the submarines.

These methods were successful. Convoys ensured that far more supply ships were reaching Britain and more U-boats were being destroyed. The most effective weapon against the U-boat in 1917 was the mine, which was responsible for the destruction of 20 U-boats. Surface patrols destroyed 16 U-boats and 6 Q ships. In 1918 convoy escorts and surface ships destroyed 34 U-boats and mines destroyed 18. In 1917 and 1918, 132 U-boats were destroyed, and although construction just about kept up with the losses, unrestricted submarine warfare was failing. The British were now building more merchant ships than they were losing and, though rationing was introduced in 1918 (see page 28), food supplies were never again as low as at the beginning of 1917. Germany's unrestricted submarine warfare damaged much of America's shipping and led directly to the USA entering the war on 6 April 1917. The extra help given by the Americans in providing escort ships for convoys and soldiers for the Western Front contributed to the Allied victory in 1918.

A German cartoon showing a couple nursing their 'baby' U-boat.

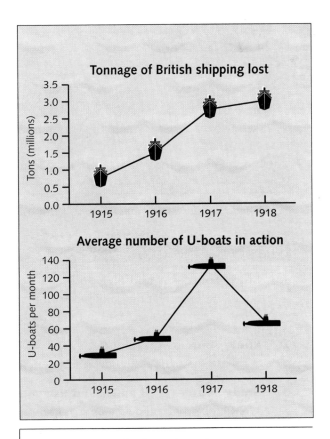

British losses and U-boats in action.

Exam-type Assessment
Conflict in the Modern World

This exercise is based on the sort of questions you could be asked on Paper 1 of your examination.

Source A

Our rations came in bags of ten. No water was brought but the ice in the shell holes was melted to obtain water. We used the water for tea for several days until one chap noticed a pair of boots sticking out and discovered they were attached to a body. We generally managed to keep warm by sleeping close together and sharing blankets. The cold however was far preferable to the mud.

A report from the Somme battlefield in 1916 by Sergeant Simon, a British soldier on the Western Front.

Source B

I want to go home, I want to go home,
I don't want to go in the trenches no more,
Where whizzbangs and shrapnel they whistle and roar.
Take me over the sea, where the German can't get
  at me;
Oh my, I don't want to die, I want to go home.

A popular soldier's song from the First World War.

Source C

12 September 1916
Tried out all the polo ponies to see if any of them would play. Played the piano and sang and played bridge until 1.15 am.

13 September 1916
Played two chukkas of polo in the afternoon.

14 September 1916
Presented some medals to soldiers at 10 am. Watched football match in afternoon.

15 September 1916
Too wet for polo; after tea we had a staff ride near camp for all the officers.

From the diaries of Brigadier-General Lucas, (a British officer on the Western Front).

Questions

1   Study Sources A and B.
Source B states that the soldiers 'want to go home'.
What reasons are suggested in the two sources to explain this?   *(4 marks)*

2   Study Sources A, B and C.
What are the main differences between Source C and the other two sources?   *(4 marks)*

3   Study Sources A, B and C and use your own knowledge.
What problems would face an historian using these three sources as evidence of the condition of British soldiers during the battle of the Somme, July to November 1916?   *(10 marks)*

Chapter 2

Conflict in the Modern World, 1919–63

The Treaty of Versailles failed in its aim of preventing future war. The USA withdrew from Europe, Britain felt that Germany had been treated too harshly at Versailles, while the French felt that Germany should have been punished far more severely. Germany recovered under Hitler in the 1930s and, encouraged by Britain's policy of appeasement, Hitler managed to extend Germany's frontiers. But his aims were not limited to overcoming the grievances of Versailles and his aggressive policies in Czechoslovakia and Poland led to the outbreak of the Second World War in 1939.

Technological improvements changed the nature of warfare. The use of aircraft and tanks in Hitler's blitzkrieg attacks led to speedy German victories in the west in 1940. Britain stood alone but firm, under the leadership of Winston Churchill, against Hitler. The RAF won the Battle of Britain and German bombing of British cities failed to bring about surrender. The Japanese attack on the US naval base at Pearl Harbor in 1941 led to the USA joining the war against Germany. America helped Britain to overcome the U-boats in the Atlantic and joined the British in the intensive bombing campaigns on German cities which helped to defeat Germany in 1945. The use of a new and more powerful weapon, the atom bomb, led to the surrender of Japan later in the same year.

After the Second World War, there followed a new war, the Cold War, which was a war of words between the two new superpowers, the communist Soviet Union and the capitalist USA. The development of nuclear weapons meant that each crisis between the superpowers could involve the destruction of the world and led to civilian protests against nuclear weapons. The nearest the superpowers came to war was the Cuban Crisis of 1962, but its peaceful solution led to an improvement in relations between the USA and the Soviet Union.

This is a Paper 1 topic and you will be required to answer a number of structured questions on it. These will test your knowledge of change in the nature of conflict throughout Units 1 to 8.

Origins of Conflict

Events leading up to the Second World War c.1919–39

The Treaty of Versailles caused resentment in Germany and a desire to gain revenge for the way the country was treated. When Hitler took power in the 1930s he restored the German military and took advantage of the goodwill and fear of war that existed in Europe to expand Germany's boundaries. By 1939 his aggressive foreign policy led to the outbreak of the Second World War.

4.1 How successful was Hitler in challenging and exploiting the Versailles Treaty?

The Treaty of Versailles

After the devastation of their territory in the First World War, the French not only wanted revenge, they also wanted to weaken Germany so that it would never be able to attack France again. Clemenceau, the French Prime Minister, wanted to make Germany pay for the damage of the war and to reduce its army, industry and trade so that it could never recover its former strength. Lloyd George, the British Prime Minister, and Woodrow Wilson, the American President, used their influence to modify the demands of the French. The result was a treaty which punished Germany, but not to the extent that Clemenceau hoped (see page 120).

Germany had no say in making the treaty and it was forced to admit that it had caused the war. This was total humiliation, which was used by Hitler in the 1930s to win the support of the German people for his aggressive foreign policy. Germany was also forced to give up some of its territory and restrictions were placed on its military forces. These terms were much tougher than the Germans had expected.

PEACE AND FUTURE CANNON FODDER

The Tiger: "Curious! I seem to hear a child weeping!"

This British cartoon shows the French Prime Minister, Clemenceau, who was nicknamed the 'Tiger', and the leaders of Britain, Italy and the USA in May 1919.

What a use could be made of the Treaty of Versailles! Each one of the points of that treaty could be branded in the minds and hearts of the German people until sixty million men and women find their souls aflame with a feeling of anger and shame; they will answer with a common cry: 'We will have arms again.'

Extract from Hitler's **Mein Kampf.**

They had hoped peace would be along the lines of Wilson's Fourteen Points calling for general disarmament and countries to be divided according to nationality.

In 1921 reparations (war damages) were fixed at £6,600 million, which the Germans said was too high, as their economy was in ruins. Germany was also refused entry to the League of Nations, a new body set up to solve future disputes peacefully. This convinced the German people that part of the League's purpose was to keep them in check.

Hitler's aims

While he was in prison in 1924 after an unsuccessful attempt to lead a rising in Munich (see page 128), Hitler began writing *Mein Kampf*, in which he set out his aims for the future. He said that he wanted:

1 To rearm Germany and recover its lost territories.
2 To unite all German-speaking people under his control.
3 To expand in the East to gain *lebensraum* (living space) for the German people.

To achieve all these aims Hitler argued it would be necessary to:

- Destroy the power of France.
- Win the friendship of Italy.
- Become an ally of Britain – by agreeing on control of colonies they disputed.

Hitler's foreign policy

Although relations between Germany and other European powers improved in the 1920s, and Germany was allowed to join the League of Nations in 1926, the effects of the Wall Street Crash in the USA caused economic difficulties across Europe. Germany suffered too. In 1933 the Germans turned to Adolf Hitler in an attempt to solve their problems. Now he had a chance to put his policies into action.

German rearmament

Hitler withdrew Germany from the World Disarmament Conference in 1933 on the grounds that no other power was prepared to disarm. He claimed that Germany wanted peace and was prepared to disarm completely if its neighbours did the same. At the same time he withdrew Germany from the League of Nations. Germany was militarily very weak and Hitler could not risk opposition. There was none. He started the build-up of the German army by introducing conscription in 1935, justifying it on the grounds that other countries were increasing their arms, so Germany had to be strong enough to defend itself. This was against the Treaty of Versailles, but no power was prepared to do anything to stop it. Britain even supported Germany's right to rearm by signing a naval agreement with Hitler in 1935, allowing the Germans to build a fleet, as long as it was no bigger than 35 per cent of the British fleet. The British attitude was that if there was to be no general agreement on disarmament, then it was necessary to get an agreement in the one area that mattered to Britain – the navy.

Origins of Conflict

The Saar Plebiscite, 1935

The industrial area around the Saar was removed from Germany by the Treaty of Versailles and put under the control of the League of Nations. A plebiscite among the German people was to be held after 15 years to decide whether it should be returned to Germany. In January 1935 90 per cent of the people voted in favour of returning to Germany. The result was never in doubt, but the Nazi Party celebrated it as a great victory. They presented it as the first of the injustices of Versailles to be removed.

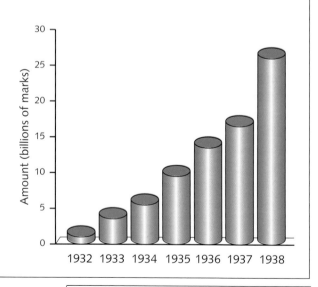

German spending on armaments in the period 1932–38.

The re-militarisation of the Rhineland, 1936

The Rhineland, the area of Germany which bordered France, was made a de-militarised zone under the Treaty of Versailles. It was still part of Germany, but the Germans were not allowed to station troops or weapons there. This was to prevent any sudden, surprise attack on France. On 7 March 1936 Hitler ordered his troops to march into the Rhineland. As this was clearly against the Treaty of Versailles Hitler feared that Britain and France would try to stop him. But nothing was done, so Hitler had his way. This action was popular with Germans and encouraged Hitler to continue pursuing his policies.

Was the Rhineland a missed opportunity?

The re-militarisation of the Rhineland is often referred to as having been the last chance to oppose Hitler without going to war. Germany's armies were too weak to take on France in 1936 and Hitler realised that he had taken a chance (see Source E). So, why was he not resisted? France had the power to drive the German army out of the Rhineland but would not act without the support of Britain. The British government did not think that Hitler was doing anything wrong – he was only 'marching into his own backyard' – so were not prepared to go to war to stop him. The French and British were more worried that Mussolini's Italian army had invaded Abyssinia and the League of Nations had done little to stop him. Hitler noticed the reluctance of the League to act against Mussolini and correctly calculated that no action would be taken against Germany.

The League of Nations condemned Hitler's action but did nothing about it. Hitler offered to make a peace treaty that would last for 25 years. This was his way of calming those countries that wanted peace, at the same time as he was getting his way. His diplomacy had triumphed. The British government believed that the Treaty of Versailles had been unfair and that the righting of wrongs would help keep the peace with Germany in the future.

Source D

German troops marching into the Rhineland.

Preparation for *Anschluss*, 1934–38

The joining together of Austria and Germany (*Anschluss*) was forbidden by the Treaty of Versailles. But it was important to Hitler who wanted to unite all German-speaking people in one country. He first tried to take control of Austria in 1934 when members of the Austrian Nazi Party murdered the Chancellor of Austria. The Nazis tried to take over the government but were prevented by the future Chancellor, Schuschnigg, and the opposition of the dictator of Italy, Mussolini. Mussolini's threats forced the Nazis to back down and prevented Hitler from interfering.

Source E

Even later, when Hitler was waging war against almost the entire world, he always termed the re-militarisation of the Rhineland the most daring of all his undertakings. 'We had no army worth mentioning. If the French had taken any action, we would have been easily defeated; our resistance would have been over in a few days.'

Albert Speer writing about how Hitler saw the re-occupation of the Rhineland by the German army.

Things to do

1 What had been the aims of the French at the Treaty of Versailles?

2 Why did they not fully achieve these aims?

3 Why did Britain and France not stop German rearmament in the 1930s?

4 Do you agree that the failure to stop Hitler re-militarising the Rhineland was a mistake?

Origins of Conflict

When the Spanish Civil War broke out in 1936 Hitler and Mussolini supported the Spanish fascist General Franco, despite having signed a treaty not to interfere. Hitler used the war to give his new forces experience of fighting – they practised dive-bombing techniques and tank formations in Spain – and to keep Mussolini occupied so that he would not oppose *Anschluss*. The Civil War brought Italy and Germany together in 1936 and they signed the Rome-Berlin Axis, which was followed by the Anti-Comintern Pact, signed by Germany, Italy and Japan, to prevent the spread of communism. The stage was set for Hitler's next step.

The annexation of Austria (Anschluss), 1938

In 1938 Hitler ordered the Austrian Nazi Party to begin a campaign in Austria for union with Germany. Riots and demonstrations followed. The Austrian Chancellor 'Schuschnigg' tried to arrange a plebiscite among the Austrian people on the union with Germany. Hitler moved German troops to the border to prevent this from taking place. Schuschnigg resigned and Seyss-Inquart, a leading Nazi whom Schuschnigg had been forced to put in charge of the Austrian police, invited the Germans into Austria to restore order. This they did, imprisoning over 80,000 opponents of Hitler. Hitler then entered Austria in triumph and union with Germany was established on 14 March 1938. A plebiscite was held and 99.75 per cent agreed with the Anschluss.

Hitler's success was another victory for his diplomacy. Mussolini had not interfered because of the Rome-Berlin Axis and there was no opposition from Britain and France who were reluctant to take any action against Hitler which might cause war. Though the plebiscite result was influenced by Nazi pressure, many Austrians greeted the union with support. They wanted to be a part of the glory and success of Hitler's Third Reich.

Anschluss was a great success for Hitler. He now looked towards Czechoslovakia as his next target, although he told the leaders of Britain and France that he had no interest in winning land in Czechoslovakia.

Source F

The reunion of Germany and Austria is our life task, to be carried out by every means possible at our disposal.

This is what Hitler said in Mein Kampf.

Source G

Hitler finally presented an ultimatum, and threatened to march into Austria if his demands were not met. When Schuschnigg left the study to take advice, Hitler could be heard shouting behind the open door: 'General Keitel. Where is General Keitel? Tell him to come here at once.' (Keitel was Chief of the German High Command). Keitel came hurrying up. He told us later that when he presented himself and asked for orders, Hitler grinned and said: 'There are no orders. I just wanted you here.'

Von Papen, the German ambassador in Vienna, describes an incident during the negotiations between Hitler and Schuschnigg over the plebiscite in 1938.

Source H

I give you my word of honour that Czechoslovakia has nothing to fear from the Reich.

Hitler speaking to Chamberlain after the Anschluss.

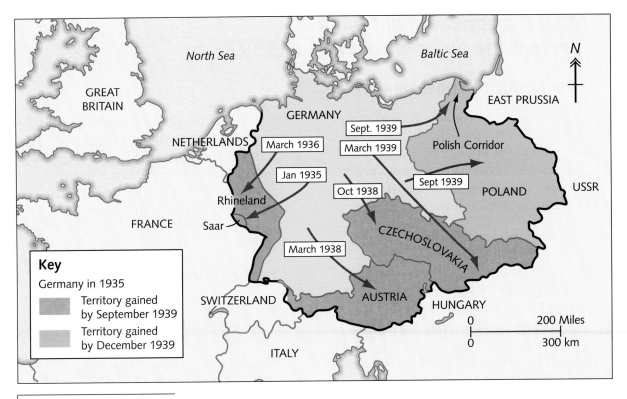

North Sea

Baltic Sea

N

GREAT BRITAIN

GERMANY

EAST PRUSSIA

NETHERLANDS

Sept. 1939

March 1939

Polish Corridor

March 1936

Jan 1935

Sept 1939

POLAND

USSR

Rhineland

Oct 1938

FRANCE

Saar

CZECHOSLOVAKIA

March 1938

Key

Germany in 1935

Territory gained by September 1939

Territory gained by December 1939

SWITZERLAND

AUSTRIA

HUNGARY

0   200 Miles

0   300 km

ITALY

Hitler's territorial gains, 1935–39.

Things to do

1   How did Hitler make use of the Spanish Civil War?

2   Read Source G. Why do you think Hitler called Keitel? What does it tell us about his methods of negotiating?

3   Do the facts suggest that Source I is a reliable portrayal of the German entry into Vienna?

Source I

The people of Vienna welcome the arrival of German troops in March 1938.

Why did appeasement fail to prevent the outbreak of war in 1939?

The policy of appeasement

When Neville Chamberlain became Prime Minister in 1937, the policy of appeasement continued to be Britain's main approach to the problem of Germany. Some historians think this was the main reason why the Second World War was not prevented.

Chamberlain's approach was to find out what Hitler wanted and show him that if his claims were reasonable, they could be discussed. Chamberlain believed that Germany had genuine grievances under the Treaty of Versailles and that if these could be solved by negotiation, Hitler would live in peace with the rest of the world. The success of appeasement, however, depended on Hitler's aims being limited and on his sincerity – he had to be trusted. France supported appeasement after 1937. The French felt safe behind their Maginot Line, a stretch of fortifications running along their border (see page 48).

There was a lot of support for appeasement in Britain: people wanted to avoid another war like the First World War with its massive loss of life and damage. Also Britain had not prepared itself for a war by rearming and was in no position to resist Hitler. Some British politicians, fearing the communist Soviet Union, saw a strong Germany as a barrier to communist expansion in Europe. There had been no opposition to the occupation of the Rhineland and the *Anschluss*. The League of Nations had failed, so Chamberlain decided to use personal diplomacy instead. He dealt directly with Hitler in an attempt to solve disputes and keep the peace.

Czechoslovakia, 1938

Czechoslovakia had an army of 34 divisions, strong mountain defences in the Sudetenland, the valuable Skoda armaments works, deposits of coal and lignite and defence agreements with Russia and France. Hitler wanted Czechoslovakia as part of his policy of *lebensraum* (living space), but he also detested the country as a democracy and a reminder of the hated peace settlement of 1919. Czechoslovakia had been formed in 1919 and its population was made up of Czechs, Slovaks and 3 million German-speakers from the old Austria-Hungary empire. Most of the German-speakers lived in the Sudetenland, and it was they who gave Hitler the excuse he needed to invade Czechoslovakia.

The leader of the Czech Nazi Party, Konrad Henlein, was urged by Hitler to demand that the Czech government make concessions to the Sudeten Germans. Henlein kept the pressure on the Czechs by asking for more and more concessions. In April 1938, German troops began massing on the Czech border. Czechoslovakia's President, Benes, mobilised his troops to resist the Germans. Britain and France wanted to avoid war so they persuaded Benes to make further concessions to the Sudetens. It became clear that Hitler would never be satisfied with improved rights for the Sudeten Germans, what he wanted was to make the Sudetenland part of Germany.

Source J

Do not misunderstand me when the government says that it is looking to our defences. I give you my word that there will be no great rearmament.

The British Prime Minister, Stanley Baldwin, in an election speech, November 1935.

Appeasement in action

On 12 September 1938 Hitler told the Sudeten Germans that he would support them. So the Sudeten Nazis began rioting but were crushed by the Czech government. On 15 September Chamberlain met Hitler at Berchtesgaden to discuss his demands. Chamberlain then persuaded the Czechs to agree to transfer to Germany those parts of the Sudetenland where the majority of the population was German. On 22 September Chamberlain met Hitler at Godesberg and informed him of the agreement. However, Hitler told Chamberlain that he wanted the whole of the Sudetenland and threatened to go to war. Chamberlain returned to Britain and prepared for war. Trenches were dug for protection from air raids, gas masks were distributed and the armed forces were put on stand-by. However, war was avoided when Mussolini persuaded Hitler to attend a four-power conference at Munich on 29 September.

Source K

Hitler said that the aim of German foreign policy was to defend Germany and to enlarge it. For the improvement of our position our first objective must be to overthrow Czechoslovakia and Austria. Hitler believed that Britain and France had already written off the Czechs.

From the Hossbach Memorandum, *notes of a secret meeting between Hitler and the commanders of his armed forces in November 1937.*

The Munich Conference, September 1938

This conference was attended by four leaders: Hitler for Germany, Mussolini for Italy, Chamberlain for Britain and Daladier for France. The Soviet Union and Czechoslovakia were not invited. It was agreed at the conference that the Sudetenland would become part of Germany immediately. The Czechs were then forced by Britain and France to accept this and German armies occupied the Sudetenland on 1 October. Peace had been obtained, Hitler had gained the Sudetenland. On the day after the Munich Agreement Chamberlain signed a separate agreement with Hitler in which the two countries promised to consult in the event of any problems and never to go to war against each other. Chamberlain returned to Britain a hero. He had his critics, such as Churchill, but he had achieved what most people wanted: he had kept peace in Europe.

A cartoon of the time, entitled 'Still hope', shows Chamberlain on his way to Munich to negotiate a settlement.

The occupation of Czechoslovakia, March 1939

Czechoslovakia had lost its strong defensive system at Munich. Moreover, the loss of the Sudeten Germans had stirred other nationalities in Czechoslovakia to demand a return to their nation states. In October 1938 Poland gained part of Czechoslovakia, as did Hungary in November. In 1939 the Slovaks were demanding more rights. The new Czech President, Hacha, appealed to Hitler for help and in the end had no choice but to invite the Germans into Czechoslovakia. On 15 March 1939 Hitler marched into Prague, the Czech capital. The state of Czechoslovakia had come to an end.

This was also the end of appeasement. The occupation of Czechoslovakia by the Germans was not opposed by Britain or France because the Germans had been invited in by the Czech government. Even so the occupation changed Chamberlain's attitude towards Hitler. Hitler could not justify the takeover by claiming that the people were German-speaking or that he was righting a wrong of the Treaty of Versailles. Hitler had broken the promise he made to Chamberlain in 1938 and was now seen as an aggressor whose aims were not limited, and who would continue to take more and more territory until he was stopped. Europe now had to take seriously Hitler's ideas on the supremacy of the Aryan race, *lebensraum* and world domination as set out in *Mein Kampf*.

Britain began building up its arms after the Munich settlement. After the occupation of Czechoslovakia the British government brought in conscription, for the first time ever in peacetime. After occupying Prague Hitler seized the province of Memel, which was mainly inhabited by Germans, from Lithuania. The British government expected Poland to be Hitler's next target. Poland occupied land (the Polish Corridor) which cut off East Prussia from the rest of Germany and there were German-speaking people living in Danzig, which had been taken from Germany at Versailles. In April 1939, Britain and France promised to help Poland if it was attacked by Germany. The problem was they were not in a position to defend Poland against Germany. Only the Soviet Union could do this.

Things to do

1 What was appeasement?

2 Some historians have criticised the Soviet Union for signing the Nazi-Soviet Pact. Source N defends the signing. Do you agree with the interpretation given in Source N? Explain your answer.

3 Do you think Hitler intended to remain on good terms with the Soviet Union after 1939? Explain your answer.

Source M

German troops entering Prague in March 1939.

The Nazi-Soviet Pact, 1939

Britain and the Soviet Union (USSR) talked of forming an alliance throughout the summer of 1939. The British delayed things as much as possible. Poland was as much afraid of an invasion from the USSR as it was from Germany, so it was not prepared to accept help from the Soviets. Hitler's policy of *lebensraum* involved conquering territory east of Germany, including the USSR. Because of his hatred of communism he would almost certainly attack the USSR. So, the world was shocked when, on 23 August 1939, the two countries signed the Nazi-Soviet Pact.

The Nazi-Soviet Pact brought war closer. Both countries agreed not to attack each other and through a series of secret clauses they divided Poland between them. Germany was to attack Poland from the west, the USSR to attack from the east. Hitler was sure Britain and France would not carry out their promise to Poland – why should they, they had backed down over Czech-oslovakia? He felt free to attack Poland.

Why did the USSR sign the Pact? Their leader, Stalin, appeared to run out of patience with Britain's failure to sign an agreement with them. He had been annoyed when left out of the discussions at Munich and was suspicious that Britain and France were trying to direct Hitler's attention to the east and away from the west.

The attack on Poland, 1 September 1939

The German army invaded Poland on 1 September 1939. Chamberlain tried to get them to withdraw and hold a peace conference. This failed and on 3 September Britain declared war on Germany, followed shortly after by France.

Source N

The Anglo-French plan was to direct Germany towards the east and involve Hitler in conflict with the Soviet Union. Munich and the negotiations of 1939 provided clear proof of the unwillingness of the British and French governments to form an anti-Hitler alliance. The treaty with Germany was a step which the USSR was forced to take in the difficult situation that had come about in the summer of 1939. The Soviet government realised Hitler's aims and understood that the treaty would only bring a breathing space which would give them time to carry through the political and military measures needed in order to ensure the country's security.

A Soviet historian writing in 1969 about the Nazi-Soviet Pact.

Summary

1919	Treaty of Versailles.
1933	Hitler takes power.
1934	Germany begins to rearm.
1935	The Saar Plebiscite.
	Mussolini invades Abyssinia.
1936	Re-militarisation of the Rhineland.
	Spanish Civil War.
	Rome-Berlin Axis.
1938	*Anschluss*.
	Munich Agreement.
1939	Invasion of Czechoslovakia.
	Nazi-Soviet Pact.
	Invasion of Poland.

Origins of Conflict

The Changing Nature of Warfare

The Second World War, 1939–45. Continuity or change?

When Germany attacked France in 1940 it was again a surprise attack through Belgium, but this time it was successful because of improved technology and tactics. Attacks on Britain by air and using U-boats followed in 1940. The entry of Japan into the war in 1941 made it more of a world war; the use of the atom bomb to bring about Japan's defeat and surrender in 1945 led to an uneasy world after the war.

5.1 How did technological developments change the nature of warfare in the period 1939–45?

The Phoney War, 1939–40

The German attack on Poland from the west and the Soviet attack from the east on 17 September 1939 were successful. By the end of September, Poland had been defeated and ceased to exist as a state. Britain and France had been unable to help the Poles. From the end of September to April the following year little progress was made in the war in the west. This became known as the Phoney War (pretend war) in Britain and as the *Sitzkrieg* (sitting war) in Germany.

The Phoney War appears to have been an attempt by Hitler to push Britain and other West European powers into backing down over Poland, as they had backed down at Munich in 1938. Hitler's strategy for fighting a war was based on a series of quick campaigns. Germany did not have the depth of resources for a long, drawn-out war.

Britain and France prepared for war during this period and a British force was sent to France to support the French. But the military preparations were half-hearted. The French

Source A

German tanks rest during the invasion of France.

felt safe from attack by the Germans because of the Maginot Line, a line of fortifications they had built in the 1930s, all along the border with Germany, stretching from Belgium to Switzerland. The French believed it was impossible for any invading army to break through this series of forts, which were linked by underground tunnels.

Conflict in the Modern World, 1919–63

Blitzkrieg in the West, 1940

The waiting in the West ended in April 1940 when Hitler invaded Norway and Denmark, conquering both countries within a few days. Britain sent a force to help, but this failed and led to the resignation of Neville Chamberlain as Prime Minister. He was replaced by the main opponent of appeasement, Winston Churchill, on 10 May 1940. On the same day Hitler launched his main attack on the West, with Belgium, Holland and France being attacked at the same time. This was a quick, surprise attack, called a *Blitzkrieg* (lightning war).

A *Blitzkrieg* depends on speed and surprise for its success. Hitler had no more forces than the Allies, he just used them better. Artillery attacks and dive bombers were used to weaken enemy resistance, then columns of tanks and armoured cars attacked at the weakest points in the Allied defences to make a breakthrough. Paratroops were sent in behind the lines to seize strategic points. Then the infantry advanced to complete the breakthrough. This was a war of movement, not a static war, like that of 1914-18.

The Germans by-passed the Maginot Line by attacking through the forests of the Ardennes in Southern Belgium, which the French thought was impossible to do. The German forces bombed the Dutch port of Rotterdam. Resistance in Belgium lasted until 28 May. The Germans swept into France through the heavily forested Ardennes, by-passing the Maginot Line and taking the French by surprise. Soon British and French forces were in retreat. 330,000 British troops were rescued from the beaches of Dunkirk, leaving the French to their fate. Paris fell on 14 June and the French surrendered on 22 June. Germany occupied the north of France leaving a puppet French government under Marshal Pétain to rule the rest of France from its new capital, Vichy. Britain was left alone against Germany.

Things to do

1   Compare the Schlieffen Plan of 1914 with the Blitzkrieg offensive of 1940.

2   Why did the Germans succeed in 1940?

3   Which countries were involved in 1940 and not in 1914?

4   Why was the Maginot Line useless?

5   How did the Nazi-Soviet Pact help the Germans in 1940?

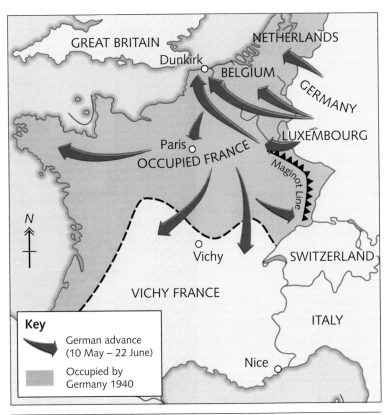

The path of the German Blitzkrieg in 1940.

Key
German advance (10 May – 22 June)
Occupied by Germany 1940

The Changing Nature of Warfare

The Blitz, September 1940 to May 1941

After defeating France, Hitler planned to invade Britain. The plan was known as Operation Sealion. To do this the German airforce (*Luftwaffe*) needed to control the skies above Britain. In the summer of 1940 the *Luftwaffe* attacked British airfields, ports and radar stations in an attempt to gain superiority in the air. Britain was defended tenaciously by its airforce, the RAF, but came very close to defeat. This was the Battle of Britain. It was a change of tactics by the Germans that saved the country from defeat in the air. Hitler decided to bomb some of Britain's most vital cities. On 7 September 1940 the first German bombing attack on Britain was launched at night against London. This marked the end of the Battle of Britain and the beginning of the Blitz, the bombing of British cities.

Hitler's change of tactics was partly in response to British bombing raids on Berlin, but the main purpose was to try to break the morale of the British people and force Churchill to sue for peace. Though the *Luftwaffe* had failed to defeat the RAF and Operation Sealion was called off, the bombing attacks on major cities continued throughout the winter causing much damage. Over a period of 77 days London was bombed every night except one. Other cities to be bombed included Bristol, Liverpool, Plymouth, Southampton, Manchester Birmingham, Coventry and Glasgow – all of them ports or industrial centres.

The bombing of Coventry in November 1940 destroyed industrial targets, such as motor-works and aero-engine factories. It also destroyed the city's Cathedral, the destruction of which became a symbol of German ruthlessness and was used by the British in the propaganda war. The raid lasted 10 hours, a third of the city was destroyed and 4,000 people were killed. The most remarkable effect of the raid was that industrial production in Coventry rose following the attack.

By the time the Blitz ended in the summer of 1941 about 43,000 people had been killed and 2 million were homeless. Hitler apparently believed that Britain had been defeated because in June 1941 he began to carry out his long-planned search for *lebensraum* (space) by breaking the Nazi-Soviet Pact of 1939 and attacking the USSR.

Source B

The ruins of Coventry Cathedral after the German bombing of the city in 1940.

The bombing of Germany

The first British bombing attacks on Germany took place in 1940 when Britain stood alone against Germany, her army defeated, and with no other way to strike at the Germans. The attacks began by targeting strategic areas, but by 1942 British aircraft were bombing entire cities in an attempt to break Germany's military power and its people's morale. The first 'Thousand Bomber' raid on Cologne in May 1942 killed about 400 Germans. British Bomber Command, led by Air Chief Marshal Sir Arthur 'Bomber' Harris, continued the bombing offensive in 1943, with 43 raids on the industrial Ruhr Basin, 33 on Hamburg and 16 on Berlin.

Because the bombing raids were at night it was impossible to hit the targets accurately and many civilian areas were damaged by mistake. The Germans used this in the propaganda war. Worse for Bomber Command was the number of planes being lost in the attacks. The attacks were seen as important in helping Britain's new ally, the USSR, and raising people's morale in Britain. German industry and transport were severely damaged by the bombings: war production did rise until July 1944, but how much greater would it have been without the bombings?

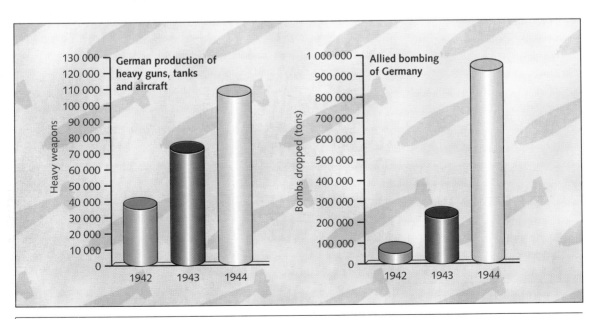

A comparison of Germany's production of weapons with the amount of bombs dropped on Germany.

Victory in the air

American bombing raids on Germany began in August 1942. Unlike the British, the Americans bombed during the day, which made the attacks more accurate, but raised the number of aircraft and crew lost. The breakthrough in the bombing raids came with the development of heavy precision bombing techniques in 1944. By late 1944 Britain and the USA controlled the air above Germany and made devastating attacks on roads, railways and industry, which contributed to the final defeat of Germany.

In February 1945, three months before the end of the war, British aircraft destroyed the city of Dresden with incendiary bombs, killing 25,000 civilians. Were these attacks on civilians justified? Even Churchill described the attacks on Dresden as 'mere acts of terror and wanton destruction'. By the end of the war about 600,000 German civilians had been killed in air raids. However, German morale did not break until the final collapse of Germany in 1945, so what part did the bombing attacks play in the final victory?

Things to do

1 Explain the meaning of the cartoon in Source C.

2 Compare the damage in Source B with that in Source D.

3 What does the graph on page 51 tell us about industrial production in Germany during the bombing raids?

4 Does this mean the bombing raids were pointless?

5 What are the arguments for and against the bombing of civilians?

Bonn	83%
Bochum (Ruhr)	83
Bremerhaven	79
Hamburg	75
Kiel	69
Kassell	69
Hagen (Ruhr)	67
Munster	65
Dusseldorf	64
Mainz	61
Cologne	61
Hanover	60
Bremen	60
Dresden	59
Aachen	59
Koblenz	58
Emden	56
Dortmund	54
Munich	54
Stettin	53
Frankfurt	52
Nuremburg	51
Essen	50

Percentage of German cities destroyed by Allied air attacks.

Source D

Dresden after being bombed by the British, February 1945.

The Battle of the Atlantic

In the First World War the Germans had almost defeated the British by using U-boats to destroy merchant shipping carrying supplies to Britain. Within a few hours of the Second World War breaking out, a British passenger liner *Athenia* was sunk by a U-boat. The Germans believed that the U-boats would have more success in 1939 than they had in 1917. The aim was to cut off Britain's supplies of food, oil and raw materials from overseas. The British countered this by organising merchant ships into convoys and using warships to defend them. But after the Germans occupied France they were free to use French Atlantic ports as bases from which their submarines attacked British ships. Britain simply did not have enough warships to protect all its merchant ships from attack. The development of sonic techniques, which could detect U-boats under water, was an advantage to the British, but the German tactic of hunting convoys in groups of up to 40 U-boats, known as 'wolf packs', was successful in the first years of the war. The 'wolf packs' attacked on the surface and at night so they could not be detected by ASDIC.

When America entered the war in December 1941 (see page 55) the fight against the U-boats changed. The USA provided warship escorts for convoys, and radar, which was invented in 1935, was used to detect submarines on the surface. By 1943 Britain had more warships and was able to give support to every convoy of its merchant ships. When U-boats were detected, some of the escort warships broke away from the convoy to hunt them. Aircraft were used more to spot U-boats and destroy them using **depth charges**. By 1943 aircraft using radar could detect enemy submarines, even in the worst weather. In 1943 the Allies for the first time were building more new ships than were being destroyed by the U-boats.

These charts show the amount of allied shipping losses and corresponding losses of U-boats in 1939–45.

(see page 55)

Source E

Britain's ability to maintain her supply lines is the decisive factor for the outcome of the war.

Admiral Raeder, Chief of German Naval Staff, speaking in 1940.

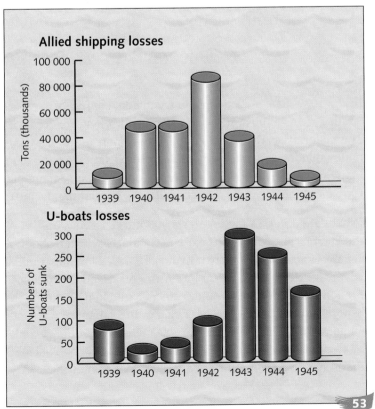

Allied shipping losses

U-boats losses

The Changing Nature of Warfare

Japan and the war

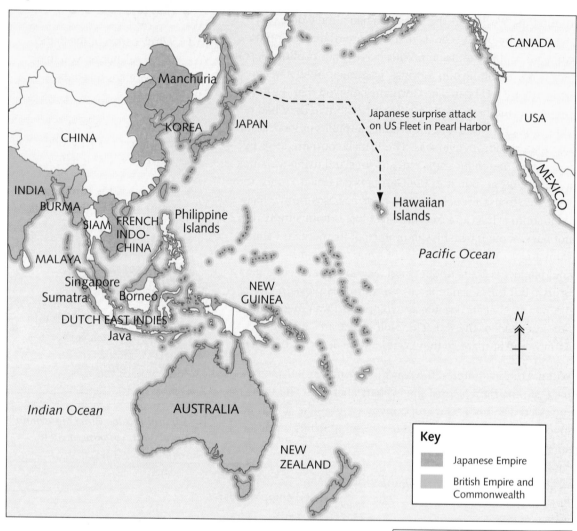

The Far East, showing the location of Pearl Harbor.

In the 1930s Japan used force to try to take control of South East Asia. Its aim was to make itself self-sufficient in raw materials so that it did not need to import them. It was this policy that led Japan to defy the League of Nations and occupy Manchuria in 1931. In 1937 war broke out between Japan and China and the Japanese launched attacks on mainland China.

Britain and the USA had interests in South East Asia and the Pacific. The Americans were particularly worried about Japanese actions in the area. In July 1941 the Japanese, taking advantage of France's defeat by Germany, seized control of French Indo-China. The Americans responded by banning the export of oil to Japan. This was vital to the Japanese who got 80 per cent of their oil from the USA. When the military, led by General Tojo, gained power in October 1941 Japan decided that it had to do something about the opposition of the USA.

Source F

Yesterday, December 7 1941 – a date which will live in infamy – the US was deliberately attacked by the naval and air forces of the Empire of Japan.

President Roosevelt speaking about the attack on Pearl Harbor.

Pearl Harbor, 7 December 1941

At 8 am on Sunday 7 December 1941, Japanese fighter planes attacked the American Pacific fleet at its base at Pearl Harbor in Hawaii. There was no declaration of war by the Japanese. The attack destroyed or damaged 8 battleships, nearly all the aircraft, around 200, were destroyed on the ground and some 2,400 servicemen and civilians were killed. Fortunately for the Americans their aircraft carriers were at sea on manoeuvres, so they escaped the attack. The Japanese lost only 29 aircraft.

Why was the attack such a surprise for the USA? The Americans had expected an attack in the Pacific during 1941, though they thought it would be at their base in the Philippines, much closer to Japan.

On 8 December the USA and Britain declared war on Japan and three days later Hitler declared war on the USA. Churchill was delighted that he now had the strength of America on his side. In the months following Pearl Harbor, however, it was the Japanese who were successful. Within six months the Japanese had captured important American and European bases, such as Hong Kong, Singapore and the East Indies. Only after the Americans had replaced their losses at Pearl Harbor did the tide turn. After several important naval victories in 1942 the Allies slowly recovered the territories they had lost to the Japanese. By early 1945 they had taken islands within bombing range of Japan and the Japanese had been cut off from their supplies of food and raw materials.

Source G

AVENGE December 7

This poster reminded Americans of what happened at Pearl Harbor.

5.2 What was the significance of the use of nuclear weapons at Hiroshima and Nagasaki?

The defeat of Japan, 1945

By July 1945 Japan's position was hopeless. Its people and industries were suffering from shortages of food and raw materials. US planes controlled the skies and could bomb Japan's major cities at will. Even so Japan refused to surrender. Its soldiers were fanatical in their resistance, and its pilots flew *kamikaze* (suicide) missions to destroy American warships. For the Japanese military, surrender meant shame. So they would fight to the death.

The USA could try to defeat Japan in different ways. It was already trying to starve the people into surrender by blockading food supplies to Japan. But this would take time. The Americans could invade Japan, but this would involve the massive loss of American lives. In capturing the Pacific Islands resistance had been so strong that there were heavy casualties on both sides. So, how many men would it cost to take Japan itself which would be defended even more fanatically?

The USSR offered to join the Americans against Japan, but events in Europe made the USA wary that the Soviets would try to occupy parts of Japan. Trying to bomb the Japanese into surrender was another possibility. The Americans carried out a massive firebomb attack on Tokyo on 10 March 1945, killing around 100,000 civilians. Attacks on other cities followed, almost doubling the civilian deaths. Still the Japanese refused to surrender.

The atom bomb

The development of the atom bomb by the Allies offered a solution to the problem of Japanese resistance to surrender. This bomb could cause such massive damage and loss of life that the Japanese would be forced to surrender. No American lives would be lost. The new American President, Harry Truman, had a difficult decision to make. Could he bomb Japan knowing that it would kill and injure many thousands of innocent people, including women and children? The worry was that the Japanese would hold its many prisoners of war as hostages in cities that might be bombed, making it more difficult to use the bomb.

President Truman ordered the bomb to be dropped. The USSR was about to join the war on 8 August, so the Americans decided to drop the bomb before then. The target was Hiroshima. The Japanese were given a final warning and the chance to make an unconditional surrender. But they ignored it. On 6 August 1945 the *Enola Gay* arrived over Hiroshima at 8.15 am. The bomb, code-named 'little boy', was dropped.

About 80,000 were killed instantly and almost as many died later from the effects of burns or radiation. Stalin declared war on Japan on 8 August and the Soviet armies invaded Manchuria, but still the Japanese refused to surrender.

Source I

My God, what have we done?

The words of one of the pilots of the Enola Gay *after the dropping of the atom bomb on Hiroshima.*

Source H

Battle	US	Japan
Leyte	17,000	78,000
Luzon	37,000	156,000
Iwo Jima	20,000	22,000

Casualty figures in battles for the Pacific Islands.

Source J

Summary

1939	Phoney War.
1940	Fall of France.
1941	Blitz ends.
	Attack on Pearl Harbor.
1942	Bombing of Cologne.
1944	Allied air supremacy.
1945	Germany surrenders.
	Atom bomb dropped on Japanese cities.
	Japan surrenders.

Hiroshima after the bomb was dropped on it.

A second bomb was dropped, on Nagasaki on 9 August, causing 50,000 deaths, which was doubled later by the after-effects. Some of the military leaders in Japan wanted to continue the war and another bomb was ready to be dropped on 18 August. The war, however, was ended by the direct intervention of Emperor Hirohito, who broadcasted Japan's surrender on 14 August. As the Japanese regarded the Emperor as a God, they obeyed him, and there was no resistance when the Americans landed, though many Japanese army officers killed themselves and *kamikaze* pilots flew their planes into the water of Tokyo Bay.

Why was the atomic bomb used in 1945?

The use of the atom bomb in 1945 has caused much debate. Many criticise the Americans for causing such widespread destruction and death. Others think that the Americans had no choice. Today, historians continue to debate the wisdom of dropping the bomb. Some argue that Japan was close to defeat and in time would have surrendered; others say that the bomb was really dropped to show the Soviet Union how powerful the USA was. There is little doubt, however, that a possible million American casualties were saved by avoiding an invasion of Japan.

Things to do

1 Was the Japanese attack on Pearl Harbor successful?

2 List all the possible reasons for the dropping of the atom bombs on Japan in 1945.

3 Compare the damage caused by the atom bomb with that shown in Sources B and E caused by the attacks on Coventry and Dresden. Explain the reasons for the differences. How does this damage compare with that in the First World War as described in Unit 2?

The Changing Nature of Warfare

Civilian Experience of War

The Home Front in Britain, 1939–45

There was no escape from the fighting in the Second World War. The development of aircraft and bombs and knowledge of the devastating air attacks gained in the Spanish Civil War meant that civilians in Britain were in danger and Britain itself could be invaded. The government needed to protect the country and its citizens.

6.1 How did the Second World War change life in Britain in the period 1939-45?

Recruitment

The government had announced the introduction of conscription after Hitler's invasion of Czechoslovakia in March 1939. It was put into effect when Britain declared war on 3 September. All men between the age of 18 and 40 were conscripted for military service, beginning with those in their early twenties. Certain occupations, such as coalminers, firemen and doctors, were exempt. In May 1940 the Emergency Powers Act gave the government complete control over 'person and property', allowing them to direct adults to work in any part of the country.

When war broke out the government expected the country to be attacked from the air and took precautions to protect its people. Air-raid wardens were appointed, some full time, but most part-time volunteers, whose job it was to make sure the blackout was followed and to prepare people for air raids. They checked that everyone carried a gas mask to protect them against gas attacks from the air. During the Blitz wardens directed the movement of people into air-raid shelters and organised the clearing up of damage.

In May 1940 the Local Defence Volunteers, later known as the Home Guard, was formed. This was part-time, unpaid volunteer work to help protect the country against invaders. It called for men aged 17 to 65 to volunteer and on the first day of recruitment 250,000 did so.

Source A

A wartime poster calling on men to volunteer for the job of air-raid warden.

Source B

Such a force is of the highest value and importance. A country where every street and every village bristles with resolute, armed men is a country against which the tactics which destroyed the Dutch resistance would not succeed.

Winston Churchill speaking in Parliament about the Home Guard, November 1940.

They met most evenings after work and were taught how to handle weapons and what action to take if the enemy landed in Britain. Lack of weapons was the Home Guard's main problem.

Women and the war

Women were far more affected by the Second World War than they had been by the First World War. They were in much greater danger from bombing raids. Women were also affected by the evacuation of themselves and their children and by rationing. Many of them did civil defence jobs, joined the armed forces and helped to reduce food shortages by joining the Women's Land Army to work on the land.

Conscription deprived industry of many of its workers. As in the First World War, women volunteered to do the work of the men who had gone to fight. But by 1941 industry was so short of workers that unmarried women were conscripted to fill the shortage. By 1943, 57 per cent of workers were female. Many of the conscripts had little choice where they worked. New munitions factories were sometimes located in the country for security reasons, and conscripted women had to move to these areas, where they were housed in local hostels. Propaganda posters glamourised the work to make it more appealing (Source D). Actually the work was often repetitive and boring, though far more skills were required in some jobs than in the First World War. Some worked at welding, forging and building aircraft and ships, as well as many other skilled jobs previously thought impossible for women.

A poster encouraging men to volunteer for the Home Guard.

A poster advertising for women to help the war effort by working in factories.

Source E

This work the women are performing in munitions factories has to be seen to be believed. Precision engineering jobs which a few years ago would have made a skilled turner's hair stand on end are performed with deadly accuracy by girls who had no industrial experience.

Clement Attlee, the Deputy Prime Minister, writing about the work women did during the war.

Civilian Experience of War

Women in service

Source F

Each of the armed forces developed its own auxiliary force for women in the Second World War: the ATS (Auxiliary Territorial Service), the WAAF (Women's Auxiliary Air Force) and the WRNS (Women's Royal Naval Service). These forces helped the men by doing backroom jobs rather than fighting. They worked alongside men and faced the same dangers, but they did not fire the guns. They operated searchlights, filled sandbags or acted as radar controllers. The WAAF repaired the planes and helped on the airfield. Women pilots were allowed to ferry planes from the factories to the airfields, but they were not allowed to fight. Women did important work supporting the men in the front line as nurses, in the intelligence service, and others did dangerous work as spies behind enemy lines.

A poster calling for women to join the Women's Land Army.

The Women's Land Army

The food shortages caused by the German U-boat attacks on British shipping in the Atlantic (see page 53) inspired the government to launch a 'Dig for Victory' campaign. The Women's Land Army, which was formed for farm work in the First World War, was re-formed in 1939 and grew to 80,000 strong by 1944. Many travelled the country doing everyday farming jobs, such as haymaking, ploughing, harvesting and looking after the animals. By 1943 production in Britain had almost doubled.

The 'Grow your Own' campaign

Women at home also played their part in the 'Grow your Own' campaign. Farms provided staple foods, such as grain, potatoes, milk and meat, with allotments providing most of the vegetables. The campaign, encouraged by poster advertisements using the cartoon characters Potato Pete and Dr Carrot, was very successful. Window boxes and lawns, public parks and golf courses were used to grow vegetables to keep the nation fed and healthy; even the moat of the Tower of London was turned into an area for allotments.

Conflict in the Modern World, 1919–63

Things to do

1 What differences do you notice between recruitment posters used in the Second World War and those used in the First World War? Why are they different?

2 How was women's work in the Second World War the same as in the First World War? How was it different?

Rationing

To make sure everyone got a fair share of food, the government introduced rationing in January 1940. Each person had a ration book filled with coupons which they used to buy the amount of food they were entitled to each week. A points system was introduced later to give people greater choice in what they could buy. The Board of Trade also issued recipes showing people how to make healthy meals using food that was available.

At first only butter, bacon and sugar were rationed, later this was extended to include meat, tea and most basic food-stuffs, though vegetables were never rationed. Clothes were rationed from June 1941 which led to shorter hemlines and fewer buttons on clothing to save on materials. The government also encouraged people to save by mending their own clothes and to use cheaper, more basic clothes and furniture. These were identified with a utility mark so that people buying them would know they were helping the war effort.

Mending your own clothes to save on materials needed for the war was encouraged by government posters like this one.

Fuel was rationed and many people gave up using their cars so that as much fuel as possible was available for the war effort. The government also encouraged people to use less hot water so that the coal that otherwise would be used for heating the water could be used for the war.

These cartoon characters were part of the campaign to encourage people to eat healthy food.

6.2 How were civilians protected by the government?

Evacuation

The government expected from the beginning of the war that the Germans would attack Britain from the air. So it took precautions to protect its civilians from bombings and gas attacks. Children were protected by being moved (evacuated) from the likeliest targets, the cities, to the countryside where they would be safe. The first evacuation was announced on 31 August 1939, the day before Hitler invaded Poland. Many parents were reluctant to be separated from their children, but accepted they would be safer. Parents were told what the children needed to take with them and where they were to assemble for the evacuation. The evacuation began on 1 September. Many city schools were closed and many teachers accompanied the children to the countryside to carry on teaching them.

At their destinations the evacuees gathered in village or school halls where they were chosen by the foster family they were to live with. The children had mixed experiences. Some were very happy, helping on farms and eating better than they had ever done.

Others had a miserable time. Some were resented as a burden by their foster families. They also missed their own families, far away in the cities. Many country families, unaware of how city slum people lived, were in for a shock. They had to deal with children who wet their beds and children who had no experience of using a knife and fork to eat with.

Source J

Everything was so clean in the room. We were given face flannels and tooth brushes. We'd never cleaned our teeth until then. And hot water came from the tap. And there was a lavatory upstairs. And carpets. And clean sheets. This was all very odd. I didn't like it. It was scary.

The memories of a Second World War evacuee.

Evacuee children on their way from the city to the countryside to escape the danger of German air raids.

Source I

THIRD

We left feeling sad for our parents and afraid that they would be killed by the bombs. We were anxious because we had no idea where we were going or whom we would live with, but at least we had been told by our parents that we would be safe. When we arrived in Sandbach, we were chosen for a variety of reasons: for the extra income they received for us, to help on the farm or with the housework. A few were very lucky because they lived with families who cared for them; for those, life was like a holiday and they did not want to leave. I was upset because I was separated from my sister.

School was a joke: we shared it with the locals so there was only half a day attendance and not enough teachers. The children whose school it was resented us being there and threatened us and made fun of us in the playground. There were many fights between the two groups. I was glad when I returned home in time for Christmas, but the following September I was evacuated with my school to Blackpool.

Ted Cummings, who was evacuated from Manchester to Sandbach in September 1939, writing about his feelings.

Homesickness and the realisation that the war had not begun saw many children drift back to their homes in the cities towards the end of 1939. The government tried to prevent this by running a campaign to encourage children and parents to stay where they were, but had little success. When German bombers started blitzing Britain's cities in 1940 a second evacuation from the cities took place, though not on the scale of the one in 1939.

TAKE THEM BACK!
TAKE THEM BACK!
TAKE THEM BACK!..

DON'T do it, mother—

LEAVE THE CHILDREN WHERE THEY ARE

ISSUED BY THE MINISTRY OF HEALTH

A government poster trying to persuade parents not to take their children back from the countryside.

Clarence and I used to sleep together and poor Clarence used to wet the bed because he was a very nervous kid. She (the foster mother) could never tell who'd done it so she used to bash the daylights out of the both of us. So, of course, the more Clarence got hit the more he wet the bed. It was then we started to get locked in the cupboard.

The film actor, Michael Caine, remembers his evacuation with his brother.

Civilian Experience of War

The Blitz

The government supplied its citizens with air raid shelters as part of its campaign to protect them from German air raids. The first shelters were delivered in February 1939. These were Anderson shelters, which were sunk into the ground in the back garden. They had enough room for a family and were safer than staying in the house. Every citizen also received a gas mask to protect them against gas attacks. Over 38 million of these were supplied. Public information leaflets (Source O) were sent to every household in July, telling people what to do if there was an air raid. The blackout came into force on 1 September. Every house had to hang thick black curtains or stick brown paper over the windows to stop the house lights being seen from outside by enemy bombers. Street lamps, traffic lights and car headlamps were also blacked out.

Most local authorities drew up civil defence plans before the war started. This was required by the Air Raid Precaution Act of 1937. The civil defence forces involved were air raid wardens, Auxiliary Fire Service, Auxiliary Police Corps, Red Cross, St John's Ambulance Brigade and the Women's Voluntary Service. They helped the main emergency services deal with the damage caused by the air attacks.

The government encouraged people to use purpose-built brick public air raid shelters, but many preferred the Anderson shelter or to stay in their own home protected in a **Morrison shelter** or in a cellar. People in London at first were not allowed to use the underground railway stations for fear they would get trapped underground. But public pressure to use them forced the authorities to give way and they became popular places to shelter.

The air attacks and their effects are described in Unit 2 of this chapter. The British people, encouraged by the Prime Minister, Winston Churchill, coped well with the bombing. However, there was looting and some opposition from citizens, particularly in London's East End which took the brunt of the early bombing.

Air raid wardens check on civilians in an Anderson shelter after a bombing raid.

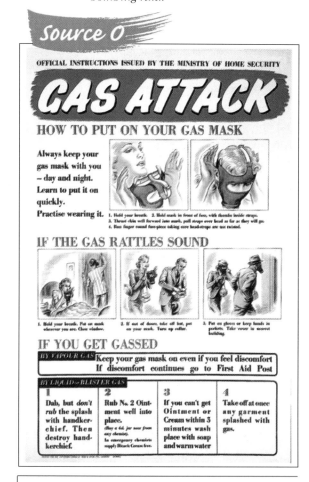

A public information leaflet telling people what to do to protect themselves against gas attacks.

Conflict in the Modern World, 1919–63

Propaganda

The Ministry of Information was responsible for the poster campaigns which encouraged people to join the voluntary services and to work hard and save in order to help the war effort. It also produced posters which warned people of the dangers of 'careless talk'. There was a fear that German spies could be working in the country so people were told not to discuss the war in public. The Ministry of Information tried to keep in touch with the people through an organisation called Mass Observation whose members carried out surveys and reported on conversations they had heard in shops and pubs.

Other wartime propaganda was concerned with encouraging people to save for the war effort and not to waste. The 'squander bug' became a regular feature of messages to the housewife implying that wasting anything was helping the Germans.

Newspapers were also censored by the government during the war. They reported on the bombings but concentrated on the heroism of the rescuers rather than the deaths and injuries in an attempt to keep up morale. Publication of the left-wing *Daily Worker* was banned in 1941 because it was claiming that the war was being fought for the bosses rather than a battle for democracy. Newsreel films were made for the cinema and broadcasts were made over the radio. Both sides tried to influence the other by transmitting propaganda over the radio. The 'Lord Haw Haw' broadcasts from Germany were disturbing to some British citizens. 'Lord Haw Haw' (William Joyce) was a Briton living in Germany who was used by Radio Hamburg to mock the British war effort and to undermine morale. The BBC also made broadcasts to Germany which included enough truth to make them appear genuine but enough rumour to disturb the German war effort.

Source P

Everybody is worried about the feeling in the East End, where there is much bitterness. It is said that even the King and Queen were booed the other day when they visited the destroyed areas.

From the diary of Harold Nicolson, a minister in the Ministry of Information, 17 September 1940.

Source Q

There were more signs of hysteria, terror, neurosis, observed than during the whole of the previous two months together in all areas. The overwhelming feeling on Friday was the feeling of utter helplessness. The tremendous impact of the previous night had left people practically speechless in many cases. On Friday evening (15 November), there were several signs of suppressed panic as darkness approached.

A Mass Observation report on the bombing of Coventry in 1940.

Things to do

1 List how some children benefited from evacuation and how others suffered from it.

2 How did the government prepare for the Blitz?

3 How does Source N show the value of an Anderson shelter?

4 What evidence is there in Sources P and Q to show that the bombing did have some effect on morale?

Origins of Conflict

Events leading to the Cold War

The USA and the USSR had joined together to defeat Germany and they ended the war as the two superpowers in the world, but their alliance did not last. The USA wanted to see the recovery of Europe, the Soviet Union was more interested in securing its frontiers. The two superpowers and their Allies argued, but there was no direct fighting, so it was called the Cold War.

7.1 Why did the USSR and USA become rivals after the Second World War?

Communism and capitalism

The USSR and the USA had been allies during the war, but their political systems were opposed to one another. The USSR was a communist state of one-party government in which there were no free elections and the state owned industry and agriculture. The USA and Western Europe were democratic and capitalist, in which governments were elected by free elections and industry and agriculture were in private ownership to be run for profit. The Soviets believed the West wanted to destroy communism, the West believed the Soviets wanted to convert the world to communism. These fears were one of the reasons for the Cold War.

Yalta and Potsdam, 1945

What happened after the Second World War encouraged these fears. The three Allied leaders (Roosevelt, Churchill and Stalin) met at Yalta in February 1945 and agreed to divide Germany into four zones, with Britain, France, USA and USSR occupying a zone each. Stalin was to have an influence over Eastern Europe, but the countries in this part of Europe were to be allowed to hold free elections to decide who governed them.

> ### Source A
>
> The Soviet government is alarmed by the attitude of the US government. The American attitude cooled once it became clear that Germany was defeated. It was as though the Americans were saying that the USSR was no longer needed.

Stalin gives his views on the attitude of Harry S. Truman, the new American President, May 1945.

The Iron Curtain.

Key
- ▨ Territory gained by USSR in 1945
- ▨ Countries under communist control
- ▨ Communist but independent
- — Iron curtain

PEEP UNDER THE IRON CURTAIN

A British cartoon, published in March 1946, commenting on the Iron Curtain between East and West.

By the time the Allied leaders met again at Potsdam in July 1945, after the defeat of Germany, relations between the West and East were much cooler. Roosevelt had died and was replaced by Truman, and Churchill had been defeated in a general election and Attlee was the new British prime minister. Truman and Stalin did not appear to get on well and the tension between them increased suspicions between the two nations.

Reparations and the atom bomb

The Allied leaders disagreed about reparations at Potsdam. The USSR wanted substantial compenstion for the great suffering inflicted on the Soviet people by Germany. Truman did not want to repeat the mistakes of the treaties following the First World War. Though they could not fully agree on reparations they did decide that each of them could take a limited amount of reparations from its zone of occupation.

When the Soviets were told at Potsdam that the USA was planning to use the atom bomb to force Japan to surrender, only 11 days before it was used, they feared that the USA would attempt to wipe out communism with the bomb.

A shadow has fallen across the scenes so lately lighted by Allied victory. From Stettin in the Baltic to Trieste in the Adriatic, an iron curtain has descended across the continent.

Extract from Churchill's speech at Fulton, USA, in March 1946.

USSR and Eastern Europe: the Iron Curtain

The USSR's actions in Eastern Europe alarmed the Americans. After the defeat of Japan, communist governments loyal to the USSR were set up in Poland, Hungary, Romania, Bulgaria and Albania. The communists' success in gaining power in these countries was in some cases achieved only with the aid of Soviet military force, not through free elections as had been agreed at Yalta. To the Americans this proved that Stalin's plan was to spread communism throughout Europe.

In a speech to an American audience in March 1946, Churchill referred to the division between West and East as the descending of an Iron Curtain between the two sides. The Iron Curtain was not a physical division, but a political and economic division between the one-party communist states of the East and the capitalist democracies of the West. Churchill's purpose was to convince the Americans that they needed to keep a military presence in Europe to prevent the spread of communism.

Origins of Conflict

The Truman Doctrine

In 1947 communists were threatening to take control in both Greece and Turkey. The USA had no wish to stand by while communism spread to other countries. In March 1947 President Truman made a speech in which he said that the USA would help any nation threatened by communism. The USA would take the lead in the 'containment' of Soviet expansion. This 'Truman Doctrine' was based on the American belief that the countries of Eastern Europe had been forced into communism by the Soviet Union and that it was America's duty to protect other democratic countries under threat. So Congress announced $400 million of aid to Greece and Turkey. This helped the Greek government defeat the communists. The Americans also installed ballistic missile sites on the Turkish border with the USSR. The Soviets were even more alarmed as they had no nuclear weapons.

Source D

Our policy is directed not against any country or doctrine but against hunger, poverty, desperation and chaos. Any country that is willing to assist in the task of recovery will find full co-operation on the part of the US government.

George C. Marshall, the US Secretary of State, speaking about his plan for aiding Europe, June 1947.

The Marshall Plan

The Truman Doctrine, with its policy of 'containment' of communism, is usually seen as the start of the Cold War. The Marshall Plan, which accompanied the Truman Doctrine, aimed at helping Europe recover from the war. The Americans feared that an impoverished post-war Western Europe would turn to communism. To prevent this they needed to help Europe recover economically as quickly as possible. To do this the Americans set up the Marshall Plan to provide economic aid wherever it was needed in Europe, including the East. As a matter of economic self-interest this also made sense for the Americans, as Europe's recovery would once again make it a strong trading partner for the USA.

The Marshall Plan set up a fund of $15 billion for Europe. The idea was that Eastern Europe could also draw on this money. However, Stalin realised this would make Eastern Europe more dependent on the USA than the USSR. He did not want that. Stalin denounced the Marshall Plan as economic imperialism, claiming that the USA was trying to spread its influence by controlling the industry and trade of Europe.

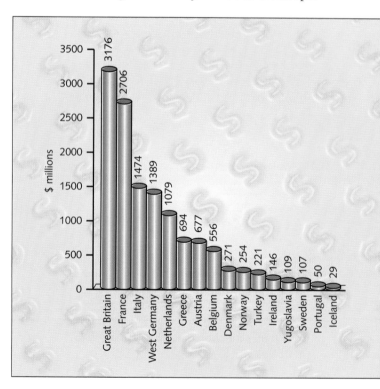

Aid received under the Marshall Plan.

How did the Cold War develop between 1945 and 1955?

The Berlin Blockade

Berlin, the capital of Germany, was divided into four zones of occupation, just like the rest of the country. As the city was in the Soviet zone, the West depended on the USSR to keep open the routes in and out of the city. But it was decisions by the West which triggered a crisis in the Cold War.

Stalin continued to extract reparations from the Soviet zone of Germany but the other zones in the West, including West Berlin, were beginning to recover because of Marshall Aid. By 1948 Britain, France and America had joined their zones together and were planning to establish a new currency to aid recovery. This was not what Stalin wanted. He saw a prosperous Germany in the West as a threat to the USSR. His response was to close all roads, canals and railways between the West and West Berlin on 24 June 1948. Stalin wanted to force the West to give up West Berlin by starving the two million inhabitants, who only had enough food and fuel to last for six weeks. Truman was faced with giving up West Berlin or going to war. But giving up West Berlin meant giving in to Stalin. To use armed force involved invading the Soviet zone of Germany. A less aggressive policy was devised to keep the people of Berlin from starving. The British and Americans flew in supplies.

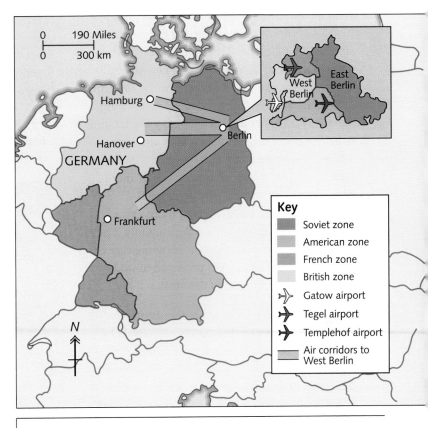

The occupied zones of Germany in 1945.

Source E

When Berlin falls, Western Germany will be next. If we withdraw our position in Berlin, Europe is threatened. Communism will run rampant.

General Clay, the American commander in Berlin, on the dangers of the Blockade.

Things to do

1 What were the fears of the West and the USSR that helped to create the Cold War? Were these fears real or imaginary?

2 Is Source B an accurate view of the Iron Curtain?

3 Which three countries received most from Marshall Aid? Why do you think these three received the most?

4 Why did Stalin not accept Marshall Aid?

5 What does Source E mean?

Origins of Conflict

The Berlin Airlift

West Berliners needed over 4,000 tons of fuel, food and other supplies each day if they were to survive the Blockade. The Allies used the three air corridors established in 1945. The airlift began slowly: the first flight was on 26 June, but on average only 600 tons a day were reaching West Berlin. By September aircraft were landing in Berlin every three minutes, day and night, and by the spring of 1949, 8,000 tons a day were being flown in. The Soviets tried to put more pressure on the Berliners by cutting off electricity supplies and offering them extra rations if they moved to East Berlin. Only 2 per cent of the population did this, showing that the people of West Berlin were prepared to undergo hardship to remain part of the West.

Stalin realised the Allies were determined to keep the airlift going. He could only stop it by shooting down the planes. Soviet planes did track supply planes in case they moved out of the permitted air corridor, but dared not shoot them down as this would be an act of war. Stalin called off the Blockade in May 1949. The West had shown how determined it was to resist communism. The Blockade was costly to the Allies and 79 British and American pilots were killed in accidents, but it ended the ill-feeling between the Americans and the defeated Germans in the West.

Any hopes for a united Germany had ended, for the time being. In 1949 the three western zones, including West Berlin, became known as the Federal Republic of Germany (West Germany), with its own elected government. The USSR responded by turning its zone into the German Democratic Republic (East Germany) which had a communist government. The Allies were now determined to build up West Berlin into a showcase for capitalism.

A 'Punch' cartoon from July 1948. It shows Stalin watching the Allied 'storks' flying supplies to Berlin during the blockade.

Source F

When we refused to be forced out of Berlin, we demonstrated to Europe that we would act when freedom was threatened. This action was a Russian plan to probe the soft spots in the Western Allies' positions.

President Truman speaking in 1949 about the Berlin crisis.

Source G

The crisis was planned in Washington, behind a smoke-screen of anti-Soviet propaganda. In 1948 there was the danger of war. The conduct of the Western powers risked bloody incidents. The self-blockade of the Western powers hit the West Berlin population with harshness. The people were freezing and starving. In the spring of 1949 the USA was forced to yield, their war plans came to nothing

A Soviet version of the Berlin crisis.

Source H

THE BIRD WATCHER

Source I

A Soviet cartoon expressing the fear that Germany would emerge again to threaten the USSR.

"WHO'S NEXT TO BE LIBERATED FROM FREEDOM, COMRADE?"

A British cartoon, dated 2 March 1948, commenting on the spread of communism in Europe.

NATO and the Warsaw Pact

The Marshall Plan was a great success and by 1950 the output of West European countries had increased by 25 per cent. The Truman Doctrine and the Marshall Plan were clear signs that the Americans had no intention of returning to the isolationism of 1919. Their action in defeating the Berlin Blockade reinforced this view and led to the formation of a military alliance in the West. In 1949 the North Atlantic Treaty Organisation (NATO) was formed, made up of the USA, Canada, Britain, France, Belgium, the Netherlands, Iceland, Luxem-bourg, Italy, Norway, Denmark and Portugal. Greece and Turkey joined in 1952 and West Germany in 1955. All members agreed to go to war if any one of them was attacked.

Stalin responded to the Truman Doctrine by strengthening his hold on Eastern Europe. All non-communists were driven from office and Stalin organised the Cominform (Communist Information Bureau) to help all European communist parties, including those in France and Italy, to work and plan together. When the Czechs showed an interest in Marshall Aid, Stalin refused to allow them to apply for it, and an election, influenced by the Soviets, confirmed the Communists as the the only political party in Czechoslovakia. After NATO was formed, Stalin set up a trading union of communist countries under the USSR called Comecon (Council for Mutual Economic Aid). When Stalin died in 1953 there was a 'thaw' in the Cold War. However, when West Germany was allowed to join NATO in 1955 Soviet fears of a recovered Germany were revived. With Germany as part of a military alliance again, the Soviets and East Europeans signed the Warsaw Pact to form a defensive alliance controlled by the Soviet Union. This was seen by the West as the USSR's response to NATO.

Things to do

1 What does Source H add to our understanding of the Berlin Airlift?

2 Why do Sources F and G differ so much?

3 Explain the meaning of Sources I and J. What evidence is there to support both these views?

Summary

1945	Conferences at Yalta and Potsdam.
1946	Iron Curtain speech.
1947	Truman Doctrine. Marshall Plan.
1948	Berlin Blockade and Airlift.
1949	Division of Germany confirmed. Formation of NATO.
1955	Formation of Warsaw Pact.

Origins of Conflict

unit 8

The Changing Nature of Warfare

The Nuclear Age, 1945–63

The use of the atom bomb in 1945 began a new period of fear and suspicion. Once the USSR had successfully tested the bomb a nuclear arms race developed between East and West. Civilians protested but the race continued. There were smaller wars and crises which involved the superpowers who came into direct opposition over Cuba in 1962.

Source A

The matter is very simple, any Soviet citizen can explain it to you. The United States is surrounding us with bases which are ready to fire atomic bombs.

A Soviet student gives the Soviet view of the arms race in 1958.

8.1 How did nuclear arms affect relations between world powers?

The nuclear arms race, 1945-63

For four years after the war, the Americans were the only nuclear power and therefore 'contained' the USSR with little fear of response. But when the Soviets successfully tested an atom bomb in 1949 this changed. Nuclear weapons were far more destructive than any weapons ever known to man. Both East and West feared for the future. The Americans and Soviets embarked on developing better nuclear weapons and better ways of delivering them to their targets. The Americans tested the first hydrogen bomb (H-bomb) in 1952. This could destroy a city the size of Moscow. The following year the USSR tested its own H-bomb which could destroy any American city.

Until 1957 nuclear bombs would have been dropped from long-range aircraft. This changed when the USSR launched a satellite, *Sputnik I*, into space using a rocket in 1957. These rockets

Western alliance and Soviet Union.

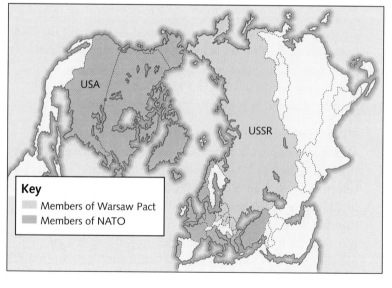

Key
- Members of Warsaw Pact
- Members of NATO

could be fitted with nuclear warheads and launched at targets thousands of kilometres away. The Americans responded by developing their own rockets. Both countries were now engaged in a 'space race', which led to the development of Inter-Continental Ballistic Missiles (ICBMs). These were land-based strategic missiles stored in concrete silos in underground bases from which they could be launched.

The race moved on in 1960 when the Americans fired a new Polaris missile from a submarine. It was now possible to fire missiles with a range of over 1,600 kilometres (1,000 miles) from anywhere under the sea. The Soviets soon followed with their own nuclear submarines.

Both sides tried to locate ICBMs in friendly countries close to their enemy. The Americans based missiles in Turkey on the border with the USSR, which explains why the USSR tried to install similar missiles in Cuba pointing at the USA. This created confrontation between the superpowers, with the world on the edge of nuclear war. Fortunately it ended in compromise, an improvement in relations between the USA and the USSR, and the signing of a Test Ban Treaty in 1963 (see page 79).

The death of Stalin, 1953

Stalin's death in 1953 led to a 'thaw' in East-West relations, with the USSR's new leaders looking to improve relations with the USA. Khrushchev, the new Soviet leader, criticised Stalin and announced a new policy for improving relations with the West. This policy was called 'peaceful co-existence'. Signs of thaw in relations were the USSR's withdrawal of its military bases in Finland and the Geneva Summit in 1955.

Spies and the Paris Summit, 1960

During the Cold War both sides used spies to discover each other's secrets. Some of these spies were caught and made the headlines throughout the world. Dr Klaus Fuchs was imprisoned in Britain for passing on information about the atom bomb to the USSR, while Julius and Ethel Rosenberg were executed in the USA for passing on secrets about the H-bomb to the Soviet Union. The USA used special spy planes (U2s) to photograph military bases in the USSR. On 4 May 1960, just days before the Paris Summit meeting between the leaders of the USSR, USA, Britain and France, President Khrushchev announced the USSR had shot down an American spy plane flying across its air space. At first the Americans denied they had a plane spying on the Soviets. But Khrushchev produced photos taken from the plane and the pilot, Gary Powers, was put on public display in Moscow.

The evidence proved the Americans were spying. At the Paris Summit, Khrushchev demanded an apology and an end to all spy flights. The American President, Dwight D. Eisenhower, refused and Khrushchev stormed out of the Summit, cancelling an invitation to the American President to visit Moscow. The Paris Summit was over. The U2 incident suspended the thaw in relations and many blamed the Americans. Gary Powers was tried for spying and sentenced to 10 years imprisonment. He was released in 1962 in exchange for a Russian spy captured by the West.

A Soviet cartoon, called 'The Art of Camouflage', comments on the USA's attitude to peace.

The Berlin Wall

Although Khrushchev declared his policy to be 'peaceful co-existence' with the West, it did not stop him challenging the Western presence in Berlin. Berlin was a huge embarrassment to the USSR. American economic aid helped transform the city into a showpiece of capitalism. While people in the west of the city enjoyed the benefits of recovery, such as being able to buy luxury goods, those in East Berlin worked long hours and suffered from food shortages. Eventually they rebelled in 1953, but were suppressed by the army.

Even more embarrassing for the Soviets was the defection of so many East Berliners to West Berlin. Over two million did so up to 1961. It was easy to escape as there was no barbed wire, minefields and watch towers between the different parts of the city, as there was on the border between East and West Germany. In 1961 the Soviets again declared that the West should give up Berlin. President Kennedy refused. This time Khrushchev decided to make it far more difficult for East Berliners to travel to and from West Berlin to work and shop.

On 13 August 1961 the East Germans erected a border of machine guns and barbed wire between East and West Berlin. President Kennedy protested, but was unwilling to risk war over Berlin. Three days later work started on building a 45-kilometre concrete wall to replace the barbed wire. The gap in the frontier between East and West was now filled. The Soviets made it clear that anyone trying to cross the Wall would be shot. Even so many were desperate enough to try. In the first year of the Wall 41 East Berliners were shot trying to cross. The Wall separated family and friends. East Berliners also saw it as a sign of their inferiority. But it did achieve one thing: it cut down the number of defectors from East to West Berlin.

Source C

The frontiers of our country will be protected at any cost. We will do everything to stop the criminal activity of the head-hunters, the slave traders of Western Germany and the American spies.

From a speech by W. Ulbricht, the Prime Minister of East Germany, 10 August 1961.

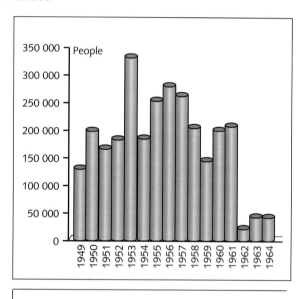

This graph shows the number of people who escaped from East Germany to West Germany, 1949-64.

Source D

The wall separating East Berlin from West Berlin. The East is to the right side of the wall.

Nuclear deterrent

In the early 1960s the Americans were still ahead in the nuclear race. Even so the Soviets had enough nuclear weapons to inflict massive destruction on the USA, even if the Americans got the first strike in. This realisation made it unlikely the superpowers would use such weapons in war against one another. This in fact has been the argument in favour of keeping nuclear weapons. This is known as the **nuclear deterrent**.

Disarmament

Nuclear weapons made it hard for countries to disarm. From 1946 to 1962 over 800 international disarmament meetings failed to reach any agreement. In the 1950s the emphasis was on 'arms control', not complete disarmament. While the superpowers distrusted one another, there could be no agreement. The Soviets actually stopped nuclear testing in 1958. But the Berlin crisis of 1961 and renewed testing by the USSR made it more urgent to find an agreement on nuclear weapons and led to a meeting between President Kennedy and Khrushchev. They agreed a set of principles and the Geneva Disarmament Conference opened in March 1962. In October 1962 the Cuban missile crisis began (see page 76).

(see page 76)

Things to do

1   Does the map on page 72 support the view of the Soviet student given in Source A? Explain your answer.

2   Why were 1949 and 1957 important years in the nuclear arms race?

3   Did the death of Stalin change the relationship between the superpowers? Explain your answer.

4   Why does Source B on page 73 show a dove on the U2?

5   Why was the Berlin Wall built?

6   Was it successful?

7   Despite the CND marches, the British government kept its nuclear weapons. Does that mean that the marches were a failure?

The civilian response: CND

Britain tested its own atom bomb in 1952 and H-bomb in 1957. Many were against this, not just because of the danger and the power of the weapon, but because of the effects of radiation on the atmosphere and the enormous cost. In 1960 Britain cancelled work on its own missile 'Blue Streak', which had cost over £100 million. Opponents of nuclear weapons argued that the money spent on developing nuclear weapons could have been better spent on improving the life of people throughout the world.

The Campaign for Nuclear Disarmament (CND) was formed in Britain in 1958 to pressure the British government to abandon the development of nuclear weapons.

It wanted the British government to decide on its own (unilaterally) to disarm. Protests and marches were held. At Easter in 1958 CND organised a march from London to the Atomic Weapons Research Establishment at Aldermaston in Berkshire. There was massive media coverage and the marchers were joined by politicians, writers, clergymen and many others. The march became an annual event. Still they did not succeed in persuading the government to stop developing nuclear weapons. The government continued to build up its nuclear arsenal in the name of defence.

The Changing Nature of Warfare

8.2 How close were the superpowers to war in 1962?

Communist rule in Cuba

The dictator Batista ruled Cuba from 1933. Cuba was a poor country largely controlled by American big business. Its main crop, sugar cane, was bought by the Americans. Batista's cruel rule was threatened in the 1950s by guerrillas led by Fidel Castro. In spite of the support he received from the USA, Batista was defeated in 1959 and Castro became ruler of Cuba. The Americans did not like Castro as they believed he was a **Marxist**, so they refused to trade with Cuba. Castro took over the possession of all land from the Americans and made an alliance with the USSR who promised to buy Cuba's sugar. The USA now had a neighbour allied to her greatest rival.

The Bay of Pigs, 1961

When John F. Kennedy became President in January 1961 he was convinced by the Central Intelligence Agency (CIA), the American secret service, that Castro could be overthrown in an attack by supporters of Batista. The rebels, with American support, landed at the Bay of Pigs in Cuba in April 1961. The attack was a total disaster. The rebels received no support when they landed and were defeated in a few days. Kennedy was severely embarrassed, realising he had been wrongly advised. Castro was now convinced that the USA was an enemy and looked even more to the USSR for support. In December 1961 Castro publicly declared himself a Marxist, convincing the Americans that Cuba had become a Soviet satellite.

Cuba now had to depend on the Soviet Union for protection. In June 1962 huge shipments of Soviet arms were received by Castro.

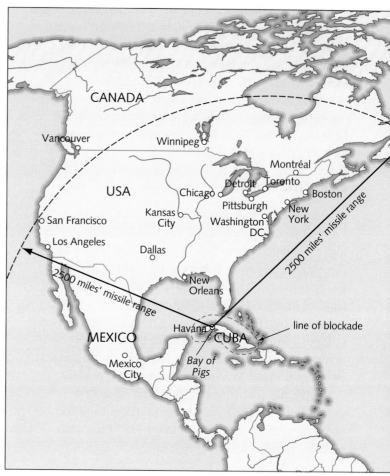

This map shows the targets in the USA that the missiles could reach from Cuba.

The first of these were classified as defensive weapons, as they were aircraft, patrol boats and ground-to-air missiles. In September however medium-range offensive nuclear missiles and bombers had arrived in Cuba. The Americans were aware of these, but the Soviets insisted they were defensive. On 14 October 1962 U2 spy planes photographed Soviet missiles in place on launch pads in Cuba. This proved the Russians had lied. The missiles had a range of around 4,000 kilometres (2,500 miles). This put most large American cities within their range of attack in minutes. More ships carrying missiles were reported to be on the way from the USSR to Cuba. What was the American President to do?

Conflict in the Modern World, 1919–63

The Cuban missile crisis

Kennedy had suffered two failures in his dealings with the Soviets. He gave the go ahead for the Bay of Pigs invasion disaster and was helpless to stop the Soviets building the Berlin Wall. Some historians think Khrushchev saw this as a sign of weakness and was trying to establish Soviet supremacy over the Americans. Placing missiles in Cuba was a test of how strong Kennedy was and how far he was prepared to go. Certainly Cuba was an ideal base for the USSR and would counteract the American bases in NATO countries, especially Turkey, which was on the southern border of the Soviet Union. This caused the Soviets great anxiety in 1962 as they had not yet developed missiles that could be fired from submarines. Another argument is that Khrushchev was simply helping Cuba defend itself from a possible attack from the USA.

Kennedy gathered around him a group of advisers who were almost in constant touch during the 13 days the crisis lasted. They proposed seven alternative policies to the President for dealing with the crisis. These were:

1   To do nothing and allow the USSR to keep its bases on Cuba.

2   Make a diplomatic protest to the Soviets.

3   To discuss the missiles directly with Castro.

4   To place a naval blockade around Cuba.

5   To launch an airstrike on Cuba with non-nuclear weapons.

6   To invade Cuba and seize the bases.

7   To launch a nuclear attack on Cuba.

The first two were ruled out because it would appear as if the USA was prepared to back down whenever Khrushchev threatened. As for the third, Castro was unlikely to negotiate with the Americans after the Bay of Pigs. The last three would cost too many lives and risk nuclear war. This left option 4. On 22 October Kennedy announced on television that he was placing a 500 mile naval blockade around Cuba to prevent Soviet missiles reaching the island. This would be enforced by the US navy. He also planned to carry out options 5 and 6 if needed, but hoped the blockade would succeed. On 24 October the first Soviet ships carrying missiles encountered American ships blockading Cuba. How would Khrushchev respond?

Source E

I have directed that the following initial steps be taken: first, a strict 'quarantine' on all offensive military equipment under shipment to Cuba. All ships, if found to contain cargoes of offensive weapons, will be turned back. It will be the policy of this nation to regard any nuclear missile launched from Cuba against any nation in the Western Hemisphere as an attack by the Soviet Union on the United States, requiring a full retaliatory response upon the Soviet Union.

From Kennedy's speech on television, 22 October 1962.

Source F

Even when people were enjoying themselves having a drink in the student bar, the conversation turned to Cuba. What would happen? Would it mean the end of the world? Everyone felt so helpless. There was nothing you could do to prevent destruction except pray. Special prayers were said in churches. The end of the crisis was greeted with a tremendous feeling of relief.

Memories of a 19-year-old British university student in 1962.

The world holds its breath

Khrushchev could have done several things. He could have ordered his ships to sail on and sent warships to accompany them so that they could defy the American blockade. But war would have broken out. He could have taken action against the USA in another part of the world, such as West Berlin or Turkey. But Khrushchev was not prepared to risk nuclear war, so he ordered his ships to turn back.

This did not end the Cuban missile crisis. There were still missile sites in Cuba which could be made ready quickly to launch an attack on the cities of the USA. President Kennedy wanted to keep talking to the Soviets and a series of letters passed between him and Khrushchev during this part of the crisis. The Americans insisted that the Soviets dismantle the missile sites in Cuba. Khrushchev sent two letters to Kennedy which he received on 26 and 27 October. In the first Russia offered to remove missile sites if Kennedy called off the blockade and promised not to invade Cuba. The second letter took things further: Khrushchev would only remove the missiles from Cuba if the Americans withdrew their missiles from Turkey, on the border of Russia.

Kennedy was determined not to give in on this issue. He was not prepared to do a deal with Khrushchev on the basis of the missiles in Turkey. While this was going on several incidents occurred which could have sparked off a war: an American U2 plane was shot down over Cuba and a Soviet ship was boarded and inspected by the US navy – it was found to be carrying nuclear bomb parts. Some of Kennedy's advisers recommended an attack on Cuba, but the President held firm against it. He ignored Khrushchev's second letter and replied to the first, telling the Soviet leader that he accepted the terms in the letter of the 26 October and giving him until 29 October to reply. If Khrushchev did not accept, American forces would invade Cuba.

On Sunday 28 October the Soviet government agreed to remove its missiles from Cuba. Khrushchev made no mention of American missiles in Turkey. The crisis was over. The withdrawal of missiles began on the 3 November and the Americans called off the blockade on 20 November.

Things to do

1 Why did the USA oppose Soviet missiles on Cuba?

2 Do you think Kennedy chose the correct option of the seven alternatives? Explain your answer.

3 What does Source F tell us about feelings in Britain about the Cuban crisis?

4 Why did Kennedy ignore Source G?

5 Who was victorious in the Cuban crisis? Give reasons for your answer.

6 Why does Source H ignore the letter of 27 October? Is Source H reliable as evidence about the Cuban crisis?

7 Is Source I an accurate interpretation of the Cuban crisis? Explain your answer.

Source G

You are worried about Cuba because it is 90 miles from America, but Turkey is next to us. We agree to remove from Cuba those means which you find offensive. The United States will for its part remove its missiles from Turkey.

Extract from Khrushchev's letter of 27 October 1962.

Results of the crisis

The Cuban missile crisis was the nearest that the world had ever been to nuclear war. The two leaders realised that the responsibility for the future of the world lay with them. Steps had to be taken to improve relations between East and West.

In August 1963 a Test Ban Treaty was signed in Moscow. This banned the testing of nuclear weapons in the air or under water. A few months before, in June, a 'hot line' direct phone link between Washington and Moscow had been set up. This would enable the two leaders to discuss matters quickly and avoid the build up of crises. On 17 October, a UN resolution banned the placing of nuclear weapons in outer space. All these points had been discussed at the Disarmament Conference which had begun in Geneva in March 1962. The conference ended with the first agreements on the control of nuclear weapons in the spirit of greater co-operation which developed after Cuba.

Both Kennedy and Khrushchev claimed to have won a victory over Cuba. Kennedy had stood up to the Soviet Union and forced them to back down. His prestige in the USA and the West increased enormously. Khrushchev posed as the peacemaker. The Secretary General of the United Nations, U Thant, had appealed to both leaders to do all they could to avoid nuclear war. Khrushchev claimed that his action in withdrawing from Cuba was in response to U Thant's appeal. His action had secured peace for the world. He could also claim a victory in that the USA had promised not to invade Cuba, which remained a useful friend for the Soviets because of its proximity to the USA. But it was also true that Khrushchev's demand for the withdrawal of American missiles in Turkey had been unsuccessful.

Source H

We agreed to remove our missiles and bombers on condition that the President promised that there would be no invasion of Cuba by the forces of the United States or anybody else. Finally Kennedy gave in and agreed to give us such an assurance. It was a great victory for us, a spectacular success without having to fire a single shot.

From Khrushchev Remembers *published in 1971.*

Summary

1945	USA use the atom bomb.
1949	USSR tests the atom bomb.
1952	USA tests the H-Bomb.
1953	USSR tests the H-Bomb. Death of Stalin.
1955	Geneva Summit.
1957	USSR launches *Sputnik I.*
1958	CND formed.
1960	U2 Incident - failure of Paris Summit.
1961	Berlin Wall. Bay of Pigs.
1962	Cuban crisis.
1963	Test Ban Treaty.

Source I

British cartoon showing Kennedy and Khrushchev struggling over the Cuban crisis with nuclear war only the press of a button away.

The Changing Nature of Warfare

Exam-type Assessment
Conflict in the Modern World

This exercise is based on the sort of questions you could be asked on Paper 1 of your examination.

Source A

The crisis over Bosnia which kept Europe on tenterhooks for six months ended recently when Britain, France, Germany, Italy and Russia accepted the annexation of Bosnia-Herzegovina by Austria-Hungary. War was avoided. Germany and Austria-Hungary won a victory but it appears that it is at a cost: Germany's action seems to have humiliated Russia and acted as a warning to Britain.

From an article on the Bosnian crisis published in a British magazine, October 1909.

Source B

Austria-Hungary and Germany won a notable diplomatic victory in the Bosnian crisis of 1908–9, but when news of the amount of support given to Austria-Hungary by Germany reached Russia, the Russian people became opposed to Germany and opposition continued to grow until 1914. After the assassination of Franz Ferdinand in 1914, the Austrians expected German support, the Russians could not afford to back down again, so war between the alliances followed.

From a book called **The Bosnian Crisis** *by a modern historian, published in 1968.*

Source C

The outbreak of war in 1914 was essentially a tragedy of miscalculation. Once the Austrians had delivered an ultimatum to Serbia, the crisis increased and the calculations of statesmen were overwhelmed by the rapid succession of events, the growth of war feeling in the various capitals and the demands of the Schlieffen Plan.

From a book called **Origins of the First World War** *by a modern historian, published in 1970.*

Questions

1 **Study Source A.**
   Give **two** facts which the British magazine is reporting in this source. *(2 marks)*

2 **Study Source A and use your knowledge.**
   What opinions are given in the source?
   Explain why they are opinions and not facts. *(5 marks)*

3 **Study Sources A, B and C and use your own knowledge.**
   Do the sources and your knowledge of events support the view that the Bosnian crisis was the main cause of the First World War?
   Give reasons for your answer. *(10 marks)*

A poster published in Britain in 1915.

A poster published in Britain in 1939.

Questions

1   **Study Sources D and E and use your own knowledge.**

(a) In what ways is Source D similar to Source E?   *(3 marks)*

(b) In what ways are these two sources different? Explain why they differ.   *(6 marks)*

(c) Suggest reasons for the publication of Source E in 1939.   *(8 marks)*

Source F

In his book *Mein Kampf*, written in 1924–25, Hitler stated that the Nazi Party had the following aims:

- the union of all Germans to form a Greater Germany;
- the cancellation of the Treaty of Versailles;
- the reunion of Austria and Germany;
- the gaining of new land in the East from Russia and her border states to provide for Germany's excess population.

In 1938 Austria was joined to Germany; at Munich later in the same year, the Sudeten Germans of Czechoslovakia became part of the German Reich. In March 1939 Hitler invaded the rest of Czechoslovakia. The Nazi-Soviet pact was signed in August 1939 and Germany invaded Poland in September 1939.

From a British school textbook written in 1993.

Source G

	Yes	No	No opinion
Should Britain promise assistance if Germany acts towards Czechoslovakia as it did towards Austria?	33%	43%	24%

Public opinion poll taken in Britain, March 1938.

	Yes	No
Hitler says he has 'No more territorial ambitions in Europe'. Do you believe him?	7%	93%

Public opinion poll taken in Britain after the Munich Agreement.

Public opinion polls taken in Britain in 1938.

Source H

People of Britain, your children are safe. Your husbands and your sons will not march to battle. If we must have a victor, let us choose Chamberlain. For the Prime Minister's conquests are mighty and long lasting – millions of happy homes and hearts relieved of their burden.

From the Daily Express September 30 1938, the day after the Munich Agreement.

Source I

We have sustained a total and unmitigated defeat. You will find that in a period of time which may be measured by years but may be measured only by months, Czechoslovakia will be engulfed in the Nazi regime. Do not suppose that this is the end, it is only the beginning. We have sustained a defeat without a war.

Winston Churchill speaking in Parliament during the Munich Debate, 5 October 1938.

Source J

WHAT'S CZECHOSLOVAKIA TO ME, ANYWAY ?

A British cartoon published in 1938.

Questions

1   **Study Source F.**
    Which of Hitler's stated aims had he not achieved by 1939? Explain your answer. *(2 marks)*

2   **Study Sources G and H.**
    Does Source G suggest that the people of Britain agreed with Source H? Explain your answer. *(6 marks)*

3   **Study Sources H and I and use your own knowledge.**
    (a) Explain how these two interpretations of the Munich Agreement are different. *(4 marks)*
    (b) Explain why they differ in this way. *(7 marks)*

4   **Study Source J and use your own knowledge.**
    Do you think this cartoonist would support or oppose the Munich Agreement? Give reasons for your answer. *(8 marks)*

Source K

From a British school textbook published in 1996.

In the early 1960s the USA had developed a special spy plane, the U-2, to fly over enemy land. These planes were equipped with cameras to photograph airfields, weapons and other military bases and were designed to fly so high that Soviet fighter jets could not reach them. On 1 May 1960 one of these aeroplanes was shot down in the centre of Russia and the pilot was taken prisoner. At first the Americans lied about the plane. Khrushchev, the Soviet leader, demanded an apology, but the Americans refused and the Soviets left the Paris Summit Conference in protest.

The Soviets were also alarmed by the number of citizens of Eastern Europe who were fleeing into the West. From 1945 to 1961 over 3 million fled into West Germany. The easiest place for this to happen was the divided city of Berlin as the frontier was unguarded. In 1961 this route for refugees was closed by the building of the Berlin Wall. The Wall became a symbol of the hatred of the two sides in the Cold War and the lack of freedom in Eastern Europe.

Source L

A statement issued by the Soviet government on 13 August 1961 explaining the need for the Berlin Wall.

The Western Powers continue to use West Berlin as a centre for plots against East Germany. In no other part of the world are so many espionage centres found as in West Berlin. These centres are smuggling their agents into East Germany to organise plots and cause disturbances. The governments of the Warsaw Pact countries propose that a procedure be established on the borders of West Berlin which will block this activity, so that effective control may be established round the whole territory of West Berlin, including its border with democratic Berlin.

Questions

1 **Study Sources K and L.**

What reasons are suggested in these two sources for the building of the Berlin Wall?

(3 marks)

2 **Study Sources K and L and use your own knowledge.**

Which of these two sources is more reliable to an historian writing about the building of the Berlin Wall? Give reasons for your answer.

(10 marks)

Chapter 3

Governments in Action:
Russia and the USSR, 1900–56

Russia saw great changes in the period 1900–56. In 1900 it was the most backward country in Europe ruled by a Tsar with complete power. Attempts to change Russia either by revolution or reform all failed in the period up to 1914. However, the First World War highlighted the weaknesses of Tsarist Russia and led to the collapse of Tsarist rule in 1917. But within eight months the new Provisional Government had been overthrown by the Bolsheviks/Communists under Lenin.

Despite a bitter civil war and severe economic problems, Lenin made sure that Communist rule in Russia survived. His successor, Stalin, set about making Communist Russia – called the USSR (Union of Soviet Socialist Republics) – a much stronger economic power with his policies of collectivisation of agriculture and the Five Year Plans for industry. The human cost and suffering to the Soviet people was immense but Stalin's reforms did allow the USSR to survive the Second World War.

Stalin also established a strong personal control of the USSR. Opponents, including those in the Communist Party, were 'purged' or 'liquidated'. In many ways Stalin's control of the USSR, was not unlike that of the Tsar in 1900. The USSR changed greatly in this period, but some things remained the same.

This is a Paper 2 topic and you will be required to answer one structured question on it.

The End of Tsarism

Russia, 1900–16

In 1900 Russia was a huge, backward country with a population of over 130 million. Its ruler, Tsar Nicholas II, ruled as an autocrat and refused to allow the Russian people to have a say in the running of the country. However, in the period leading up to the First World War, there were serious challenges to his authority and significant growth in support for revolutionary opponents of his rule. By 1917 Nicholas had lost control of his country. Tsarist rule in Russia was over.

1.1 How strong was the Tsarist regime in 1914?

The government of Nicholas II

Nicholas II became Tsar in 1894 at the age of 26. He was modest and deeply religious, and took his responsibilities as Tsar of Russia seriously. However, he knew very little about his people. He never travelled around the country meeting them and relied on his advisers telling him what was going on. Nicholas believed in autocracy — government by one man. He believed his powers came from God. Therefore he did not tolerate criticisms of his rule. He ruled with the help of his wife, Tsarina Alexandra, and they were determined that their son, Alexis, should inherit their power.

Source A

Tsar Nicholas II and Tsarina Alexandra in 1903.

Only Nicholas had the power to make laws in Russia. He appointed ministers, but they were often no more than advisers and were sometimes inefficient and corrupt. As there was no elected parliament in Russia, local councils (*zemstva*) had to look after matters such as schools and hospitals. When there were calls for an elected parliament, Nicholas dismissed them as a 'senseless dream'.

Nicholas' rule was enforced by the secret police (Okhrana). Critics of the Tsar were arrested, imprisoned and often sent to labour camps in Siberia. Newspapers and books were censored and controlled to prevent criticism. The Russian Orthodox Church also supported the Tsar and preached to its congregations that it was a sin to oppose him. In spite of his complete control there was opposition to Nicholas' rule.

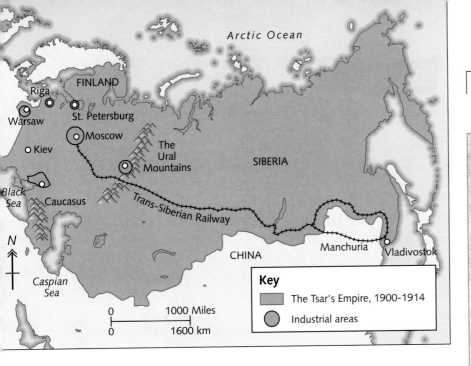

Russia in 1900.

Key
The Tsar's Empire, 1900-1914
Industrial areas

0   1000 Miles
0   1600 km

Opposition to Tsarist rule

The **Liberals** were middle class, educated Russians, such as doctors, lawyers and teachers. They wanted an elected parliament to help the Tsar run the country. In 1905 they formed the Constitutional Democratic Party (the Cadets). Other groups were more extreme.

The **Social Revolutionaries** (SRs) wanted the peasants to overthrow the Tsar and set up a republic. All the land of Russia would then be handed over to the peasants to farm together in communes. The SRs were prepared to use violence and assassination to further their cause.

The **Social Democrats** (SDs) also wanted to overthrow the Tsar. However, they believed the revolution would be made by the urban workers. They followed the ideas of Karl Marx and were called Communists. The party, however, was divided. In 1903 it split into two groups. The Bolsheviks ('majority group'), led by Lenin, believed that revolution in Russia should be planned secretly by a small group of committed individuals who would seize power. The Mensheviks ('minority group'), led by Trotsky, believed revolution should be a mass movement involving anyone. The Bolsheviks eventually dominated the party.

One major difficulty for these revolutionary groups was that their leaders were often in prison or in exile. Lenin, for example, lived in exile in London for years. Trotsky was exiled in London and Paris and other revolutionaries were in Switzerland. The 1903 Party Conference was held in a warehouse in Brussels.

Revolution in Russia seemed just a dream. But it was much closer than anyone realised.

Source B

How long have you been a member of the Communist Party? Since 1894.

Have you ever belonged to any other parties? No.

What sentences were you given for revolutionary activities? 1887 prison; 1898-1900 Siberia; 1900 prison.

How long did you spend in prison? Several days and 14 months.

How long at hard labour? None.

How long in exile? Three years.

How long a political refugee? 9-10 years.

Extract from Lenin's answers to a Communist Party questionnaire.

Things to do

1   The government of Russia was an autocracy. Explain what this means and how it worked in Russia.

2   **(a)** What were the different aims and ambitions of the groups opposing the Tsar?

   (b) Is there anything on which they agreed?

The End of Tsarism

The causes of the 1905 Revolution

In the years after 1902 there was economic depression in the towns and bad harvests in the countryside. This led to demonstrations, strikes and violence. These were brutally crushed by the Tsar's army, which only increased bitterness. In July 1904, the Minister of the Interior, Plehve, who controlled the police, was assassinated by revolutionaries. In the same year Russia and Japan waged war against one another. Nicholas welcomed the war as an opportunity to increase his popularity, but Russia's forces suffered humiliating defeats. The war revealed the weaknesses, not the strengths, of Tsarist rule. These events and the people's growing resentment at the Tsar's autocratic rule help explain why unrest in 1905 led to revolution.

Bloody Sunday: the marchers' path to the Winter Palace is blocked by troops.

Bloody Sunday, January 1905

On 22 January 1905, about 200,000 people in St Petersburg, carrying pictures of the Tsar, marched to the Winter Palace to petition him to help improve their working conditions. Led by Father Gapon, they sang hymns as they marched. But the Tsar was not in St Petersburg and the marchers' way to the Palace was blocked by troops. Fighting broke out and the troops opened fire. Official figures put the number killed at 96, but actually hundreds were killed.

The 1905 Revolution

'Bloody Sunday' was crucial. The Tsar was blamed for the massacre. As news of it spread, strikes and violence broke out all over Russia. Strikers in towns demanded shorter hours and higher wages. Peasants attacked landowners' property, looting and burning their houses and seizing the land for themselves. There was a naval mutiny in June. Sailors on the battleship *Potemkin* seized the ship and sailed across the Black Sea to Romania. In September, the Tsar was forced to sign a humiliating peace with Japan. Part of the peace treaty involved losing Port Arthur and Korea to the Japanese.

This aroused even more anger and despair among the Russian people. In October Russian workers began electing soviets (workers' councils) to plan strike action. It was clear the Tsar was losing control. Even some of his own army were supporting the revolutionaries. He was forced to make changes to the way Russia was governed.

The October Manifesto and the end of the 1905 Revolution

Nicholas issued the October Manifesto by which he granted freedom of speech, the right to form political parties and agreed to the election of a parliament (Duma) by the people. The Cadets accepted the Manifesto and claimed a great victory. The more extreme revolutionary groups however rejected it. They wanted to overthrow the Tsar and install a completely new system of government. So revolutionary action continued. But by now the Tsar had recovered some of his authority and ruthlessly put down opposition. Revolutionary leaders, such as Trotsky, once more fled Russia. By the end of the year Nicholas was again in complete charge of Russia.

The Dumas

The elections for the first Duma were held in April 1906. But by now the Tsar had regained so much of his power that he was able to impose the Fundamental Laws. These allowed Nicholas to dismiss the Duma and call new elections whenever he wanted. Only he could appoint ministers and in an emergency he had the power to govern by decree without consulting the Duma.

The Dumas were a huge disappointment. The first one was dismissed by the Tsar after 75 days because of opposition to some of his policies. The second lasted just three months because it also opposed the Tsar. The third was mostly filled with supporters of the Tsar, so lasted its full five-year term. The fourth Duma, elected in 1913, also had a Tsarist majority, but its term was cut short by the outbreak of war in 1914. No Duma managed to pass any meaningful laws to improve the position of the poor in Russia.

The October Manifesto and the creation of the Duma promised so much. It was soon clear, however, that the Tsar was not prepared to give up any of his powers. The autocracy continued.

Sire – We, working men and inhabitants of St Petersburg, our wives and our children and our helpless old parents, come to You, Sire, to seek for truth, justice and protection. We are near to death.... We ask but little: to reduce the working day to eight hours, to provide a minimum wage of a rouble a day.... Do not refuse to help Your people.

The Workers' Petition, 1905.

The rioting in Our Empire fills Our heart with deep grief. We grant freedom of person, conscience and assembly. We include in the Duma those classes that have been, until now, deprived of the right to vote. No law shall go into force without the approval of the Duma.

Extract from the October Manifesto.

I created the Duma not to have it instruct me but to have it advise me.

The Tsar speaking in 1908.

The End of Tsarism

Stolypin and reform

Peter Stolypin became Prime Minister of Russia in 1906. He was tough on civil disturbances. But he also realised the Tsar needed to win the support of the people. With this in mind he made it possible for peasants to buy land from their neighbours and join the strips of land to form larger single farms. He set up a peasants' bank to provide loans. In this way a new rich landowning class was created – called the Kulaks. They would work the land more efficiently and would be loyal to the government. By 1914 about 15 per cent of the peasants had bought more land. But the change also brought problems. It created poorer peasants who were forced to sell their land and become labourers. So some peasants were happier, others more discontented.

Despite these reforms, Stolypin's toughness in dealing with opposition to the Tsar made him hated by many of the people. With so many executions during his rule the hangman's rope was called 'Stolypin's necktie'. Stolypin was assassinated in 1911.

Peter Stolypin.

Russia in 1914

By 1914 the Tsar seemed to be well in control of Russia. There were still some strikes and demonstrations but the army was loyal and troops crushed any disturbance. The Okhrana (secret police) rooted out trouble-makers and revolutionaries. Nicholas' opponents were also weak. Leaders of the revolutionary groups were in prison, in Siberian labour camps or living in exile in other countries. Lenin, then in Switzerland, doubted if he would ever return to Russia or live to see it change by revolution.

However, things were about to change dramatically with the outbreak of the First World War.

Things to do

Look at the information in this unit. Draw up two lists, one of the strengths of the Tsar's position in 1914, the other of the weaknesses. Compare the lists. Do you think that in 1914 the Tsar was in any danger of being overthrown? Give reasons for your answer.

Summary

The causes of discontent in Russia between 1900 and 1914:

- The autocracy of the Tsar.
- Economic depression.
- Failure of the Russo-Japanese war.
- Use of the army and Okhrana to crush opposition.
- Failure of the Dumas.

1.2 Why did the rule of the Tsar collapse in March 1917?

Military defeat

In 1914 Russia went to war with Britain and France against Germany and Austria-Hungary. The outbreak of war in 1914 was greeted with enthusiasm and increased patriotism. St. Petersburg was renamed Petrograd, the 'Russian' name for the city, because the original name sounded too German. Crowds gathered outside the Winter Palace to cheer the Tsar. In other parts of Russia the strikes ended. In the Duma members swore to support the Tsar. It seemed as if the people were prepared to give Nicholas another chance.

But the Russian army suffered defeats at Tannenburg and the Masurian Lakes and the Germans invaded Russia. The Russian army was large but poorly equipped, with not enough ammunition and weapons (nearly a third of Russian soldiers marched into battle without rifles) and basic supplies, such as boots, medical supplies and food. Leadership was also weak, with officers drawn from the nobles and winning promotion more because of their birth than their military skills.

Effects of war on the Russians

The war affected those at home, who had to put up with serious food shortages. With millions of peasants conscripted into the army there was not enough people to produce food. Whatever food there was frequently did not make it to the cities where it was most needed because the railways were being used to transport troops and supplies to the front. Problems increased as food prices rose and wages stayed the same. Millions of Russian refugees flooding into the towns to escape from the advancing German armies created overcrowding and greater pressure on food supplies. Unemployment rose as factories closed down because of the shortage of manpower, coal and other raw materials.

Russia was in chaos. People were dying of starvation and cold. There was more despair as news from the front told of Russian defeats and the deaths of loved ones.

Source H

Thousands of students and working men, carrying portraits of the Tsar, singing the national anthem and hymns, went towards the Winter Palace. Here, [they] fell on their knees singing 'God save the Tsar.' Never during the twenty years of his reign had the Tsar been so popular as at that moment.

A Russian describing the outbreak of war in 1914.

Source I

Russian prisoners of war under guard in May 1915.

The Tsar and the war

The people's support for the Tsar at the beginning of the war soon evaporated. As long as he remained in Petrograd it was difficult to blame him personally for the defeats suffered by the Russian army. However, in 1915 he took personal command of the armed forces even though he had little military experience. He did this because he believed it was his duty and that the army would fight better if he was leading it. The decision had two important consequences.

First, Nicholas was blamed for the continued defeats of the Russian army. Second, he was now out of Petrograd and therefore not running the government.

The day-to-day running of Russia was now in the hands of Tsarina Alexandra. This was a mistake. Alexandra was of German birth and was suspected, wrongly, by the people of being a spy. She was also incapable of governing Russia. She would not work with the Duma and came to depend more and more on Gregory Rasputin (see case study).

Things to do

Look at the evidence in the case study and the sources. Why do you think Rasputin's relations with the royal family helped to weaken the Tsar's rule?

Case Study: Rasputin

Gregory Rasputin, a self-styled monk and 'holy man', was of striking appearance and claimed to have hypnotic powers. He became well known in St Petersburg, especially among upper-class women who came to him for advice and healing. Through them he met the Tsarina. After he appeared to heal a life-threatening injury to the heir to the throne, Alexis, the Tsar and Tsarina were convinced Rasputin had been sent by God to look after their family and the Russian people.

Rasputin's influence grew under the protection of the Tsar, who even asked his advice in the appointment of ministers and officials. Rasputin used his power to place his friends in important positions. When war broke out his influence increased, especially after the Tsar took charge of the army.

The Tsarina became completely dependent on Rasputin and ministers were appointed and dismissed on his direction.

She even wrote letters to her husband containing Rasputin's advice on how to run the war.

Rasputin's power and influence aroused envy and made him powerful enemies, particularly among the nobles. It was a group of nobles, led by Prince Yusopov, who assassinated him in December 1916.

Rasputin's influence weakened the royal family's standing in Russia but his murder came too late to save them.

The Tsar blesses his troops.

A cartoon of Rasputin with the Tsar and Tsarina.

The move towards revolution

By 1917 Russia was in chaos.
The German army advanced across the country, sweeping aside the Tsar's forces. The Russians were increasingly disillusioned with the war. The economy was getting worse, especially the shortage of food and its high prices. The winter of 1916-17 was severe and the railways were badly disrupted by ice, making it difficult to get food and fuel to the towns. Bread queues were familiar sights. The government was increasingly unpopular and the murder of Rasputin did little to change this. Nicholas was losing control.

Conditions were now ideal for revolution. Russia was about to be engulfed by two revolutions within nine months. The first, in March 1917, ended not only the rule of Nicholas II, but also the rule of the Tsars in Russia.

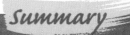

The effects of the First World War on Tsarist Russia:

- Russian army suffered military defeat.
- Russia invaded by Germany.
- Economic disruption.
- Starvation.
- Weak government.
- Growing unpopularity of Tsar and Tsarina.
- Russian people disillusioned.
- Revolution and collapse of Tsarist rule.

The End of Tsarism

The Revolutions of 1917

Russia, 1917

The year 1917 was momentous in Russian history. There were two revolutions. The first, in March, overthrew the Tsar and replaced him with a Provisional Government. When the Provisional Government failed to end the war, it too became unpopular. The second revolution, in November, overthrew the Provisional Government and replaced it with Bolshevik/Communist control of Russia.

2.1 Why did the Provisional Government last for only eight months?

Source A

A queue of hungry people outside a bread shop, in 1917.

The March Revolution and the abdication of the Tsar

With a severe winter, food shortages and rising prices, and the war going badly the Tsar's government was under pressure in the first two months of 1917. By March the government had lost control.

Workers demanding higher wages went on strike at the Putilov engineering works in Petrograd on 4 March. Three days later 40,000 were on strike and the factory closed down. As the strike spread there were clashes between striking workers and the army, with some of the strikers being killed.

As law and order broke down the Tsar, who was at the front, was told what was happening,

but he chose to ignore the warnings and ordered the Duma to stop meeting.

The key date in the Revolution was 12 March. Soldiers in Petrograd refused to fire on demonstrators and joined them instead. Soldiers and strikers then marched together to the Duma to demand a new government.

Nicholas now realised how serious matters had become. He tried to return to Petrograd but his train was stopped outside the city. His generals made him aware of how grave things were and advised him to abdicate, which he did on the 15 March. Within a week he and his family were arrested and removed to Siberia.

The Provisional Government and the Petrograd Soviet

The Duma formed a Provisional Government to run the country until elections could be held to choose a permanent government.

At the same time the Petrograd Soviet (a council representing the interests of workers and soldiers) met and other soviets were set up throughout the country. The Petrograd Soviet had more power in the city than the Provisional Government and set about organising the distribution of food and housing and running the rail services. More important, it took control of the armed forces of the city.

The weaknesses of the Provisional Government

At first the Provisional Government was popular, particularly through its granting of basic rights, such as freedom of speech and the right to strike. But problems soon emerged. The government itself was made up of members of different political parties – SRs, Cadets, Liberals and Mensheviks – with different views on how Russia should be governed. This often made it hard to make decisions. The Petrograd Soviet by contrast was more united and had a clearer idea of what it wanted to do.

Two issues made the Provisional Government more unpopular. The first was land. The government rejected the idea of peasants owning the land they worked until an elected permanent government was formed to decide on the matter. This infuriated the peasants, many of whom refused to wait and seized the land for themselves.

More crucial was the war. The government decided to go on fighting fearing that any peace treaty worked out with the Germans would end in Russia having harsh conditions imposed on it. This decision was unpopular with the army and the people. Soldiers demoralised by defeat were deserting in even greater numbers. People were suffering food and fuel shortages and were desperate for the war to end. In this climate of discontent an alternative to the Provisional Government emerged – Lenin and the Bolsheviks.

Source B

The situation is serious. Petrograd is out of control. The government is paralysed; the food and fuel supplies are completely disorganised. Discontent is general and on the increase. There is wild shooting on the streets; troops are firing at each other.

Telegram from the President of the Duma to the Tsar, 11 March, 1917.

Source C

The Soviet of Workers and Soldiers' Deputies has decided:

- In all military units committees should be chosen.
- The order of the Provisional Government shall be carried out only when they do not go against orders and decisions of the Soviet.
- All weapons must be under the control of the committees. They must not be handed over to officers.
- All ranks and titles in the army are abolished.

Order No. 1 of the Petrograd Soviet Army, issued on 14 March 1917.

Things to do

1. Explain why the Tsar was forced to abdicate.

2. Why did the Provisional Government become unpopular?

The Revolutions of 1917

Lenin's return and the *April Theses*

A painting showing Lenin addressing a crowd greeting him on his return to Petrograd in April 1917.

The Revolution in March caught the revolutionary groups unprepared, just as the 1905 Revolution had.

The Bolsheviks' leaders were in exile – with Lenin in Switzerland and Stalin in Siberia. So, the Bolsheviks were leaderless. Lenin made it back to Russia as fast as possible – with the help of the Germans! The Germans saw that with the Bolsheviks in power Russia would withdraw from the war, releasing German troops from the Eastern Front for fighting in the west. Even if the Bolsheviks failed to seize power the turmoil in Russia could only help Germany's war aims.

Lenin made it to Petrograd on 16 April, having travelled through Germany by train in a sealed carriage provided by the German government. He announced that the Bolsheviks would not co-operate with the Provisional Government, but would work for its overthrow. He also declared that Russia should withdraw from the war and that land would be distributed to the peasants. These announcements were published as the *April Theses*. They were summarised in slogans: 'Peace, Bread and Land' and 'All Power to the Soviets'.

The *April Theses* were popular with the people. Lenin also gave leadership to the Bolsheviks and a clear direction.

Week by week food became scarcer. The daily allowance of bread fell from a pound and a half to a pound, then three-quarters, half and a quarter of a pound. Towards the end there was a week without any bread at all. On the freezing front, miserable armies continued to starve and die without enthusiasm.

The American writer, John Reed, describes conditons in Petrograd in October 1917.

The July Days

In July the Provisional Government ordered a military attack on the Germans. It ended in a massive defeat. News of this reached Petrograd and soldiers, sailors and workers demonstrated against the government on 16 and 17 July. The Bolsheviks eventually joined the demonstrators and their Red Guards joined in the rioting that followed.

Troops loyal to the government put down the rising and a warrant was issued for Lenin's arrest. Though he managed to escape to Finland other Bolshevik leaders were arrested.

The July Days failed and the Provisional Government held on to power through the support of the army. However the problems of the Provisional Government persisted, with more military defeats and food shortages.

Governments in Action: Russia 1900–56

2.2 How were the Bolsheviks able to seize power in November 1917?

The Kornilov Affair

The commander of the Russian army, General Kornilov, tried to seize power and install a military dictatorship in September 1917. But he had little support and his troops were persuaded not to fire on fellow Russians. Kornilov was arrested and the rising crumbled.

This was another example of the unpopularity of the Provisional Government. In contrast, the Bolsheviks won popularity because they had refused to help Kornilov and were prepared to fight him, with arms supplied to their Red Guards by the government. Afterwards the Red Guards held on to the weapons.

Summary

The Provisional Government failed to survive because:

- It was weak politically. It was not elected and was made up of different parties.
- It was challenged by the Petrograd Soviet.
- It was unpopular because it refused to hand over land to the peasants.
- It continued the war and was blamed for the defeats of the Russian army.
- It failed to solve food shortages and other economic problems.
- The Bolsheviks offered alternative policies which were more popular.

Source F

Leon Trotsky.

Bolshevik preparations

The Bolsheviks prepared for revolution throughout the summer and autumn. They were gathering more support and conditions in the country were not improving. In the elections to the Petrograd Soviet they won an overall majority.

Trotsky was elected chairman of the Petrograd Soviet and played a crucial role during this time, with Lenin still in Finland. He organised the Bosheviks' preparations for revolution. Agents were sent to factories to drum up support among the workers. Trotsky also organised the Red Guards, who were formed into units with specific roles in the revolution.

Lenin wanted the revolution to happen as soon as possible and secretly returned to Petrograd on 23 October to meet the Bolshevik Central Committee. He persuaded them to go along with his plans. They eventually agreed, though Trotsky did persuade Lenin to delay the action until 7 November.

The Bolsheviks were ready for revolution on 6 November. They planned to seize control of Petrograd. They achieved this within 36 hours and overthrew the Provisional Government.

The November Revolution

The main events of 7 and 8 November are as follows:

7 November

2am	Railway stations, bridges, power station, waterworks and newspaper offices taken over.
3.30am	Cruiser *Aurora* sails to Nicholas Bridge.
4am	Capture of Telephone Exchange and Telegraph Agency.
7am	Provisional Government trapped in Winter Palace.
10am	Bolsheviks announce overthrow of the government.
	Kerensky, the Prime Minister, flees Petrograd.
6.30pm	Bolsheviks demand surrender of members of Provisional Government. No reply.
9.40pm	*Aurora* fires blank shot at the Palace. Troops desert the government.
11pm	Guns in Peter and Paul fortress fire on Palace.

8 November

1.50am	Palace stormed by Red Guards. Ministers arrested.
	Congress of Soviets meet to elect a new government. Fourteen of the 25 ministers are Bolsheviks.

So far the Revolution was confined to Petrograd. What Lenin and the Bolsheviks now had to do was to keep control of Petrograd and extend the Revolution to the rest of the country.

Source G

The night dragged on. From everywhere we expected reinforcements but none appeared. For various excuses the Cossack regiments stayed in their barracks. Meanwhile the night hours passed.

Alexander Kerensky, leader of the Provisional Government, writing in 1927 about the November Revolution.

Things to do

1. Look at Source D and the information in the *April Theses*. If you had been a Russian in April 1917 what would you have found attractive about them?
2. How did each of the following help the Bolshevik preparations for revolution: economic conditions, Trotsky, Lenin?

A painting of the storming of the Winter Palace, the headquarters of the Provisional Government.

Summary

The Bolsheviks were successful in seizing control of Petrograd because:

- They took control of the Petrograd Soviet.
- Lenin persuaded them to attack the Provisional Government when it was weak.
- They were well prepared.
- The Provisional Government had little support in Petrograd.

The Revolutions of 1917

Creation of a Communist State

Russia, 1917–24

The Bolsheviks had taken control of Petrograd in November 1917. It took a further three years before that control extended to the rest of Russia and it was only achieved after a bitter civil war. Conditions for the Russian people remained poor and Lenin's policy of War Communism made things worse. Only with a New Economic Policy (NEP) did some improvements come.

3.1 How did Lenin impose Communist control on Russia?

Setting up a Bolshevik government

On 8 November the Bolsheviks set up their new government. Most of the commissars (ministers) of the government were Bolsheviks. Lenin himself was chairman of the Council of Commissars – in effect the leader. Trotsky was Commissar for Foreign Affairs and Stalin Commissar for Nationalities (that is, all the non-Russians living within the state of Russia).

Lenin announced an immediate end to the war, and peace talks with the Germans began in December. He also issued a land decree. This seized land owned by the Tsar, the Church and rich landlords and handed it to the peasants. They would form committees in their local areas to divide it up among themselves. These measures made the Bolsheviks popular throughout Russia in the days following the Revolution.

Source A

A Communist poster
'Lenin, Father of the Working People.'

The Constituent Assembly

Before the Provisional Government fell from power, Kerensky promised an election to choose a permanent parliament, the Constituent Assembly. Lenin allowed the elections to go ahead.

Lenin renamed the Bolshevik Party as the Communist Party and tried to broaden its appeal to the mass of Russian people. However, most voters were peasants and were supporters of the SRs, which won 370 out of the 700 seats.

Lenin's Communist Party won 175 seats and with the support of other groups it could muster over 200 seats, but this was not enough to give it a majority. Lenin therefore shut down the Assembly after only one day. He was not prepared to hand over, or even share, his power with any other group. It was the first step in setting up a dictatorship by the Communist Party.

The Communist dictatorship

Although the Revolution had been fought to end the Tsar's autocracy, Lenin's control was as strong as that of the Tsar. In December 1917, he set up the Cheka, a secret police force. The Cheka's agents worked in factories and villages all over Russia to spy on people. Anyone suspected of being anti-Communist would be arrested, tortured and could be shot without trial. When opponents tried to assassinate Lenin in 1918, he launched a Red Terror campaign against his enemies that summer. It is said that over 50,000 opponents of Communism were arrested and executed during this period.

Peace: the Treaty of Brest-Litovsk

Lenin was determined to end Russia's involvement in the war whatever the cost. He feared the war would bring about the overthrow of Communist rule, just as it had the Provisional Government. The Russian army in any case had been weakened by poor morale, massive desertions and a breakdown in discipline. It was incapable of resisting the Germans. Defeat seemed inevitable. Peace negotiations with Germany ended on 3 March 1918, and the Treaty of Brest-Litovsk was signed. The terms were harsh. Russia lost a huge amount of land on her western frontier, which contained one-sixth of the population (over 60 million people), three-quarters of her iron and coal and over one-quarter of her farmland, some of it the best in Russia. The Communists had paid a high price but Lenin knew he could not fight the Germans and his opponents in Russia at the same time.

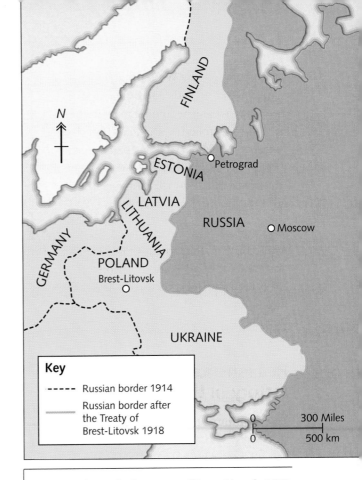

Russia's losses in the Treaty of Brest-Litovsk, 1918.

Things to do

What were the advantages and disadvantages to Russia of the peace treaty with Germany? Do you think that Lenin was right to agree to it?

The civil war

After four years of war against invading German forces, Russians in 1918 faced an even worse war – a civil war in which Russian fought against Russian over how the country should be ruled.

Lenin's Red Army was forced to fight a war against the 'Whites'. His opponents were a collection of supporters of the Tsar and groups like the SRs and Mensheviks, who had not supported the Tsar. The Whites also had the support of foreign powers: Britain, France, Japan, the USA and Czechoslovakia all sent troops to fight against the Communists. There were a number of reasons for this. Britain and France, in particular, were furious at Russia's withdrawal from the First World War, which allowed German troops to move from the Eastern Front to fight on the Western Front. Lenin had also cancelled Russia's debts to other countries.

Creation of a Communist State

In the civil war the Whites had larger armies than the Reds and by the end of 1918 they were threatening to overwhelm the area controlled by the Reds. But the Red Army held out and by 1920 the main threat from the Whites was over. The civil war dragged on into 1921. Against the odds the Communists had won.

The war was cruel and violent. Both sides committed atrocities and seized grain and animals from the people. As a result the peasants, who had hoped for so much from the Revolution, continued to starve.

Reasons for the Communist victory in the civil war

The Communist victory owed much to Trotsky who was in charge of the war effort. He built up the Red Army by enforcing conscription on men over 18 years. Being short of officers to lead the troops, Trotsky used experienced former Tsarist officers. Trotsky also imposed tough discipline on the Red Army: deserters were shot and if a regiment refused to fight every tenth man was executed. Trotsky kept in touch with the fighting by travelling to the different fronts in a special train.

The Communist victory was also as a result of the weaknesses of the Whites. The Whites were divided in their aims, whereas the Reds had a single aim – the survival of the Communist government. Some of the Whites wanted to restore the Tsar, some wanted a constitutional government, some wanted more socialist revolution. All that bound them together was a desire to defeat the Reds. The White armies were also dispersed across Russia and their leaders failed to work together. The Red Army could pick them off one at a time. Foreign military support for the Whites was not as great as expected. The call for foreign help lost the Whites support among their own people, some of whom saw this as a betrayal of Russia. Many peasants also turned against the Whites, fearing a White victory would mean loss of land they had gained in the Revolution.

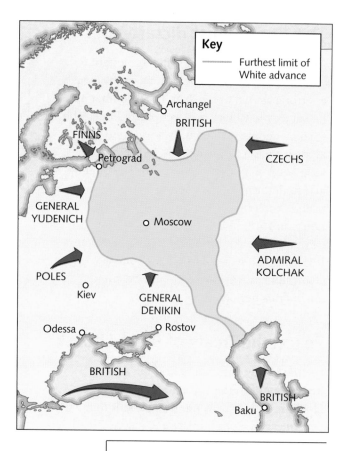

Russia in the civil war, 1918–21.

Things to do

Why did the Communists win the civil war?

The Communists imposed their control on Russia by:

- Setting up a Communist-controlled government.
- Introducing popular measures, especially the land decree.
- The use of force by the Cheka to remove all opposition.
- Ending Russia's involvement in the First World War.
- Victory over the Whites in the civil war.

Case Study: the assassination of the Tsar, July 1918

After his abdication in March 1917 Nicholas and his family were arrested, removed to Siberia, and then held at the Red-controlled town of Ekaterinburg. During July 1918, with a Czech army, part of the White forces, closing in on Ekaterinburg and the possibility that Nicholas would be freed to become a rallying point for White forces, the Communists decided to murder the royal family.

The White account of the murder is that on 16 July the Tsar and his family were taken to the basement of the house in which they were prisoners and were shot. Those who did not die instantly were finished off with bayonets. Eleven members of the royal households were murdered: the Tsar, his wife Alexandra, his son and four daughters, the family doctor and three servants. The bodies were then taken to a mine where they were soaked in acid and burned.

The Communists announced the Tsar had been executed but the rest of the family had been sent to safety. The Communist version of events never explained what eventually happened to the royal family, though an American, Anna Anderson, did in later years claim she was Nicholas' daughter, the Grand Duchess Anastasia, and that she had escaped from Russia.

In 1991 a burial pit in a bog was found in Ekaterinburg containing several bodies. The remains were examined using DNA tests and dental records and in 1994 the conclusions were made public. The bodies were those of the Tsar, his wife and three of their daughters. They had been shot and bayoneted. The report appeared to confirm most of the accepted accounts of the murders. There was no sign of the bodies of the Tsar's son, Alexis, and one of his daughters, Maria. Later, however, charred remains were found and identified as the missing son and daughter.

The room where the assassination took place.

Source C

Shortly after one o'clock am, they were taken from their rooms. It seemed as if all of them guessed their fate, but not one of them uttered a single sound. I heard the firing and I returned to the house. I saw that all members of the Tsar's family were lying on the floor with many wounds in their bodies. The blood was running in streams. The heir [Alexis] was still alive and a soldier went up and fired two or three more times at him.

A Red Army soldier describes the murder of the royal family.

Things to do

Look at the evidence in the case study. What do you think happened to the Tsar and his family? Give reasons for your answer.

3.2 How successful was Lenin in creating a new society in Russia?

War Communism

Lenin's greatest problem in fighting the war was to make sure the Red Army had enough food and supplies. This involved producing more weapons and food. To achieve this Lenin extended state control over the economy. This he called War Communism.

The state now took control of the factories, and appointed managers to run them. Factory workers had to work hard and long hours and trade unions were banned. Food was rationed and ration cards were only issued to those in work.

To get enough food to feed the Red army and the industrial workers, the Cheka seized all surplus grain from the peasants. The peasants resisted. They hid food, but they risked punishment if caught. Many peasants preferred to grow less grain than give it away free to feed the people in the towns. Grain production fell even more as a result. To make matters worse, drought and severe famine hit the country in 1921, and over four million Russians starved to death.

The Kronstadt Revolt

War Communism made the Communist government very unpopular. Discontent among peasants led to violence in the countryside. In towns workers went on strike, in spite of the penalty for striking being death.

The most serious opposition to the government came in March 1921. Sailors at the Kronstadt naval base revolted. They accused the Communists of breaking their promises of 1917 by failing to help the workers. Lenin ordered the Red Army to put down the revolt. This caused 20,000 casualties and the leaders of the revolt were executed.

The Kronstadt revolt made Lenin realise how unpopular War Communism was and that he had to improve the economic situation in Russia. Failure to do so might end in the overthrow of the Communist government.

Starving children during the famine of 1921.

Governments in Action: Russia 1900–56

Source D

Parties which were sent into the countryside to obtain grain by force might be driven away by the peasants with pitchforks. Savage peasants would slit open a belly, pack it with grain, and leave him by the roadside as a lesson to all.

A Communist describes unrest in the countryside.

Things to do

Look at sources D and E and the section on the Kronstadt Revolt. What reasons do they suggest to explain why Lenin ended War Communism?

Source E

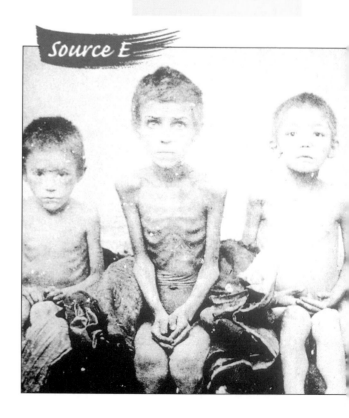

New Economic Policy

Lenin therefore introduced the New Economic Policy (NEP). State control of the economy imposed by War Communism was relaxed under the NEP. Smaller industries and factories were returned to private ownership. What was then produced was sold on the open market for profit. Grain was no longer seized from the peasants. Instead, they had to give a fixed amount to the government in tax, retaining for themselves any surplus, which could be sold in the open market at a profit. Important industries, such as coal, steel, railways and the banks, remained under state control.

Lenin hoped that the NEP would help increase industrial production and farm output, and put Russia back on its feet economically. He called the NEP 'a breathing space'. Most of the Communist Party saw the need for change and were prepared to go along with the NEP. However, there was some opposition to it from within the Party. Many Communists thought that returning the idea of profit to trade and business was against Communist principles.

On the whole the NEP was a success. Factories and peasants responded to the change by increasing their production of industrial goods and grain. The end of the civil war certainly helped. In fact the NEP was marked by seven years of relative stability compared to the previous seven years of world and civil war.

The NEP though did create problems. Some peasants – the Kulaks – became rich at the expense of others who often became hired labourers. Traders and businessmen in towns, called 'Nepmen', made huge profits by buying goods and food cheaply and selling them at much higher prices. To many this was a betrayal of Communism and a return to the old system.

Things to do

1 What was the New Economic Policy?
2 How successful was it?

Output (in millions of tons)			
	1913	1921	1928
Coal	29.0	9.0	35.0
Oil	9.2	3.8	11.7
Iron	4.2	0.1	3.3
Steel	4.3	0.2	4.0
Grain	80.0	37.6	73.3

Production in the USSR, 1913–28.

The creation of the USSR

By the end of the civil war in 1921 the Communists controlled most of the Tsar's former empire. As areas were captured they were turned into socialist republics. In 1924 all of these socialist republics came together as the Union of Soviet Socialist Republics (USSR). In theory the new state was a democracy with parliaments elected by the people. In practice the Communist Party was the only party, so the USSR was run by a dictatorship of the Communist Party.

By the time Lenin died in January 1924, having dominated Russia since 1917, he had made sure the Communist Party kept control of the country. He achieved this partly by introducing popular policies, but mainly by force and terror.

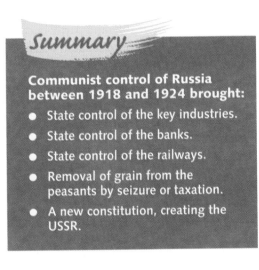

Summary

Communist control of Russia between 1918 and 1924 brought:

- State control of the key industries.
- State control of the banks.
- State control of the railways.
- Removal of grain from the peasants by seizure or taxation.
- A new constitution, creating the USSR.

The Rule of Stalin

The USSR, 1924–53

Between 1924 and 1941 the USSR underwent more changes. Stalin emerged as the new leader and set up a personal dictatorship which removed all opposition which he felt threatened him.

Stalin wanted to make the USSR a great economic power. To achieve this he reorganised industry and agriculture through the Five Year Plans. They brought further suffering to the Russian people but made it possible for the USSR to survive the Second World War.

4.1 How far did Stalin set up a personal dictatorship in Communist Russia?

The struggle for power with Trotsky

Joseph Stalin.

When Lenin died in 1924 a successor had not been appointed. Trotsky was most likely to succeed given that Lenin in his **'Political Testament'** had warned the Party against appointing Stalin (Source B).

However, Stalin was in a strong position. Trotsky was unpopular with some members of the Party, partly because he had not joined the Bolsheviks until 1917 and partly because he was arrogant. In contrast Stalin was a loyal Party member.

Each man had different ideas on communism's future. Trotsky believed it could only survive if other countries became communist. The only way this could be done was to have a 'permanent revolution', which involved encouraging and helping revolution in other countries. Stalin believed communism in Russia must survive by itself, that it was up to the Russian people, guided by the Communist government, to turn Russia into a modern, powerful state.

This approach was called 'Socialism in one country'. It was more popular with the people because it involved them doing something about their own futures.

Stalin was also General Secretary of the Communist Party, another strong advantage. He was responsible for making appointments to posts in the Party. This meant he could remove his opponents and replace them with his supporters.

Comrade Stalin, having become General Secretary, has great power in his hands, and I am not sure that he always knows how to use that power with sufficient caution. Therefore, I propose to the comrades that a way be found to remove Stalin from that post.

An extract from Lenin's 'Political Testament', 1923.

Governments in Action: Russia 1900–56

The removal of Trotsky

After Lenin's death Stalin built support in the Central Committee of the Communist Party, the ruling body of the Party. The Party Congress of 1924 elected Stalin to the leadership of the Party. Trotsky's influence then swiftly declined. He was dismissed as Commissar for War in 1925 and the following year he was dismissed from the Central Committee. In 1927 he was expelled from the Communist Party and in 1929 exiled from the USSR.

Trotsky's exile took him to Mexico, where in 1940 he was assassinated by an agent of the Soviet secret police.

The removal of other Communist leaders

Stalin did not want to share power and so moved against other leading Communists who might threaten him. He got rid of left-wingers Kamenev and Zinoviev from the Central Committee in 1926 and the right-winger Bukharin in 1929. By removing his main political opponents and building up so much support within the Party Stalin had become the unchallenged leader of the Communist Party and the USSR.

Source C

Stalin's face is seen everywhere. His name is spoken by everyone. His praises are sung in every speech. Every room I entered had a portrait of Stalin hanging on the wall. Is it love or fear? I do not know.

A foreigner describes the glorification of Stalin in the USSR.

Things to do

Explain why it was Stalin rather than Trotsky who succeeded Lenin as ruler of the USSR.

Stalin's control of the USSR

The 1936 Constitution confirmed Stalin's and the Communist Party's control over the USSR. There was the appearance of democracy, with two chambers of parliament – the Soviet of the Union and the Soviet of Nationalities – with elections to them every four years. But there was only one political party – the Communists – so the elections were never contested. Real power was with the Central Committee of the Communist Party and its chairman, Stalin.

Stalin also controlled other parts of Russian life. The Churches were persecuted and religious services were banned. Priests were arrested and sent to labour camps. Art, music and literature were censored and directed to glorify the achievements of the Communist Revolution and the people of Russia. This was called 'Socialist Realism'.

In all these ways, the USSR was a totalitarian state, with the Communist Party having total control over the lives of the people.

The cult of personality

Hero-worship of the leader is another feature of the totalitarian state. This is called the 'cult of personality'. Propaganda was used to make people aware that Stalin was playing a part in every part of their lives – work, home, leisure. The message was that Stalin was looking after the people. Paintings, posters, statues, films, all glorified him.

History was also re-written to show Stalin as Lenin's most trusted adviser during the Revolution. All mention of Trotsky was removed from Russian history.

In this way Stalin not only strengthened the Communist dictatorship of the USSR, he also established a personal dictatorship.

The Rule of Stalin

Case Study: the Purges and Great Terror

By the 1930s, even with his main opponents removed, Stalin still felt insecure. To eliminate the criticism and opposition Stalin embarked on a policy of purges, which went on from 1934 to 1938. Millions of communists and non-communists were arrested and either executed or sent to labour camps.

Many of the arrested 'confessed' under torture to whatever charges were trumped up against them. The most important figures in the Party were tried in public, in what was known as 'show trials'.

The accused were always found guilty of treason and executed. This was what happened to Kamenev and Zinoviev in 1936 and to Bukharin in 1938. Thousands of other Party members were denounced and expelled. The Purges enabled Stalin to gain complete control of the Communist Party.

Stalin also purged the armed forces to make sure they stayed loyal to him. Nearly 90 per cent of the army's top officers and every admiral in the navy were purged. This ensured the loyalty of the armed forces' to Stalin. However, it left Russia short of experienced officers to lead those forces in war against Nazi Germany.

This 'Great Terror' also extended to ordinary Russians, millions of whom were arrested. Without even being tried they were executed or sentenced to labour camps in far-off Siberia or the Arctic, where millions were worked to death or died of cold and hunger. The Terror was carried out by the secret police, the NKVD (formerly the Cheka), aided by informers who were encouraged to denounce their fellow-workers, neighbours, friends, and even their own families. The Russian people lived in terror.

Source D

By 1939 it was clear even to Stalin that the Purges and Terror were destroying Russian society and they were scaled down. No one knows how many suffered during this time. Some have estimated that 20 million people were sentenced to labour camps, over half of them dying there. The country lost many of its scientists, doctors, teachers, engineers, as well as military officers.

A French cartoon of the 1930s showing a Russian with banner saying 'We are really happy'.

The prisoners were charged with every conceivable crime: high treason, murder, espionage and all kinds of sabotage. They had all signed written statements confessing to the crimes and incriminating themselves and each other. ... Yet what they said bore no relation to the truth. It became clear that the purpose of the trial was to show them not as political offenders, but as common criminals, murderers and spies.

A British diplomat describing a show trial.

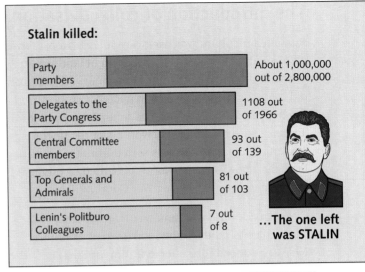

Stalin killed:

Party members	About 1,000,000 out of 2,800,000
Delegates to the Party Congress	1108 out of 1966
Central Committee members	93 out of 139
Top Generals and Admirals	81 out of 103
Lenin's Politburo Colleagues	7 out of 8

...The one left was STALIN

The purge of the Communist Party.

Things to do

1 Use Source C and the evidence on Stalin's control of the USSR to explain the cult of personality.

2 Use Source D and the evidence in this section to explain why Stalin used show trials to remove his opponents in the Communist Party.

3 Look at Source E and the chart above. What were the results of the Purges for: Stalin, the Communist Party, the Russian people?

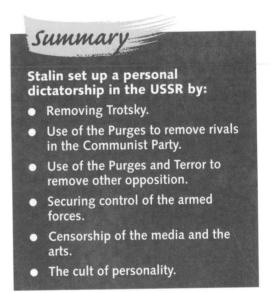

Summary

Stalin set up a personal dictatorship in the USSR by:

- Removing Trotsky.
- Use of the Purges to remove rivals in the Communist Party.
- Use of the Purges and Terror to remove other opposition.
- Securing control of the armed forces.
- Censorship of the media and the arts.
- The cult of personality.

4.2 To what extent did Stalin make Russia a great economic power?

The need for economic growth

Under the NEP Russian industry made up much of the ground lost during world and civil war. Even so, in 1928 the country was still backward compared to other major powers.

Stalin wanted the USSR to be strong industrially, mainly because it would make it more able to resist invasion. Industry had to expand, especially heavy industries, such as coal, steel and oil. New factories and new towns would have to be built. To feed the workers and their families more food would be needed, so agriculture had to be made more efficient to meet this demand. For its industry the Soviet Union needed to buy machinery from other countries and to do this it needed to raise money from the export of grain to the West.

The Rule of Stalin

The introduction of collectivisation

Russian agriculture was backward in 1928. Most farms were small following the distribution of land among peasants after the Revolution. Peasants were still using old methods of farming. When a food crisis occurred in the late 1920s Stalin was forced to introduce rationing. To make sure the industrial workers of the towns had enough to eat grain was seized from the peasant farmers. They were furious and hoarded or produced less, just as they did during War Communism.

Given that industry depended on an efficient agriculture to produce the food needed, Stalin in 1929 announced the collectivisation of Russian agriculture as the way to increasing its efficiency.

The collective farm

Among the different kinds of collective farms, the most common was the Kolkhoz, where peasants joined their land together to form a larger farm. All their animals were also given over to the farm. It was run by a committee and the peasants worked together and shared everything. Each farm produced a set amount of grain and sold this to the state at a low price. Anything they produced over this amount was for them to keep or sell. The state provided tractors and other machinery to help the peasants farm more efficiently.

The process of collectivisation

Stalin linked collectivisation to socialist policy to try and persuade the peasants to join the collective farms. In doing this he identified an enemy of the poor – the Kulaks, rich peasants who had prospered under the NEP. He claimed he was taking land from the 'greedy, capitalist Kulaks' and giving it to the poor peasants.

The Kulaks were arrested and 'liquidated' – that is, shot or deported to labour camps in Siberia.

Many peasants were still not convinced about collectivisation and rather than hand over their crops, stock and buildings they destroyed them.

By 1930 over half the farming land was collectivised, but Stalin was worried about continuing resistance

Source F

The history of old Russia has consisted in being beaten again and again because of our backwardness. It is our duty to the working class to increase the pace of production. We are 50-100 years behind the advanced countries. We must make up this gap in ten years. Either we do it or they crush us.

Extract from a speech by Stalin in 1931.

Source G

Stock was slaughtered every night. As soon as dusk fell the muffled, short bleats of sheep, the death squeals of pigs, or the lowing of calves could be heard. Bulls, sheep, pigs, even cows were slaughtered, as well as cattle for breeding .... 'Kill, it's not ours any more ... Kill, they'll take it for meat anyway ... Kill, you won't get meat on the collective farm ...' And they killed. They ate until they could eat no more.

An extract from the Russian novel, **Virgin Soil Upturned,** *by M. Sholokhov.*

Source H

Collectivisation achieved its main aims. The government could now take food from the peasants at incredibly low prices. Also it acquired an increased working force for industry. Mechanisation, especially tractors, released millions of young peasants for industries in the cities.

A modern British historian writing about collectivisation.

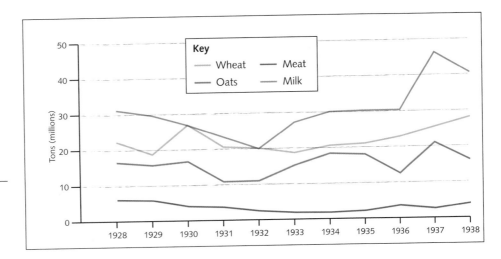

Key
— Wheat   — Meat
— Oats   — Milk

Russian agricultural production, 1928–38.

from many farmers. So he made changes to the system. Peasants could keep their own houses and a small plot of land for their own use. This encouraged more peasants to join the collective farms, though some still refused. By 1937 nearly all the farmland in the USSR was organised into collective farms.

Things to do

Use Source G and H, the graph above, and the evidence in this section to make a judgement on whether collectivisation succeeded.

Results of collectivisation

Collectivisation had limited success. Grain production did not increase; actually it fell between 1929 and 1933. Bad harvests and peasants' destruction of crops in protest at collectivisation caused famine in 1932-33, with millions dying of starvation. Grain production did, however, increase after 1933 as the collectives became more organised.

Collectivisation had a high human cost. The Kulaks were eliminated, with almost five million being executed or deported, and over 13 million peasants died during collectivisation, many of them from the famine.

Source I

A painting of Stalin with industrial workers.

The Rule of Stalin

Industry: the Five Year Plans

Stalin believed industry could only develop through strong state control and planning. This was to be achieved by a series of Five Year Plans. During these the state would decide what and how much would be produced.

Gosplan, the state planning agency, was responsible for the Plans. It set the targets an industry had to meet in five years. Each factory in an industry would have its own target to contribute to the overall target of that industry. Success in meeting targets was rewarded, failure was punished.

Between 1928 and 1941 there were three Five Year Plans. The first concerned heavy industry – coal, iron and steel, oil and electricity. Though it failed to meet its targets, substantial industrial growth was achieved. At the end of the second Plan, 1933-37, which also involved heavy industry, even more industrial growth had taken place. The third Plan began in 1938 with the idea of producing more consumer goods. However, it was disrupted by the threat of war with Nazi Germany and the need to divert industry to the making of arms for war.

Source J

A quarter of a million people – communists, Kulaks, foreigners, convicts and a mass of peasants – were building the largest steelworks in Europe in the middle of the Russian steppe at Magnitogorsk. Here men froze, went hungry and suffered, but the construction went on with a disregard for individuals.

An extract from a book by an American engineer who worked in the USSR in the 1930s.

Things to do

Study Sources J, K and the graph on page 113. What evidence do they give to show the effects of the Five Year Plans on Russian industry?

Source K

Magnitogorsk, a new industrial city in Russia.

The growth of industry

Russian industry changed and expanded enormously because of the Plans. Old industrial areas were re-developed and expanded, and new ones were created to the east, in the Urals and Siberia, well away from areas most likely to be attacked by enemies, such as Germany.

New towns were built, such as Magnitogorsk in the Urals and Komsomulsk in Siberia. In eight years Magnitogorsk was transformed from a tiny village to a massive industrial city producing steel.

Other achievements included the construction of a hydro-electric dam on the River Dneiper, which by itself produced more electricity than was produced in the whole of Tsarist Russia.

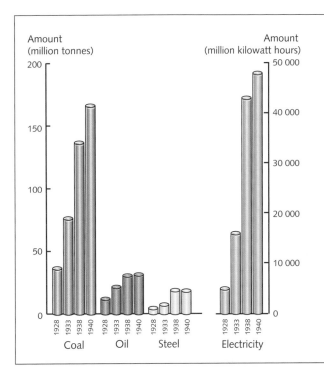

Industrial production, 1928-40.

Results of the Five Year Plans

In all the key industries – coal, iron and steel, oil, electricity – the USSR grew to be a major industrial power in ten years. Though it was still well behind the most powerful Western countries, it was no longer an easy target for invaders, particularly the Germans.

The human cost of this achievement was high. Forced labour killed millions of people. In the towns and cities, unable to cope with the mass influx of new workers from the countryside, slums and poor sanitation flourished. There wasn't enough food and rationing was common. Working conditions were poor and hours of work long. Improvements were made by the government, with more schools being built and social insurance schemes introduced. However, these could not meet the level of demand.

De-Stalinisation

Stalin died in 1953 but it was not until 1956 that he was officially criticised in the USSR. His eventual successor, Khrushchev, took the opportunity at the 20th Communist Party Congress in 1956 to criticise Stalin's cult of personality, his dictatorship and the Purges and Red Terror. This was a period of de-Stalinisation, in which Stalin's place in Russian history was diminished.

Summary

The achievements of Stalin's economic policy were:

- Collectivisation of all farmland in USSR.
- Production of more grain for export.
- Increased industrial production in all key industries.
- Expansion of Russian industry to new areas.

The cost of Stalin's economic policies were:

- Elimination of the Kulaks.
- Disruption of agriculture because of peasant opposition to collectivisation.
- Poor condition of life in cities and towns.
- Death of millions of Russians through famine, starvation, overwork and forced labour.

Exam–type Assessment
Russia and the USSR, 1900–56

This exercise is based on the sort of questions you could be asked on Paper 2 of your examination.

Source A

A cartoon of Russian Society in 1900. The workers at the bottom protest at their lack of freedoms. Next, the capitalists say 'We do the eating'; the army say 'We shoot you'; the clergy say 'We fool you'; and the nobles say 'We govern you'. The royal family at the top say 'We rule you'.

Questions

1   Study Source A.
What is the cartoon saying about Russian society? *(4 marks)*

2   Summary Essay.
Why did the First World War weaken the Tsar and Russia and bring the collapse of his rule? *(15 marks)*

A painting called 'The Inevitable' showing a Red Guard standing in the throne room of the Tsar in the Winter Palace.

Questions

1   Summary Essay.

The Provisional Government ruled Russia for only eight months – from March to November 1917. Explain why it lasted for such a short time.   (*15 marks*)

2   Study Source B.

Use your knowledge of the events of 7/8 November 1917 to explain whether you agree with the title of the painting.   (*7 marks*)

Source C

- Every scoundrel who incites anyone to retreat or to desert will be shot.

- Every soldier who throws away his rifle will be shot.

Orders to the Red Army from Trotsky.

Source D

	1928	1933	1938	1940
Coal (million tonnes)	36	76	136	166
Oil (million tonnes)	11.7	21.4	30.2	31
Steel (million tonnes)	4.2	6.9	18.1	18
Electricity (million kilowatt hours)	5,000	16,000	43,000	48,000

Industrial production in Russia, 1928–40.

Questions

1   Study Source C.
Use your knowledge to explain why the Reds won the civil war of 1918–21.   (*6 marks*)

2   Summary Essay.
Explain the changes in economic policy in Russia in the period 1918–24.   (*15 marks*)

3   Summary Essay.
Explain how Stalin set up a personal dictatorship in the Communist Party and in the USSR between 1928 and 1941.   (*15 marks*)

4   Study Source D.
Use your knowledge to explain how Russian industry grew in the period of the Five Year Plans, 1928 to 1940.   (*6 marks*)

Chapter 4

Governments in Action:
Germany, 1918–39

In 1918 Germany suffered defeat in the First World War. The Treaty of
Versailles, which formally brought peace to Europe, proved humiliating to
Germany. It weakened the Weimar Republic, the new government in Germany,
and brought challenges to it. The impact of the Treaty played an important part
in shaping post-war Germany, it also brought economic hardship with hyperinflation in 1923. Extremist groups developed and one of these, the Nazi Party,
destroyed the Weimar Republic and took control of Germany in 1933, following
the impact of economic depression between 1929 and 1933.

Hitler and the Nazi Party were brought to power by the votes of the German
people. However, in a short time, a fascist dictatorship was established in which
the Nazi Party controlled all aspects of German life such as education, the law,
religion and the media. Those who disagreed, or who were not accepted by the
Nazis, were persecuted – none more so than the Jewish people. Hitler brought
benefits to the German people, most importantly in employment, but the
Germans paid a heavy price for such gains.

**This is a Paper 2 topic and you will be required to answer one
structured question on it.**

The Weimar Republic

Germany, 1918–33

The Weimar Republic, which governed Germany after the Kaiser abdicated, was blamed for signing the Treaty of Versailles and all the problems that followed. It looked like it might survive after the success of the Stresemann years, but its failure to deal with the depression of 1929 led the German people to reject it in favour of extremist parties. The Nazi Party took control of Germany and by 1933 the Weimar Republic was dead.

1.1 How far do the early problems of the Weimar Republic suggest that it was doomed from the start?

The abdication of the Kaiser

In 1918, the final year of the First World War, conditions in Germany were poor. There was starvation and hunger among the people. The army was demoralised. In November, the sailors at Kiel mutinied, refusing to obey orders to leave the port for battle with the British navy. The Kaiser failed to send the army to crush the mutiny. The result was that it spread – to other sailors, to soldiers and to workers who went on strike. Within days there were strikes and risings all over Germany as the country fell into chaos. The Kaiser found himself without support, even from his army generals. On 9 November he abdicated and fled to Holland. On 11 November 1918 Germany signed the armistice with the Allies. The war was over.

However, the Kaiser had departed so suddenly that a new government had not been appointed or elected. The lead was taken by Friedrich Ebert, the head of the Social Democratic Party.

An ex-soldier begs in the streets of Berlin in 1923.

This was the largest single party in the Reichstag (the German Parliament) so it could claim that it represented the people. Two days after the Kaiser's abdication, Ebert declared a new German Republic with an elected parliament.

The Spartacist Revolt

Not all Germans accepted the new republic. Some wanted a social revolution like the Russian Revolution of November 1917 (see pages 98–9). These were Communists or Spartacists, named after the Roman slave who had led a revolt in ancient Rome. Led by Rosa Luxemburg and Karl Liebknecht, the Spartacists demonstrated against the new government in January 1919. Ebert called out the troops and 16 people were killed.

Governments in Action: Germany, 1918–39

Then in January 1919, the Spartactists attempted a revolution in Berlin. Badly planned and poorly supported, the revolution was crushed by the Free Corps – ex-soldiers who had returned from the war. Luxemburg and Liebknecht were arrested, beaten and murdered on 15 January 1919.

The creation of the Weimar Republic

On 19 January 1919, four days after the defeat of the Spartacists, a general election was held for a new parliament. The Social Democrats were elected as the largest party and Ebert was appointed the first President of the German Republic. However, it was felt that Berlin was too unsafe for the government to meet there. Instead, it moved to the safer town of Weimar.

Revolts in Berlin and Bavaria

Any hopes that the newly elected government would be accepted by all Germans were quickly ended. In March 1919 the Communists organised riots and strikes in Berlin. Again the Free Corps destroyed this opposition.

A further threat to the Weimar Republic was the setting up of a Socialist Republic in Bavaria in November 1918. On 7 April it was made a Soviet Republic like Russia with Munich as its capital. Food, money and houses were taken from the rich and given to the workers. The government sent soldiers to besiege Munich. In May the soldiers, helped by the Free Corps, broke into the city. The revolt was crushed and its leaders massacred. The Weimar government had established its control of Germany by defeating opposition with the help of the Free Corps. Now it had an even greater problem to face – the peace treaty to end the First World War.

Source B

Spartacists defend their position, Berlin 1919.

The Treaty of Versailles

On 28 June 1919, the German government signed the Treaty of Versailles – the 'Diktat', the dictated peace. Germany was not involved in negotiating the treaty and was forced to accept its harsh terms under threat of invasion by the Allies (see page 120).

The Germans lost some of their territory and industry and were forced to pay huge reparations. Their military forces were cut and restricted to certain limits and they were forced to accept the blame for the war. The treaty also greatly weakened the Weimar Republic and it became unacceptable to many Germans. Its politicians were the 'November Criminals' who had signed the treaty and 'stabbed Germany in the back'.

Things to do

Look at Source B and the evidence in this section. Explain why the Weimar government was able to defeat the opposition to it in 1919.

The Weimar Republic

Case Study: the Treaty of Versailles

Summary of the main terms of the Treaty.

1 Territorial losses

- Alsace-Lorraine returned to France.
- West Prussia and the Polish corridor lost to Poland (thus splitting Germany in two).
- Eupen and Malmedy given to Belgium.
- North Schleswig given to Denmark.
- Part of Upper Silesia given to Poland.
- Port of Danzig made a free city under the League of Nations.
- Memel taken over by the League of Nations.
- Saarland taken over by the League of Nations for 15 years. France given control of the Saar's coalfields.
- Overseas colonies became mandates.
- Germay lost 13 per cent of its land and 12 per cent of its population.
- Losses of industrial areas: Alsace-Lorraine, Silesia, the Saarland.

2 Military restrictions

- Army limited to 100,000 soldiers.
- Navy limited to 6 battle-ships and no submarines.
- Airforce disbanded.
- Rhineland 'demilitarised'.

3 War Guilt

- Article 231 blamed Germany for the war.

4 Reparations

- Germany forced to pay reparations to Allies (later set at £6,600 million).

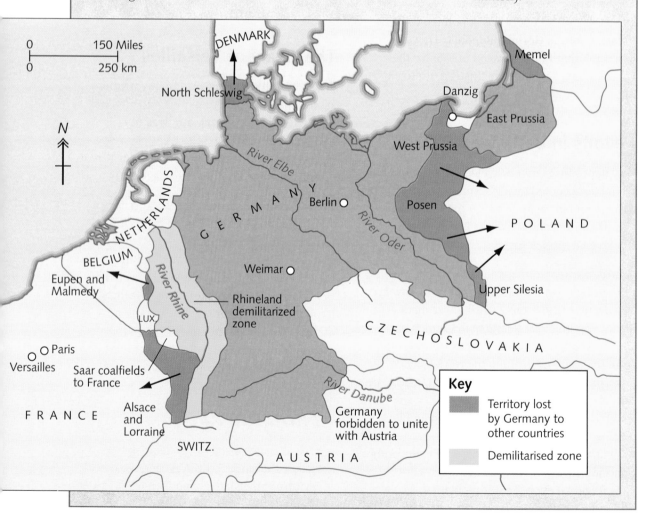

The Kapp *Putsch*

The Treaty of Versailles had ordered the reduction of the German army. Many of the soldiers who had been demobbed joined the Free Corps. These had supported the government in defeating socialist and communist risings, often with great violence. In early 1920 the Allies put pressure on the government to break up the Free Corps, who, led by Wolfgang Kapp marched into Berlin to seize power. This was a *putsch* – an attempt to take power by force. Kapp was supported by the army and the police in Berlin. By this time Ebert and his government had returned from Weimar to Berlin. Now they left Berlin and fled to Dresden. From here the government appealed for support from the workers in Berlin. The workers supported the government and organised a general strike. Within a day there was no water, gas, coal or transport in Berlin. The *putsch* quickly collapsed and Kapp fled to Sweden. Ebert and the government returned to Berlin. Order had been restored. The Weimar government now hoped for a period of calm to allow the new constitution to be put into operation.

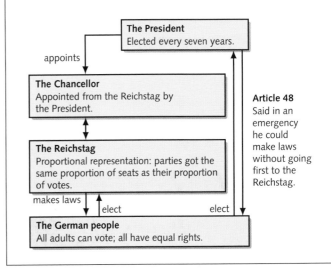

The Constitution of the Weimar Republic.

Things to do

1   Look at the evidence on the Spartacist Revolt, the Bavarian Rising and the Kapp *Putsch*. How did the Weimar Republic defeat all three? What does your answer tell you about the strengths and weaknesses of the Weimar Republic?

2   Explain why you would hate the Treaty of Versailles if you were a German in 1919.

The Weimar Constitution

A constitution is a set of rules which show how a country is to be governed. The Weimar Constitution was one of the most democratic constitutions ever introduced. Every German over the age of twenty could vote and all had equal rights. The head of state was the President, elected every seven years. The German Parliament, the Reichstag, was elected by a system called proportional representation – that is, political parties had the same proportion of seats in the Reich-stag as their proportion of votes. So a party with 30 per cent of the votes in an election had 30 per cent of the seats in the Reichstag.

Yet the Constitution had weaknesses. The President was given powers to take control of Germany in an emergency, which could make him a dictator. Proportional representation allowed a large number of parties to win seats in the Reichstag. This meant that no one party had a majority of seats, so governments had to be coalitions of a number of parties. The result was weak governments which often changed as parties left or entered the coalition. It also allowed a number of parties who were against the Weimar Republic to gain seats in the Reichstag – the Nazi Party was an example.

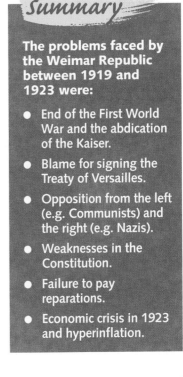

Summary

The problems faced by the Weimar Republic between 1919 and 1923 were:

- End of the First World War and the abdication of the Kaiser.
- Blame for signing the Treaty of Versailles.
- Opposition from the left (e.g. Communists) and the right (e.g. Nazis).
- Weaknesses in the Constitution.
- Failure to pay reparations.
- Economic crisis in 1923 and hyperinflation.

Children playing with worthless money, 1923.

Economic crisis of 1923

Germany managed to pay the first instalment of the reparations but was unable to pay the next instalment, due in 1922. The French refused to accept this, believing that Germany was unwilling to pay reparations rather than unable to pay them. So in January 1923, French and Belgian troops invaded the Ruhr, Germany's richest industrial area. They took over the coal mines, factories and steel works as compensation for the reparations payments. The German government responded by ordering the workers in the Ruhr not to work for the French – to put up 'passive resistance'. Violence broke out and in the next six months over 100 German people were killed by French troops.

Passive resistance also failed as Germany became even poorer because of the refusal to work for the French. The German government decided to print more money to pay the reparations but this only made things worse.

Hyperinflation

The effect of a government printing money is that the value of the money goes down and prices go up. As more and more money is printed, so prices rise higher and higher. More money then has to be printed to meet the increasing prices. As a result, money becomes worthless. This is called hyperinflation.

Hyperinflation affected the German people in different ways. For those in work, wages rose higher and higher – sometimes twice a day. Workers were seen collecting their weekly wages with wheelbarrows. However, the price of goods always tended to rise faster than wages. People on fixed incomes suffered the most. The rises in prices meant that their incomes were now too low to live on.

As soon as I received my salary I rushed out to buy what I needed. My daily salary was just enough to buy one loaf of bread and a small piece of cheese .... A friend of mine, a vicar, came to Berlin to buy some shoes with his month's wages for his baby. By the time he arrived, he only had enough to buy a cup of coffee.

A German woman writing about the effects of hyperinflation.

They struggled to buy food and clothes, and to heat their homes. Many of these people were pensioners and they now faced starvation. People with savings in the bank also suffered as the money they had saved was now worthless. Surprisingly, some Germans gained from the hyperinflation. But those who had debts or had taken out loans could now pay the money back with ease.

However, many more Germans suffered from the hyperinflation than gained from it. They laid the blame for their problems on the government. The Weimar Republic became even more unpopular. Some of this anger turned into violence. For example, in November 1923, the Nazi Party tried to seize power in Munich (see Unit 2 on the Munich *Putsch*). Yet the Weimar Republic survived. This was largely because of the work of Gustav Stresemann who was Chancellor for a few weeks in 1923, and then Foreign Minister until his death in 1929.

(see Unit 2 on the Munich *Putsch*)

Things to do

1 Look at the evidence in this section. How did the 1923 economic crisis affect the people of Germany?

1.2 Why did the world depression of 1929 to 1933 destroy the stability of the Stresemann years and lead to the collapse of the Weimar Republic?

The recovery of Germany between 1924 and 1929

Stresemann realised that swift action was needed in order to save Germany from ruin. The passive resistance campaign in the Ruhr was called off and the government agreed to start paying reparations again. As a result, French troops left the Ruhr. The government also stopped printing more paper money. They abolished the old mark and instructed people to hand in their old notes. This was then replaced by a new currency, the Rentenmark. These actions were needed to solve the immediate crisis in Germany. However, Stresemann also realised that other measures were required if Germany was to overcome its economic problems. He realised that Germany needed help and support from other countries.

Stresemann was able to persuade Britain, France and the USA to work out a new plan for paying reparations in a way that would not be so crippling for Germany. The Dawes Plan of 1924 was the result. It stated that the amount of reparations Germany would pay each year would vary according to what it could afford to pay. A further change to this plan came in 1929 with the Young Plan. This reduced the amount of reparations Germany needed to pay each year and extended the time it had to pay them.

The German economy was now more stable. Foreign businessmen, especially from the USA, were prepared to invest their money in Germany. As a result, new factories were built and new machinery was placed in them. New houses were built. All this meant more jobs were created.

However, there were still weaknesses in the German economy. Industrial production went up compared to the early 1920s but it only reached its pre-war level by 1928. Unemployment was still relatively high – in 1928 over a million Germans were without jobs. Above all, the German economy depended on loans from abroad. These could be withdrawn at any time.

The Weimar Republic

The Great Depression

A further problem for the Weimar Republic also continued – the political one. The Social Democrats remained the largest party in the Reichstag but they never had enough seats to govern on their own. Governments could only be formed by coalitions of parties working together. Sometimes these worked, but usually they did not last long because of party differences. As a result there were frequent changes in government. The Weimar Republic had also not yet won over the German people. An indication of this came in 1925 when Hindenburg was elected President. The great hero of the First World War was an outspoken critic of the Weimar Republic.

Despite these problems, there were signs that Germany was becoming more stable. It was unfortunate for the Weimar Republic that, at this point, another depression hit the country.

In October 1929, Stresemann, the most able minister in the government, died. Shortly after, the American financial market on Wall Street in New York crashed. The effects of the collapse were felt not only in the USA, but across the world. Germany was hit particularly badly because of the scale of its loans from America after 1924. American bankers and businessmen whose stocks and shares had collapsed now wanted their money back from German businesses. They demanded repayment of their loans and, of course, were not in a position to lend any more money. The result was a disaster for Germany. Businesses closed down as loans were repaid and trade slumped. Unemployment shot up. By 1932 six million Germans were unemployed. Millions of others became homeless, and set up camps on the outskirts of towns. They became dependent on charity food and soup kitchens to avoid starvation.

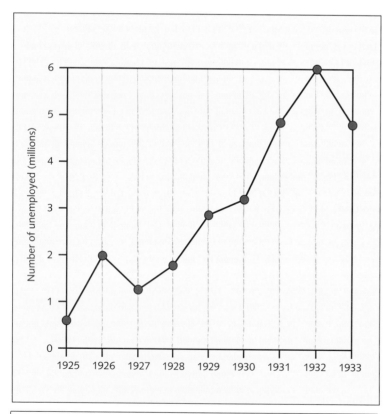

Unemployment in Germany 1925-33.

Source E

Men standing hopelessly on the street corners of every industrial town in Germany; houses without food or warmth; young people without any chance of a job. All these things explain the bitterness which burned in the minds of millions of ordinary Germans.

A description of the effects of unemployment in Germany in 1932.

The Weimar government and the Depression

The government was taken by surprise at the speed and extent of the Depression. It also had very few answers as to how to deal with it. To increase government expenditure to help the poor could only be done by printing money – and after 1923 this was unthinkable. So the government introduced a series of limited measures which often made things worse. It raised taxes to obtain money to help the needy, but this caused further problems for the businesses and companies being taxed. It reduced the wages of public officials, but this made life more difficult for them. Finally, it reduced unemployment benefit at a time when the growing numbers of unemployed needed all the help they could get. These policies also caused the collapse of the government as political parties withdrew from the coalition. It proved impossible to put together another coalition of parties that could form a government. In such a political emergency, the Constitution allowed the President to take control of the government. So the 84-year-old Hindenburg became the ruler of Germany.

This Nazi election poster of 1932 says 'Our last hope: Hitler!'

The Depression brought out all the weaknesses of the Weimar Republic which seemed to be incapable of doing anything to end the Depression. It is not surprising that the German people began to listen to parties promising to do something. In particular, they began to look to the Nazis.

Summary

The Great Depression of 1929–33:

- It ended the recovery of Germany from the 1923 depression.
- It was caused by Germany's dependence on American loans.
- It brought unemployment and hardship to the German people.
- It was blamed on the Weimar Republic and increased its unpopularity.
- It increased the support of extreme parties who promised to end it.

Things to do

Explain why the German people turned away from the Weimar politicians.

The Weimar Republic

Hitler and the Growth of the Nazi Party

Germany, up to 1933

The Nazi Party rose to power by organising itself and developing ideas that appealed to the German people. The depression of 1929 gave them the chance to aim for power. Hitler convinced many Germans that the Nazis could solve the country's problems and won increasing support in elections. Eventually Hitler became Chancellor, one step from gaining total control of Germany.

2.1 How did the Nazi Party develop its ideas and organisation in the period up to 1929?

Hitler's life in Vienna

Adolf Hitler was born in Austria in 1889. His father, a customs officer, died when he was fourteen, his mother when he was eighteen. With little education and no job, Hitler drifted to Vienna, the capital of Austria. He wished to become an art student but the Academy of Art would not enrol him. He was forced to live in poverty in hostels for tramps and take whatever jobs he could find. He developed an interest in politics and supported nationalist parties. He also came to dislike foreigners and, especially, Jewish people. He became convinced that it was Jews who had caused him to be a failure in Vienna. This early political interest would become important later on.

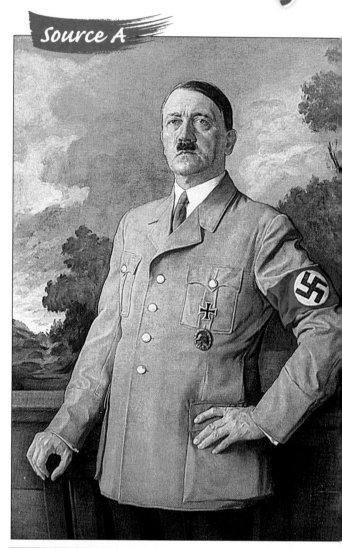

Source A

Adolf Hitler.

Source B

The news came through that we were about to surrender, I broke down completely. Darkness surrounded me. I buried my head between the blankets and the pillow. I had not cried since the day that I stood beside my mother's grave.

Hitler's reaction to the German surrender in 1918.

Governments in Action: Germany 1918–39

Hitler and the First World War

In 1913 Hitler left Austria to avoid military service. He went to live in Munich. When war broke out he immediately volunteered to join the German army. He was on active service throughout the war and was wounded twice. He was promoted to corporal and won the Iron Cross, First Class – the highest award for a German soldier. In 1918 he was gassed. It was in hospital that Hitler learned that Germany had surrendered and signed the armistice. He was bitter and angry and, like many other Germans, he blamed the defeat not on the German army but on Communists and Jews – the 'stab in the back' idea examined in Unit 1.

After the war Hitler returned to Munich. However, he stayed in the army and was used to spy on political parties to find out if they were a threat to the new government. One of the parties he spied on was a newly formed one, the German Workers Party.

The foundation of the Nazi Party

The German Workers Party was small. Hitler found he agreed with its ideas and decided to join. He became its seventh member. Before long, he was its leader and began to reorganise the Party to increase its popularity.

One of the first things he did was to change its name to the National Socialist German Workers Party – shortened to the Nazi Party. In 1920 he drew up the party programme which summarised the ideas of the new party (see Source C). In 1921 he set up a private army, the SA (Stormtroopers), also known as the Brownshirts because of their uniforms. The SA consisted of young men and some former members of the Free Corps. Their role was to protect Nazi speakers at rallies. In practice they usually went much further and beat up opponents. For example, Social Democrat and Communist meetings were often broken up by violence. Hitler also devised a symbol for the new party – the swastika. The Party began to publish its own newspaper to put forward its ideas.

The Nazi Party was based in Munich, the capital of the German state of Bavaria. Hitler was well known here, mainly because of large public meetings held throughout the state. However, the Nazi Party was relatively small in Germany as a whole. Even so Hitler was confident that Nazi ideas would appeal to the German people. In 1923, as economic crisis and hyperinflation hit Germany and brought despair to millions of Germans, he became convinced that now was the time to seize power.

Source C

1 We demand the union of all Germans to form a greater Germany.
2 We demand the abolition of the Peace Treaty of Versailles.
3 We demand land and territory for the nourishment of our people.
4 None but those of German blood may be members of the German nation.
....
25 We demand the creation of a strong central government in Germany.

From the Twenty-Five Points of the Nazi Party programme, 1920.

Things to do

1 Study Source C. Who might be attracted by each of the points set out in the source.

The Munich *Putsch*, November 1923

Although the Nazi Party was small and its support was largely limited to Bavaria, Hitler thought that the conditions in Germany in 1923 and the unpopularity of the government gave him a good chance of success. He expected support from the right-wing Bavarian government, led by Gustav Von Kahr. He also thought that the German army could be persuaded to desert the government and support the Nazis. He was encouraged in this by General Ludendorff who had shown sympathy with Nazi ideas.

On 8 November 1923, as Kahr addressed a meeting at a beer hall in Munich, Hitler arrived with 600 Stormtroopers. He stopped the meeting and tried to persuade Kahr at gunpoint to support the *putsch*. The arrival of Ludendorff at this point appeared to win over Kahr. The next day the SA seized key positions in Munich and Stormtroopers from other parts of Bavaria began to arrive. However, Kahr had been freed after agreeing to support the *putsch* and had alerted the army and the police.

As the Nazis marched to the city centre, their route was blocked by armed police and soldiers. Firing broke out – 16 Nazis and 3 policemen were killed. Hitler, Ludendorff and other Nazi leaders were arrested.

The *putsch* failed largely because Hitler over-estimated his support and the army and police stayed loyal to the government.

In February 1924 Hitler was put on trial on a charge of treason. He used the trial as a public platform to put forward his ideas and to condemn the Weimar Republic. The trial made Hitler a national and international figure. Despite the seriousness of the charge, Hitler was sentenced to only five years imprisonment. He served less than nine months. The other leaders received even lighter sentences.

Source D

Things to do

Look at Source E and the evidence on the Munich *Putsch*. Was the putsch a failure or success for Hitler? Give reasons for your answers.

Police about to disperse Hitler's supporters in Munich, 9 November 1923.

Mein Kampf

While in prison Hitler wrote a book about his life and ideas called *Mein Kampf* ('My Struggle'). This became the 'bible' of the Nazi movement. It contained many of the ideas which Hitler later put into practice. The ideas in *Mein Kampf* were nothing new. However, they did give a clear indication of what the Nazi Party stood for. When Hitler came to power, the book became compulsory reading for all Germans – at home, in school and, even, in church.

The Nazi Party, 1924-29

The years between 1924 and 1929 were difficult ones for the Nazi Party. After the Munich *Putsch*, the party was banned by the government and its supporters began to drift away. On Hitler's release from prison in December 1924 the ban was lifted and the party re-formed.

However, it struggled to attract the support of the German voters. These were the Stresemann years (see Unit 1), when employment was high, business was doing well and Germany at last seemed to be recovering from the war and its effects. The extremist policies of the Nazi Party were not attractive in such stable conditions. This decline in the Nazi Party is seen in its performance in elections. In May 1924 it won 32 seats in the Reichstag, in December this had fallen to 14 seats, and in 1928 there was a further fall to 12 seats.

Yet the Nazi Party did not fade away in these years. A number of developments of importance took place. Hitler increased his control of the Party, Nazi organisations were set up and public meetings and rallies were held throughout Germany. It was activities like these which brought an increased membership to the Nazi Party. In 1925, it had 27,000 members, in 1928 over 100,000.

Even so, this was a long way off becoming a major national party which could take power in Germany. Something was needed to push the Nazi Party forward. It was at this point in 1929 that Germany was hit by a severe economic depression.

Source E

I am not a criminal. There is no such thing as high treason against the traitors of 1918. History will judge us as Germans who wanted only the good of their people and fatherland.

From Hitler's speech at his trial, 1924.

Source F

- Germany should be ruled by a strong leader with total power – the Führer.
- The Aryan race of which the Germans are part are a 'master race'. All other races are inferior to them.
- Jews have weakened the German race and brought Germany's defeat in the war. They must be destroyed.
- Communism must also be destroyed.
- The Treaty of Versailles must be destroyed and the land which Germany lost must be returned.
- Germany needs more land to live and work in (*lebensraum*). If necessary, it must take this by force.

The main ideas of Mein Kampf.

Summary

The development of the Nazi Party from 1919 to 1928:

1919 – Hitler joined the German Workers Party.

1920 – Hitler became its leader and renamed it the National Socialist German Workers Party – the Nazi Party.

1921 – SA was set up.

1923 – The Munich Putsch.

1924 – Hitler imprisoned; wrote *Mein Kampf*.

1928 – Nazi Party won 12 seats in the Reichstag.

2.2 How was Hitler able to use the world depression to extend support for the Nazis between 1929 and 1933?

The Nazi Party and the Great Depression

Support for the Nazi Party was due to the growing belief that it was a party with a leader who could do something about Germany's problems.

The Nazis promised much: jobs for the unemployed in state-financed public works programmes, help for employers to increase their profits, help for farmers and shop-keepers. They also promised that Germany would be great again. The Nazis were prepared to promise anything to win votes. Only the Jews and Communists, who were blamed for all Germany's problems, were left out of the Nazis' plans for Germany.

The Nazis were also well organised. They were disciplined and portrayed Hitler as a strong leader who would 'save' Germany. Mass rallies enabled Hitler to speak to thousands of people at one time. Joseph Goebbels, who was in charge of propaganda, ran a 'Hitler over Germany' campaign, which involved flying Hitler from one rally to the next, allowing him to make speeches all over Germany. This was supported by a poster campaign, strong in emotional appeal (Source G).

The SA also played an important role. They beat up opponents, especially the Communists, and smashed up their election meetings. This made it very difficult for the Communists to run a free election campaign. In contrast to the strong campaign of the Nazi Party, the Social Democrats and other parties who supported the Weimar government seemed to have little to offer.

Nazi election gains, 1930–32

Nazi election campaigning was effective. In 1930 they won 107 seats and in July 1932 this had increased to 230 seats. Although this fell to 196 in the November election, they remained the largest single party in the Reichstag.

In the presidential elections of April 1932 Hitler stood against Hindenburg for the presidency of Germany. Hindenburg won with 19 million votes against Hitler's 13 million.

Unlike the Munich *Putsch*, the Nazis were using the democratic process to win power. By the summer of 1932 Hitler was in a position to demand that he should become Chancellor of Germany.

Source G

A Nazi election poster of 1932 saying 'Women! Millions of men out of work! Millions of children without a future! Save our German families. Vote for Hitler.'

Things to do

Look at Source G. How far does it help us to explain why so many Germans turned to the Nazis between 1930 and 1932?

Hitler becomes Chancellor

Hindenburg disliked the Nazi Party and its leader. He refused to make Hitler Chancellor despite the fact that after the July 1932 elections the Nazis were the largest party in the Reichstag. Instead, he used his emergency powers to appoint the leader of the smaller Centre Party, von Papen, as Chancellor. However, one of Hindenburg's advisors, von Schleicher, told him that the army opposed von Papen and might take action unless he was replaced. Hindenburg was forced to back down but again he did not summon Hitler.

In December 1932 he asked von Schleicher to become Chancellor. Von Schleicher failed to get much support in the Reichstag and resigned after only eight weeks. Finally, in January 1933, Hindenburg summoned Hitler to his office and invited him to become Chancellor. Even then Hindenburg showed his distrust of Hitler. He persuaded Hitler to accept von Papen as Vice Chancellor and put von Papen's supporters into the government. In this way Hindenburg expected to be able to control Hitler. However, he had underestimated Hitler's political ability. Hitler accepted the arrangement but immediately called another election to the Reichstag. He wanted to get full control of the Reichstag by making the Nazis the majority party.

The new elections were called for March 1933. The Nazis began a violent campaign using the SA to disrupt Communist meetings. However, before the election could take place, a dramatic event happened – the Reichstag building went up in flames.

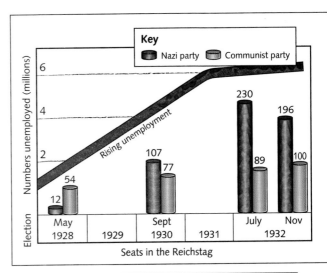

Growth of support for the Nazi Party in Reichstag elections.

Hitler as Chancellor being presented to President Hindenburg.

Case Study: the Reichstag fire and its results

On 27 February 1933, the Reichstag building was set on fire. Inside the building a young Dutch Communist, Marinus van der Lubbe, was found by the police with matches in his pocket. He was charged with the crime and later confessed. At his trial he was found guilty and then executed. Firm evidence still does not exist to prove the case. Van der Lubbe was known to have been of limited intelligence and his interrogation by the Nazi-controlled police force may well have resulted in a forced confession. It is possible, although again not proven, that the Nazis themselves planned and set fire to the Reichstag.

There was an underground passage that ran from the SA offices into the Reichstag building, and so access to the Reichstag would have been easy. A few days before the fire the SA had picked up Van der Lubbe after hearing him boast that he planned to set fire to the Reichstag. It would have been easy to set him up to take the blame.

If there is a doubt over who was responsible for the Reichstag fire, the results of are not in doubt. Hitler immediately claimed that the fire was proof of a Communist plot to take control of the government. It was the signal for a bloody uprising.

Source I

The Reichstag buildings on fire, 27 February 1933.

At a luncheon on the birthday of the Fuhrer in 1942 the conversation turned to the topic of the Reichstag building. I heard with my own ears when Goering interrupted the conversation and shouted: 'The only one who really knows about the Reichstag is I, because I set it on fire!

The Nazi general, Halder, speaking at the Nuremberg War Crimes trial, 1945.

Source K

This act of arson is the most outrageous act yet committed by Communism in Germany. The burning of the Reichstag was to have been the signal for a bloody uprising and civil war.

Statement by Hitler, issued the day after the Reichstag fire.

He persuaded President Hindenburg to sign an emergency decree, the Law for the Protection of People and the State. It ended all the freedoms guaranteed in the Constitution and gave the police total control. Working with the SA the police arrested Communist leaders and detained them without trial. Communist meetings were broken up, and their newspapers closed down. Other political opponents of the Nazis also suffered.

At the same time as all this violence, the Nazi propaganda machine encouraged the German people to vote for the Nazis. There were mass rallies, torchlight parades and radio broadcasts.

The 1933 election

The election results of March 1933, not unexpectedly, brought victory to the Nazis. More people voted for them than ever before (44% of the voters) and the Party won more seats (288) than ever before. However, the Nazis still did not have control of the Reichstag – 359 seats went to parties other than the Nazis. But they were now helped by one of the smaller parties, the Nationalist Party. It decided to join with the Nazis. Its 52 seats were added to the 288 of the Nazi Party, and this gave the Nazis control of the Reichstag.

Hitler was finally in a position where he could move for complete power.

Things to do

Look at Sources I, J and K, and the evidence in the case study on the Reichstag fire. Who do you think set fire to the Reichstag? Give reasons for your answer.

Summary

The Nazi Party's rise to power, 1929–33:

1929	Depression hit Germany.
1930	Nazis win 107 seats in the Reichstag.
1932	**April** Hitler wins 13 million votes in election for President. **July** Nazis wins 230 seats in the Reichstag. **November** Nazi Party wins 196 seats in the Reichstag.
1933	**January** Hitler appointed Chancellor. **February** Reichstag fire. **March** Nazi Party won 288 seats in the Reichstag.

Establishment of a Nazi Dictatorship

Germany, 1933–34

After Hitler became Chancellor he moved Germany from a democracy to a dictatorship. Any opposition to the Nazi Party was eliminated and opponents were imprisoned. Nazis were appointed to important positions in the state. They became ministers in the government, civil servants, judges and officials in the state parliaments. Hitler even eliminated a key organisation within his own party, the SA, because he felt that it was becoming a threat to him. Finally, the death of President Hindenburg allowed Hitler to become the Führer – the Leader. The Nazis were now in complete control. Germany had become a totalitarian state.

3.1 How did Hitler change Germany from a democracy to a Nazi dictatorship in the period 1933 to 1934?

The Enabling Law

The elections of March 1933 and the decision of the Nationalist Party to join with the Nazis had given Hitler control of the Reichstag. He lost no time in using this to his advantage. On 23 March he introduced an Enabling Law which would allow him to have complete power in Germany. However, this law needed to be approved by the Reichstag. Because it also changed the Constitution of the German Republic, it had to be approved by a two-thirds majority in the Reichstag. Hitler did not have this – the Nazis and the Nationalist Party together held just over half the seats. Great pressure was now put on the other parties in the Reichstag. The first step was to ban the 81 Communist members of the Reichstag from taking their seats. This was done easily by using the emergency powers Hitler had already been given by the Law for the Protection of the People and the State. The next largest party in the Reichstag was the Social Democrats. Its members were threatened and attacked by the SA as they turned up on the day of the vote for the Enabling Law. Many did not even turn up. Other parties gave in to Nazi pressure. The result was that the Enabling Law was passed by 444 votes to 94. Over a hundred members of the Reichstag were absent for the vote.

Source A

Our leader, Otto Wels, gave our good wishes to the persecuted and oppressed in the country who were already filling up prisons and concentration camps because of their political beliefs.

Hitler was furious. The SA and SS who surrounded us shouted at us 'Traitors' and 'you'll be strung up'.

A Social Democrat describes the scene when the Enabling Law was passed.

The Enabling Law destroyed the Weimar Constitution. It gave Hitler the power to pass any laws without consulting the Reichstag and without the approval of the President. He could even make treaties with foreign countries on his own authority. After March 1933, and for the rest of Hitler's rule of Germany, the Reichstag did not meet very often, and then only to hear a speech from Hitler. In November 1933 new 'elections' were held to the Reichstag. The Nazis were the only party allowed to stand.

The removal of opposition

With the powers given to him by the Enabling Law, Hitler now moved against any opposition to the Nazi Party. The Communists had already been destroyed. In June 1933 the Social Democrat Party was banned. Other political parties soon followed. This removal of political parties became formal in July when Hitler introduced the Law against the Formation of New Parties. This stated that the Nazi Party was the only party allowed to exist in Germany. It also laid down severe punishment for anyone who tried to set up another party. Germany was now a one-party state. Trade unions, which tended to be anti-Nazi, were also abolished and their offices destroyed. The leaders of political parties and trade unions were arrested and imprisoned. Many were to die in labour camps.

At the same time Hitler also ensured that Nazis were placed in important positions in the state and the government, and that opponents of the Nazis were removed. When Hitler became Chancellor, there were only three Nazis in his government. Now all the ministers were Nazis. Nazi officials were also put in charge of the local governments which ran the states of Germany. Many civil servants, who administered the government departments, were Nazis or sympathised with the Nazis. Those who did not were removed from office. The same was true for the judges.

All these actions gave Hitler complete control of Germany and its political, administrative and legal systems. However, Hitler now identified one more threat to his power – and it came from within his own party.

Source B

The Law against the Formation of New Parties.

Article I: The National Socialist Party is the only political party in Germany.

Article II: Whoever tries to maintain another political party or form a new party will be punished with penal servitude and imprisonment up to three years, if not a greater penalty.

The Law against the formation of New Parties, July 1933.

Things to do

Look at Sources A and B and the evidence in the section. What methods did Hitler use to remove the opposition to the Nazi Party?

Case Study: the Night of the Long Knives

Now that Hitler was in control of Germany, he did not need the SA. Hitler also realised that the SA might be a threat to his control. It was an undisciplined body, with many of its members no more than thugs. Its leader, Ernst Roehm, held views that were more socialist than those of Hitler. He wanted to remove big business and allow the state to take over the major industries. Hitler had won the support of the leading industrialists in his rise to power and, at this stage, could not afford to lose that support.

Above all, Roehm wanted the SA to take control of the German army. This alarmed Hitler because it would make Roehm more powerful than he was. Throughout 1933 Hitler had met with the army leaders to win their support for the Nazi take-over. Now he was in danger of losing that support. Hitler had to make a decision – whether to support Roehm and the SA or the army. Hitler decided to support the army.

He moved quickly against the SA. On 30 June 1934, the Night of the Long Knives took place. Hitler claimed that the SA was plotting to seize power. He ordered the SS to arrest them. Over the next few days hundreds of leaders of the SA were arrested. Many, including Roehm, were shot. Hitler also took the opportunity to remove other opponents. For example, von Schleicher, the former Chancellor, was murdered. In July, Hitler explained his actions to the Reichstag. It accepted that he had 'saved the nation'.

The event removed any opposition to Hitler from within the Nazi Party.

Source C

THEY SALUTE WITH BOTH HANDS NOW.

A British cartoon published after the Night of the Long Knives in 1934.

The Death of Hindenburg

The one person with a higher position than Hitler in the German state was the President, Hindenburg. On 2 August 1934, Hindenburg died at the age of 87. Immediately, Hitler declared himself President as well as Chancellor and took the new title of 'Führer and Reich Chancellor'. On the same day the officers and men of the German army swore an oath of personal loyalty to Hitler. The only Germans with the power to oppose and remove Hitler, the army, had promised to support him.

The Nazi control of Germany was now complete.

Source E

I swear by God this sacred oath that I will give complete obedience to the Führer, Adolf Hitler ... and will be ready as a brave soldier to risk my life at any time for this oath.

The German army's oath of loyalty to Hitler.

Things to do

1   Explain the meaning of the following:
    Enabling Law;
    Führer;
    Law against the Formation of New;
    Parties;
    Night of the Long Knives.

2   Look at Sources C and D and the evidence in the case study. What reasons are given by Hitler for the removal of the SA? Why do you think he removed the SA?

Source D

It became clear that my SA were planning a revolution to seize power. I alone was able to solve the problem. In order to save the state the SA had to be destroyed.

Hitler explains his reasons for removing the SA.

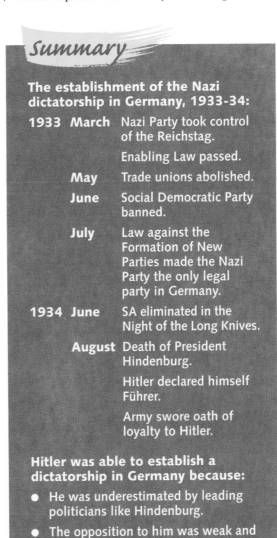

Summary

The establishment of the Nazi dictatorship in Germany, 1933-34:

1933	**March**	Nazi Party took control of the Reichstag.
		Enabling Law passed.
	May	Trade unions abolished.
	June	Social Democratic Party banned.
	July	Law against the Formation of New Parties made the Nazi Party the only legal party in Germany.
1934	**June**	SA eliminated in the Night of the Long Knives.
	August	Death of President Hindenburg.
		Hitler declared himself Führer.
		Army swore oath of loyalty to Hitler.

Hitler was able to establish a dictatorship in Germany because:

- He was underestimated by leading politicians like Hindenburg.
- The opposition to him was weak and divided.
- The Nazis used violence to crush political opposition.
- He removed any opposition to the Nazi Party and within the Nazi Party.

Establishment of a Nazi Dictatorship

Nazi Rule in Germany

Germany, 1934–39

*Germany was now under the control of a Nazi dictatorship.
The Nazis ruled through control, persuasion and propaganda.
Control of the German people was enforced by the SS and the Gestapo
who acted against anyone opposing the Nazis. This also included
persecution of those Germans not accepted by the Nazis as true Aryans.
In some ways Germans benefited from Nazi rule, such as the creation
of more jobs. But the benefits came at the price of freedom.*

4.1 What were the main features of the totalitarian dictatorship of Nazi Germany?

The one party state: law and order

Nazi Germany was a police state. This meant that the power of the authorities was supreme. These powers were used not only to prevent crime and punish criminals but also to arrest and punish people simply because they had said or done something against Hitler and his party. The organisation which enforced law and order was the SS.

When it was first set up, the SS (or *Schutz-Staffel*) had been a small private bodyguard for Hitler. Later, it had played a major part in the removal of the SA in the Night of the Long Knives. By 1934 it consisted of 50,000 highly trained men. Its leader was Heinrich Himmler, a devoted Nazi totally loyal to Hitler. Under him the SS was given unlimited powers. It could search houses, confiscate property and arrest people without charging them with any offence. It could send people to concentration camps without a trial. These camps were run by a branch of the SS called the Death Head Units. Conditions were brutal and harsh and, as one prisoner later wrote, 'death took place daily'.

By 1939 there were many camps in Germany and prisoners were being used as slave labour. Later, during the war, these camps would also become extermination camps.

Another branch of the SS was the Gestapo, the state secret police. The Gestapo had the power to arrest anyone it wanted. It could also spy on people, read their mail and tap their telephones. The Gestapo was helped by a system of informers whereby local party members were encouraged to spy on their neighbours and fellow workers, and to report anything that might be anti-Nazi. Children were even encouraged to spy on their parents. The Gestapo became the most feared organisation in Germany.

The old systems of law and order still remained but were now under Nazi control. The police were controlled by the SS and all judges were reappointed after taking an oath of loyalty to Hitler. The courts could, therefore, be used for political as well as criminal cases.

Case Study: Persecution

The Jews

The people who suffered most under Nazi rule were the Jews. Hitler blamed them for Germany's defeat in the First World War by 'stabbing the German army in the back'. Nazi ideas on the Aryans as a master race excluded the Jews. The Nazis believed that Jews were an inferior race who should not be allowed to mix with true Germans. In their minds the inter-marriage of Jews and Germans over the years had weakened the German people. The Jews were also resented for their influence in Germany. Although they were less than 1 per cent of the German population, Jews were prominent in the professions as lawyers, bankers and doctors. The Jews were an obvious target – they were the scapegoats for all Germany's problems in the 1920s.

Once in power, the Nazis made life difficult for the Jews. In 1933 a boycott of all Jewish shops and businesses was ordered. In 1934 Jewish shops were marked with a yellow star to show that they were Jewish. Jews were also dismissed from important jobs in the civil service, education and the media. In parks and public transport, Jews had to sit apart from other Germans. These actions were humiliating for the Jews. However, they were just the start of the persecution.

In 1935 Hitler passed the Nuremberg Laws. The Citizenship Law stated that Jews were no longer German citizens. As a result, they could not be employed in any public position nor would they be protected by

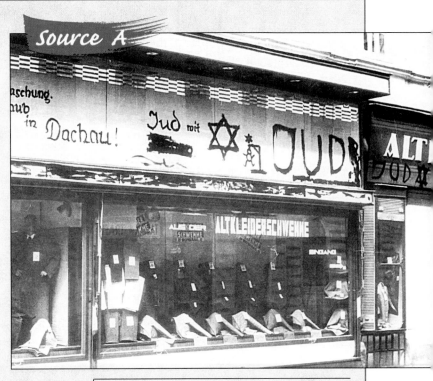

Source A

Jewish shops were boycotted as part of the Nazi persecution of Jews.

the law. The Law for the Protection of German Blood and Honour banned marriages between Jews and non-Jews and outlawed sexual relations between the two groups outside of marriage.

Persecution was now official, directed by the state. Many Jews saw the warning signs and started to leave Germany. However, most Jews stayed and for them life became much worse. They found it difficult to buy the necessities of life – food, clothes, medicine – because German shopkeepers would not serve them. They were dismissed from their jobs and unable to get other work. They were banned from entering public places, such as hotels and cinemas. Jewish doctors, dentists and lawyers were forbidden to look after Germans. Between 1935 and 1938 more Jews left Germany, and even more would have done so if other countries had been prepared to accept them.

In November 1938 a Jew shot dead a Nazi official in Paris. Hitler ordered the SS to begin a campaign of terror against the Jews on *Kristallnacht* (the Night of Broken Glass). In a week of violence, Jewish shops, synagogues and homes were destroyed and looted. Thousands of Jews were arrested, nearly a hundred were killed. This was followed by a collective fine on the Jews of one billion marks. Jews were further humiliated by being forced to clean the streets on their hands and knees. This was followed by the mass arrest of Jews at the beginning of March 1939. Within weeks 30,000 Jews had been sent to concentration camps.

The Second World War brought the Nazi treatment of the Jews to its terrible conclusion. Hitler began his 'Final Solution' with its aim of the total extermination of the Jewish people. Six million Jews died in the Nazi Holocaust.

Other groups

Not only the Jews were persecuted under Nazi rule. Anyone who did not fit into the ideal of an Aryan was suspect. The result was that many Germans found themselves excluded from the 'master race', and therefore persecuted.

Gypsies were an obvious target. They did not look like Aryans and, because they were homeless and tended not to have permanent jobs, they were not 'socially useful'.

Black people were another 'inferior race' and a target of persecution, even though there was relatively few of them in Germany.

Others who suffered because they were not 'socially useful' included tramps and beggars, alcoholics, the mentally and physically disabled. Many of them were sent to concentration camps. Other measures were also taken. In 1933 the Nazis passed a Sterilisation Law. This allowed the sterilisation of people with certain illnesses, especially mental illness. The law was extended to other groups. By 1939 the Nazis had also begun a euthanasia programme to kill the mentally ill, including babies and children.

The Church

Hitler tried to get the churches to encourage their congregations to support the Nazis. At first Hitler tried to reach agreement with the churches. In 1933 a concordat was signed with the Catholics by which the Church promised to keep out of politics and, in turn, the Nazis would not interfere with the Church. A harder line was taken against Protestant churches. They were brought together in one Reich Church – a Nazi-dominated church. Ministers who opposed this, such as Martin Niemoller and Paul Schneider, were arrested and put in concentration camps.

Things to do

Look at evidence in the case study. Explain the different ways that Jewish people suffered under the Nazis.

Education

Hitler wanted to create a 'Thousand Year Reich', in which the Nazis would rule forever. He believed this could only be done by winning the support of the young people of Germany. Hitler therefore began a programme of indoctrinating young people, getting them to believe in Nazi ideas. This could be done by controlling the education system.

Teachers were instructed and trained to put across Nazi ideas in their lessons. They had to belong to the German Teachers' League, a Nazi organisation. Any teachers who refused were dismissed.

The teaching of school subjects was controlled in order to indoctrinate the young. For example, in history children were taught about the failures of the Weimar Republic and its betrayal of Germany. The Nazi Party was shown as saving Germany. Biology was used to explain Nazi ideas on race, that Germans were the 'master' Aryan race and that others were inferior. Physical education was stressed and extra time was found for it in the time-tables of schools. It was important to have fit, healthy young people.

Some subjects were taught to girls only to prepare them for the role of wife and mother. They studied domestic science and child care.

Children were not only indoctrinated through the education system, they were also indoctrinated through the Hitler Youth Movement.

Hitler Youth Movement

The Hitler Youth Movement was organised and run by members of the SS. Its aim was clear: to indoctrinate young people into accepting Nazi ideas, to train them for future service and to ensure that they were loyal and obedient to Hitler.

The Movement was set up in 1925. After 1933 young people were encouraged to join it and other youth organisations were forced to shut down. After 1935 it was compulsory to join it. By 1939 eight million young Germans belonged to the movement. As they became older they progressed through different groups in the movement.

Source B

PERIODS	Monday	Tuesday	Wednesday	Thursday	Friday	Saturday
1. 8:00–8:45	German	German	German	German	German	German
2. 8:50–9:35	Geography	History	Singing	Geography	History	Singing
3. 9:40–10:25	Race Study	Race Study	Race Study	Race Study	Party Beliefs	Party Beliefs
4. 10:25–11:00	Break – with sports and special announcements					
5. 11:00–12:05	Domestic Science with Mathematics – Every day					
6. 12:10–12:55	The science of breeding (Eugenics)–Health Biology					
	2:00–6:00 Sport each day					

A 1935 timetable for a girl's school in Nazi Germany.

Things to do

Look at Source B and the text. How did the Nazis use education to 'indoctrinate' young people?

The movement was attractive to young people. They wore smart uniforms and paraded through their towns. They took part in a range of leisure activities, such as sport, gymnastics, walking and weekend camps. The older members were trained to use rifles. Every young person had a 'performance book' in which the marks gained in these activities were recorded. Those with the best marks were sent to special schools – the Adolf Hitler Schools – where they were trained to be the future leaders of Germany.

Women

In the new Nazi order, women were encouraged to have children. The Nazis were worried about the declining birth rate in Germany and believed that Germany needed more people if it was to become great again. So they encouraged marriage through the Law for the Encouragement of Marriage, which was introduced in 1933. This granted newly married couples a loan of 1,000 marks. To encourage married couples to have children they allowed them to keep 250 marks for each child they had. Mothercraft classes were introduced. Homes for unmarried mothers were set up to allow unmarried women to become pregnant, often by a 'racially pure' member of the SS. These measures to encourage more children worked. The birth rate rose throughout the 1930s.

Women were also encouraged to stay at home to look after their husbands and children, and many women teachers, civil servants and doctors were dismissed from their jobs. Women were given advice on what to cook and were even advised on how to appear: no make-up, hair arranged in a bun or plaits, and slimming was discouraged because it was not good for childbearing.

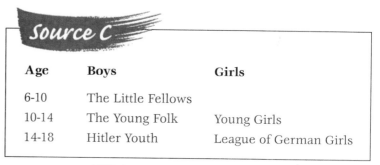

Source C

Age	Boys	Girls
6-10	The Little Fellows	
10-14	The Young Folk	Young Girls
14-18	Hitler Youth	League of German Girls

The organisation of the Hitler Youth Movement.

Source D

A 1930s painting representing the Nazi image of the ideal family.

Things to do

Look at Sources C and D. What message do they give to young people and women about their places in Nazi Germany? Give reasons for your answer.

Propaganda

The Nazis continued to use propaganda to encourage the German people to have the same ideas and beliefs of the Nazi Party and to ensure they stayed loyal to Hitler. Joseph Goebbels was responsible for propaganda as the Minister for Propaganda and National Enlightenment. He used all the resources of the state to carry out his task.

Goebbels made sure that newspapers only printed stories that were favourable to the Nazis. Newspaper editors were even told what the headlines should be. Newspapers that did not support the Nazis were closed down – over 1,500 were closed by 1934.

The Nazis saw the advantages of radio for reaching mass audiences. Goebbels took control of all the local radio stations and used them to send out the Nazi message. Cheap radio sets were produced so that every German household could afford one. They were called the 'People's Receivers'. They were made so that foreign stations could not be picked up, so that the only view of the world they received was the Nazi one. Loudspeaker pillars were set up in streets and public squares all over Germany to make sure that people could hear the radio wherever they were.

The cinema also reached a mass audience and the Nazis made use of it in their propaganda campaign. The German film industry made over a hundred films a year. They included comedies, adventures, love stories and many political films. Special films carrying the Nazi message were made for the young. A typical programme at the cinema would also include newsreels and documentary films with a Nazi slant.

Mass rallies, which had been used by the Nazis in their rise to power, became even grander and more spectacular. The most famous was the Nuremberg rally held every year for a week in August. There were army parades,

Source E

As the time for the Führer's arrival drew near, the crowd grew restless. Suddenly the beat of the drums increased and a fleet of black cars rolled into the arena. The stadium looked like a sea of swastikas. Hitler began to speak. The crowd hushed into silence, but the drums continued their steady beat. Hitler's voice rasped into the night and every now and then the crowd broke into a roar of cheers. Some began swaying back and forth, chanting 'Sieg Heil' over and over again. I looked at the faces around me and saw tears streaming down people's cheeks.

A description of a Nuremberg rally.

gymnastic displays, bands and choirs, firework displays and fly-pasts by the airforce. Above all, it had Hitler to address the mass of people gathered in the arenas. The Nazis also used the 1936 Olympic Games in Berlin as a massive propaganda event to demonstrate the superiority of the Aryan race. The black American athlete Jesse Owens winning four gold medals, however, dampened some of the Nazi celebrations.

All German culture was controlled by the Nazis. Goebbels formed the Reich Chamber of Culture. Musicians, actors, writers and artists had to be members of the Chamber before they could work or perform. Membership depended on supporting the Nazis. Many could not accept this and left Germany.

Music had to be German and composers like Wagner, Beethoven and Mozart were in favour. German folk songs and marching music were also encouraged. The work of Jewish composers however was banned, as was jazz because it was black American music.

Nazi Rule in Germany

*Gruppe
Nieder-Sachsen*

A Nazi rally at Nuremberg during the 1930s.

Books written by Jews or by authors opposed to the Nazis were banned. In 1933 students were encouraged to burn huge piles of banned books looted from libraries.

The theatre, cinema and art were all censored in the same way.

By force, persuasion and propaganda the Nazis firmly controlled the German people. Yet something more was required for the Nazis to retain power. They had to deal with the economic problems which helped them to power.

Governments in Action: Germany, 1918–39

Things to do

1 Look at Sources E and F. Why do you think the Nuremberg rallies made such a great impression on the German people?

Summary

The main features of the Nazi dictatorship were:

- Creation of a police state.
- Control of law and order by the SS and Gestapo.
- Arrest and internment of political opponents.
- Persecution of the Jews, gypsies and other groups.
- Control of the Church.
- Indoctrination of young people by education and the Hitler Youth Movement.
- Brainwashing of the German people by propaganda.
- Censorship of all forms of culture.

4.2 To what extent did the German people benefit from Nazi rule in the 1930s?

Economic policy

When Hitler came to power in 1933, Germany was still in the economic depression which had begun in 1929. It was Nazi promises to end the Depression that won them so much support. Hitler was now expected to make good these promises. The control of economic policy was the responsibility of Dr Schacht, who was Minister of the Economy from 1934 to 1937. His 'New Plan' for Germany had clear aims: to reduce unemployment, to build up the armaments industry and to make Germany self-sufficient.

Increasing employment

In 1933 six million Germans were still out of work. It was vital that the Nazis find them jobs. National Labour Service was immediately set up. This was for young men between 18 and 25 years. They did various jobs, such as digging ditches and planting forests. The men had to wear uniforms and live in camps. They were given pocket money rather than wages. These schemes were then extended to ambitious public works programmes organised by the German Labour Front. New motorways (autobahns) were built, as were hospitals, schools, sports stadiums and other public buildings. These schemes created thousands of jobs.

However, the greatest fall in unemployment was brought about by rearmament. In 1935 Hitler ignored the Treaty of Versailles and started to rearm Germany. He then introduced compulsory military service (conscription). The army alone increased by over one million men between 1935 and 1938. To support this rearmament, an armaments industry grew up to make the weapons and equipment needed. This also employed thousands of men.

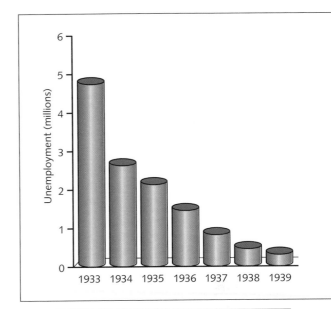

Unemployment in Nazi Germany during 1933–39.

There were other ways the Nazis reduced the statistics of unemployment. Women were forced out of work to look after their homes and families. Jews were dismissed from their jobs but they were not recorded as unemployed. More and more people were being sent to labour camps and concentration camps but were not recorded as unemployed.

So unemployment in Germany fell. By 1939 the Nazis were even declaring that there was a shortage of labour.

Things to do

1 Look at the graph above and the evidence in the section on increasing employment. Give at least five ways in which the Nazis reduced unemployment. Which way do you think was the most successful?

The German Labour Front and Strength through Joy

All German workers were forced to be members of the German Labour Front run by Dr Robert Ley. This controlled the workers in a number of ways. Trade unions were abolished. Strikes were made illegal. Workers could not bargain for higher wages and there was no limit on the number of hours they had to work in a week. Workers could not leave a job without the permission of the Front.

The Nazis also tried to control people's leisure time. A branch of the German Labour Front, called 'Strength through Joy', organised people's leisure activities so that free time was not 'wasted'. Cheap holidays were arranged including foreign travel and Mediterranean cruises. 'Strength through Joy' was also involved in the plan to manufacture a car cheap enough for workers to buy. This was the *Volkswagen* ('People's Car'). Workers could pay for it on a hire purchase scheme into which they paid weekly sums in advance. Actually, very few German workers managed to buy a Volkswagen and the whole scheme was a failure.

Improving the economy: self-sufficiency

Hitler wanted to make Germany self-sufficient – that is, the country should be able to produce its own food and raw materials so that it did not have to depend upon other countries. This policy was called autarky. A Four Year Plan was drawn up in 1936 with the aim of making Germany self-sufficient in four years. More raw materials, such as coal, oil, iron and other metals were produced and synthetic (artificial) raw materials, such as rubber, fuel and textiles, were developed. New factories and industrial plants were built.

The Four Year Plan was expensive and needed massive state investment in industry. By 1939 it had not succeeded in making Germany fully self-sufficient. Over a third of its raw materials was still being imported from other countries.

Nazi economic policy also aimed to strengthen the military power of Germany. This is clear from the rearmament programme, the building of autobahns and the attempt to achieve self-sufficiency. When it was obvious that Germany could not achieve full self-sufficiency, the Nazis decided to take over countries with the raw materials and food it needed. This was the policy of *lebensraum* (living space). Nazi economic policy and foreign policy began to overlap.

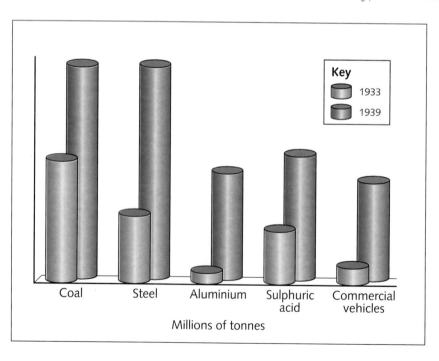

Industrial growth in Nazi Germany.

Nazi rule in the 1930s

The German people benefited from Nazi rule. The economic problems which had affected the nation from 1929 to 1932 ended. In their place there was employment and financial stability. The Nazis also restored Germany's honour and pride. There was more optimism and self-confidence.

However, the price was heavy. The German people lived in a police state where their whole lives were controlled by the Nazis – their education, their religion, their work, even their leisure time.

It is difficult to judge exactly what the German people thought about Nazi rule. There was very little open opposition or underground resistance, and what did exist was soon destroyed. The powers of the SS and the Gestapo terrified most Germans from saying or doing anything against the Nazis. The censorship and propaganda of the Nazis meant that people did not have the information on which to make reliable judgements.

On balance, it would seem that most Germans were prepared to accept Nazi rule in the 1930s. They were now to be faced by even bigger changes as Hitler took the nation into war.

Source G

5 Mark die Woche musst Du sparen – Willst Du im eignen Wagen fahren!

KdF-Wagen: Über Anschaffungspreis und Zahlungsweise erteilen Auskunft alle Betriebswarte und Dienststellen der NS.-Gemeinschaft „Kraft durch Freude" Gau München-Oberbayern

A poster of 1938 encouraging German workers to 'Save five marks a week and get your own cars'. The Volkswagen ('People's Car') was introduced by the Nazis.

Summary

In their economic policy, the Nazis:

- Reduced unemployment by public works and the rearmament programme.
- Controlled German workers in the German Labour Front and National Labour Service.
- Controlled the leisure time of German workers in 'Strength through Joy'.
- Tried to make Germany self-sufficient (autarky) in raw materials.
- Used economic policy to prepare for war.

Things to do

Look at the graph on page 146, Source G, and the evidence in the text on improving the economy. Do you think the Nazis improved the economy? Give reasons for your answer.

Nazi Rule in Germany

Exam-type Assessment
Germany, 1918–39

This exercise is based on the sort of questions you could be asked on Paper 2 of your examination.

One fine day I dropped into a café to have a coffee. As I went in I noticed the price was 5000 marks – just about what I had in my pocket. I sat down, read my paper, drank my coffee, and spent altogether about one hour in the café, and then asked for the bill. The waiter duly presented me with a bill for 8000 marks. 'Why 8000 marks?' I asked. The mark had dropped in value in the meantime, I was told.

A German writer remembers the economic crisis of 1923.

An election poster of 1932. It says 'Our last hope: Hitler'.

Questions

1   Study Source A.

Use your knowledge to explain how Germany came to be affected by hyper-inflation in 1923.

(6 marks)

2   Summary Essay.

Why did the Depression of 1929–33 lead to the collapse of the Weimar Republic?

(15 marks)

Questions

1   **Summary Essay.**

   Explain how the Nazi Party developed in the period 1920–9.   (*15 marks*)

2   **Study Source B.**

   Use your knowledge to explain why this poster would be attractive to
   many German people in the election of 1932.   (*6 marks*)

A Nazi poster of the 1930s. It is entitled 'Long Live Germany'.

Questions

1   **Summary Essay.**

   Explain how the removal of opposition in the period March 1933 to
   August 1934 allowed Hitler to have complete control of Germany.   (*15 marks*)

2   **Study Source C.**

   What interpretation of Nazi Germany is given in the poster?   (*4 marks*)

A Hitler Youth Poster from the 1930s.

Questions

1   **Study Source D.**
    Use your knowledge to explain how the Nazis used the Hitler Youth Movement
    to win over the young people of Germany.   (*6 marks*)

2   **Summary Essay.**
    Explain what the Nazis tried to achieve in their economic policy between
    1933 and 1939. How successful were they?   (*15 marks*)

Chapter 5

Governments in Action: USA, 1919–41

When the First World War ended so did American involvement in European and world affairs. Although President Wilson played a major part in drawing up the Treaty of Versailles, America adopted a policy of isolation after the war.

For many Americans the 1920s and 1930s was a period of suffering and intolerance. Immigration was reduced and racism increased. This reached its peak in the activities of the Klu Klux Klan. Conditions for black people and groups like farmers were never good. The USA also saw the introduction of Prohibition and, with it, the violence of organised crime.

However, throughout the 1920s the USA enjoyed a period of economic prosperity. This allowed many Americans to achieve a life-style European workers could only have dreamed about. It lasted only a relatively short time. Depression hit the USA in 1929 as the stock market collapsed. The result was mass unemployment. The 1930s saw President Roosevelt in his New Deal try to bring 'relief and recovery' to the American economy. Although the New Deal had its successes, including creating millions of jobs, it was the Second World War which finally ended the Depression in America.

This is a Paper 2 topic and you will be required to answer one structured question on it.

The Growth of Isolation

The USA, 1919–22

*In 1919 the USA was a confident, powerful country. It was the strongest
economic power in the world with technology and mechanisation envied by other
countries. However, the First World War had had an effect on Americans. It forced
them to look at their relations with the rest of the world and to look at their own
society. The result was a move to isolation, seen not only in the rejection of the
League of Nations but also in changes in immigration and trade policies.*

1.1 How did the USA react to the end of the First World War?

The USA in 1919

By 1919 the USA had grown into
one of the world's greatest powers.
Throughout the 19th century
the USA was seen as a 'land of
opportunity'. Between 1850 and
1914 over 40 million people left
Europe and emigrated to the USA.
One result of this was that the USA
had become a mixed society – it
has been estimated that people
from 100 different nationalities
were living in America in 1914.

In the First World War American
forces played a key part in the
campaigns of 1918 and the extra
resources they brought helped
in the final defeat of Germany.
The USA did not enter the war
until April 1917 and so lost just
100,000 men. Unlike the other
powers involved in the war,
the USA was strengthened by it.
Throughout the war, the countries
of Europe had paid the USA to
provide them with their war needs
– food and raw materials as well
as weapons. The USA had also
gained many of the overseas
markets of European countries.

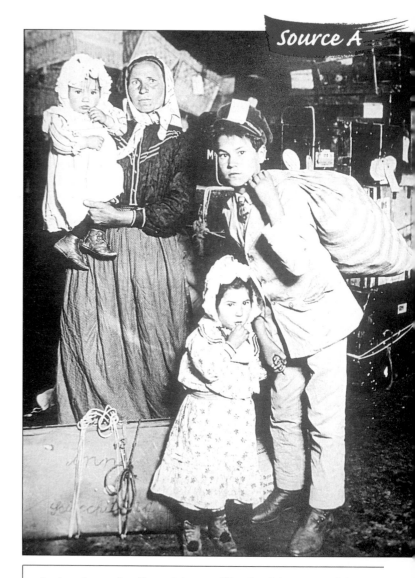

Source A

An immigrant family arriving at Ellis Island in New York in 1905.

Governments in Action: USA 1919–41

USA reaction to the end of the First World War

President Woodrow Wilson had taken the USA into the war. He also played an important role in the peace talks. The Fourteen Points drawn up by him in 1918 were the basis for the peace settlement. Wilson saw it as the USA's duty to help preserve world peace and proposed an international body to do this.

So the Treaty of Versailles committed all countries which signed the Treaty to join the 'League of Nations'.

The mood of isolation grows

However, the mood of the American people was different from Wilson's. To many Americans the war was a remote one fought thousands of miles away about issues that did not really concern them. They did not want more American soldiers to be killed trying to keep peace around the world. They were afraid that America's entry into the League of Nations would lead to just that. Furthermore they were worried that the USA, as the strongest and richest country in the world, would end up paying the cost of keeping world peace. It would be better to keep out of other countries' problems.

Rejection of the Treaty of Versailles and the League of Nations

President Wilson hoped that the USA would sign the Treaty of Versailles and join the League of Nations. Unfortunately for Wilson, his party – the Democrats – did not have control of Congress. Their opponents, the Republicans, rejected the Treaty of Versailles and with it America's entry into the League. Wilson refused to accept defeat and though he did not run again for President in the election campaign of 1920 the Democrat candidate, James Cox, fought for Wilson's ideas. His opponent, the Republican Warren Harding, campaigned with a slogan of 'America First'. He also talked about a return to 'normalcy', a word he had invented, but one which was attractive to Americans – the idea of life getting back to normal, to what it had been before the war. It is not surprising that Americans voted in Harding as the new President. The rejection of the Democrats meant the final rejection of the Treaty of Versailles and the League of Nations. America was to follow a policy of isolation.

Things to do

1 What was the impact of the First World War on America?

2 Why did some people
   a) want America to be isolated?
   b) oppose isolationism?

3 What can you learn about American society in 1918 from Source B.

Source B

The First World War revealed some alarming facts in regard to our foreign population.

1 Many immigrants neglected to become American citizens.

2 Radical labor agitators were suspected of 'taking their orders from Moscow'.

3 Over one thousand newspapers in the United States were printed in foreign languages.

4 Over 10 per cent of the people here could not speak English.

5 American labor leaders were disturbed over the incoming foreigners who were used to working for low wages.

Adapted from an American school textbook published in 1961.

1.2 How did the policies of the American government encourage isolation?

Isolation did not only apply to foreign affairs; it also meant limiting foreign trade and immigration.

Tariffs against foreign goods

Action was taken to make sure that foreign goods would not be able to compete with home-produced goods on the US market. In 1922 Congress introduced the Fordney-McCumber tariff. A tariff (or tax) was placed on foreign goods coming into the USA. This made them more expensive than the same American products and so 'protected' American industry. This policy worked well in the 1920s and helped to bring about the 'Boom' conditions (see pages 156–8). However, there was a danger: foreign governments retaliated by putting high tariffs on American goods exported abroad, which made them harder to sell.

Restricting the flow of immigrants

It was inevitable that the mood of isolation would bring with it some re-thinking of the open-door policy of immigration. This was starting to happen before 1919. It was partly the result of the war and an increased feeling of nationalism in the USA. There was also an increasing fear that new immigrants, especially from poor countries, would provide cheap labour. This would take jobs from Americans. There was a further fear that new immigrants would bring with them political ideas, such as communism, which were against the spirit of democracy that existed in the USA. This fear, called the 'Red Scare', became especially strong after the communist revolution in Russia in 1917.

In 1917 Congress passed an Immigration Law which required all foreigners wishing to enter the USA to take a literacy test. They had to

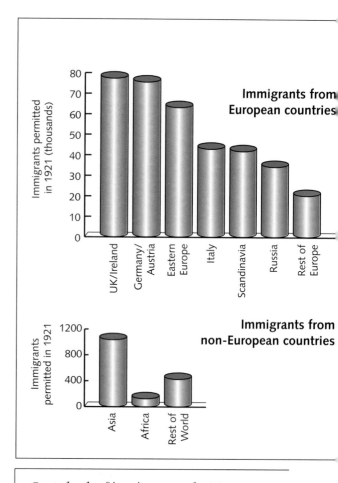

Quota levels of immigrants to the USA, 1921.

prove they could read a short passage in English before they would be allowed into the country. Such a test prevented people from the poorer countries of Europe and Asia entering the USA, as they could not afford to learn English in their own country.

In 1921 the Immigration Quota Act was introduced. This limited the maximum number of immigrants allowed into the USA to 357,000 each year. It also stated that the number of people emigrating to the USA from any country should not exceed 3 per cent of the number from that country already living in the USA in 1910. This 'quota' system

Governments in Action: USA 1919–41

worked in favour of people from western and northern Europe because they had a larger number of immigrant American citizens in 1910. This was almost certainly the idea.

In 1924 the quota limit was further reduced to 2 per cent of the population in 1890. In 1929 the number of immigrants into America each year was reduced to 150,000 – under half of the 1921 figure. In addition, no immigrants from Asia were allowed.

More distrust of foreigners

For those foreigners fortunate enough to be allowed into the USA, there were still problems to face. The fact that many could only find low-paid jobs in the cities meant that they lived in poor housing. Immigrant ghettos began to appear where violence and crime were high. This only increased Americans' distrust of foreigners and led to growing intolerance. The 'Red Scare' of the early 1920s added to these suspicions. Sacco and Vanzetti were victims of the anti-immigrant feelings of the time.

Things to do

1   Use the information in this section to explain:
    (a) how the US government reduced the number of immigrants.
    (b) how the government encouraged immigration from some countries but not others.

2   Explain the following terms: isolation, tariff, immigration, normalcy, quota system.

Case Study: the Sacco and Vanzetti Case

Nicola Sacco and Bartolomeo Vanzetti were immigrants from Italy. They were self-confessed anarchists and openly said they hated the American system of government.

In 1920 they were arrested and charged with the murder of two guards in an armed robbery. The evidence against Sacco and Vanzetti was based on four points. They were both carrying loaded guns when they were arrested. The bullets in Sacco's gun matched the size of the bullets which killed the guards. Sixty-one eye-witnesses identified them as the killers. Finally,

Vanzetti had a proven conviction for armed robbery in 1919.

The defence pointed to the fact that the 61 prosecution eyewitnesses could not agree on the details of the crime or even on the descriptions of the killers. The defence also produced 107 witnesses who swore to seeing the two men somewhere else at the time of the crime – although most of these witnesses were recent Italian immigrants.

The jury found both men guilty of murder. Appeals were made against the verdict. Petitions were organised by people convinced that the two

men had been found guilty because they were foreigners. All failed. Sacco and Vanzetti were executed in 1927.

In 1977 the verdict against the men was declared unjust because the judge presiding over the case was strongly opposed to the political views of Sacco and Vanzetti.

Things to do

What does the Sacco and Vanzetti case tell us about the USA in the 1920s?

The Growth of Isolation, 1919–22

unit 2 The Promised Land?

The USA in the 1920s

The 1920s was a time of contrasts in America. There was economic prosperity which allowed many Americans to buy a wide range of consumer goods and invest in shares. At the same time there was poverty which meant that many could not share in the boom. There was intolerance, especially towards black people, violence and organised crime.

2.1 How far did the USA achieve economic prosperity in the 1920s?

During the 1920s the USA experienced increasing economic prosperity – a boom – in which many Americans, though certainly not all, shared. A plentiful supply of raw materials, the boost provided by the First World War and the policy of protection all helped America become the richest country in the world.

Source A

The operations are sub-divided so that each man and each machine do only one thing ... the thing is to keep everything in motion and take the work to the man, not the man to the work.

Henry Ford speaking in 1926 about mass production.

Mass production

Mass production helped boost the number of goods made. The principle behind the system of mass production was simple and effective. Huge new factories were built in the towns of America. In the factories, assembly lines were set up. The parts of the product being made travelled along the lines so that a worker did the same small job in fitting the part for which he was responsible on to the product. By the end of the assembly line the product was complete. The job was quick and straight-forward and production rose dramatically.

The car industry

The motor car industry was one of the first to use the method of mass production. One of its pioneers was Henry Ford. Ford had the idea of making a car for the ordinary man and his family. In 1911 the first Model T was produced by methods of mass production.

The use of mass-production methods meant that by the 1920s a Model T was being produced every ten seconds.

Source B

The assembly line in the Ford Motor Company.

Governments in Action: USA 1919–41

156

This allowed Ford to reduce his prices: in 1911 a Model T cost $1,200; by 1920 it was $295. One Model T was identical to another – the same colour, the same engine size. This did not bother the American people. The 'Tin Lizzie', as it was known, became the most popular car in America. By the mid-1920s one out of every two cars sold was a Model T.

It was not only the car industry which expanded during the 1920s, although it did help other industries to grow – steel, rubber, glass, leather and oil were all in greater demand because of the car industry. The construction industry provided roads for the increased traffic. Consumer goods were also produced using mass-production methods: radio sets, telephones, refrigerators, vacuum cleaners, washing machines, ovens. These new 'gadgets' were attractive to the American people and sales rocketed.

The cycle of prosperity.

Cycle of prosperity

This growth created a 'cycle of prosperity'. The increased production of consumer goods created increased employment. This meant that people had more money to spend on consumer goods, especially as their prices were falling. This in turn created an increased demand for goods and encouraged further increased production. So the cycle went on.

Government policy

Other factors also helped to maintain the boom. The Republican governments of the 1920s encouraged the growth of business by a policy of non-interference (called *laissez-faire*) and did not place any controls on industry or financial institutions. They also lowered taxes on people's incomes and on company profits: this gave people more money to spend on consumer goods and companies more money to invest in new factories and buildings.

Credit facilities

The ability to buy consumer goods was greatly helped by the introduction of hire purchase – buying on credit. This allowed people who did not have enough cash to pay the full cost of a product to obtain it by paying for it in instalments over a period of time. Mail order also increased the market for goods beyond the towns and cities into the more remote country areas.

Advertisements appeared in magazines, newspapers, on the radio, in cinemas and on billboards – all trying to convince Americans that they should 'keep up with the Jones'' and buy the products that every other American now had.

The Promised Land? – the USA in the 1920s

Confidence

Throughout the 1920s there was a feeling of confidence among the American people, which encouraged them to buy goods by cash or by credit. It encouraged them to invest some of their wages in companies by buying shares. Even this could be done on credit by buying 'on the margin'. A person could buy shares by paying 10 per cent of their total value in cash and borrowing the remaining 90 per cent from the banks. Share prices soared as more and more were bought. It seemed that the good times were here to stay.

Americans who did not share the prosperity

However, in reality there were still many Americans living in poverty. The new wealth in the USA was not shared by everyone. Some sections of the population suffered more than others.

Farmers

Farmers had a hard time in the 1920s – and almost half the American people were engaged in agriculture. New machines like tractors and combine harvesters helped farmers to produce more food. But they produced more than the American people needed. As a result of this surplus, food prices dropped and many small farmers suffered from lower incomes. As incomes fell, farmers found it difficult to keep up with their mortgage payments – some farmers were evicted, others were forced to sell their land. Farm labourers also found themselves out of work and drifted to towns or areas such as California where the fruit farms promised work.

> This cartoon comments on the situation of farmers in the 1920s.

Black people and immigrants

Black people had a similar experience. Almost one million black farm workers lost their jobs in the 1920s. Many moved from their homes in the south to the cities of the north. Here they were able to find jobs, but they were usually the lowest paid. The same was true for new immigrants.

Workers in older industries

Not all industries benefited from the boom. For example, the coal industry suffered as new forms of power – oil, gas, electricity – became more widely used. The overproduction of coal led to wage cuts or, worse, loss of jobs as mines closed down. Other older industries, such as cotton and textiles, suffered in a similar way.

Things to do

1 Why did the USA have a consumer boom in the 1920s?

2 Which people did not share the boom of the 1920s? Why not?

Source C

2.2 Was the USA a free society in the 1920s?

Although many Americans prospered in the 1920s there was also a dark side to life. This was seen most clearly in the intolerance and racism of the Ku Klux Klan and the organised crime which exploited the unpopularity of Prohibition.

Ku Klux Klan

The Ku Klux Klan stirred up racial and religious hatred in what they believed was a moral crusade to save the USA. It would only accept as true Americans those people who were WASPs (white, Anglo-Saxon, Protestant) – that is, people who had originally come from northern Europe and whose families had lived in America for several generations. All other people were condemned as not being true Americans: Jews, Catholics, immigrants from southern Europe (such as Italians), from eastern Europe (such as Russians), from Asia and, especially, black people.

During the 1920s membership of the Ku Klux Klan grew from 100,000 members in 1920 to 5 million members in 1925.

Members of the Klan were often poor whites who felt that their jobs were threatened by black people and immigrants who were willing to work for lower wages. However, the Klan also had rich and influential members including state politicians. The Klan was strongest in the southern states where there was a large black population and a history of oppression of blacks.

Extracts from the **Kloran,** *the Klan's book of rules*

Source E

A Ku Klux Klan parade in 1925.

Things to do

Look at Sources D and E. What do they tell us about the Ku Klux Klan?

The Promised Land? – the USA in the 1920s

Klan members held ceremonies in which they dressed in long white robes and hoods and Klansmen spoke to each other in secret codes known as 'Klonversations'.

Torture and violence were used against people who were not 'true Americans', with black people suffering the most. Victims were beaten, whipped, tarred and feathered, or lynched (where victims were put to death without trial). Their homes were set on fire and their property destroyed.

In many cases, the Klansmen were not punished for these activities. They were often protected by the authorities – the police or judges – who were themselves members of the Klan. It was also true that juries made up of white people were reluctant to find people guilty of Klan activities.

However, there were successful prosecutions against the Klan, especially for the most violent activities. The trials were widely reported and helped to produce a reaction against the Klan. After 1925 its membership fell and, while it continues to exist in the USA, the Klan has never again achieved the influence it had in the early 1920s.

Prohibition

In January 1920 the USA introduced Prohibition – the making, selling or transporting of alcoholic drink in the USA became illegal. This was made part of the American Constitution in the 18th Amendment. A separate law, called the Volstead Act, defined an alcoholic drink as any drink which contained more than one-half per cent of alcohol.

Prohibition marked the final success in a long campaign by groups such as the Women's Christian Temperance Union (1875) and the Anti-Saloon League (1895) to have alcohol banned. They claimed that alcohol brought poverty, broke up marriages, caused crime and insanity, and disrupted industry. By 1917, 18 American states had banned alcohol and in 1920 the ban became national.

A poster published by the Anti-Saloon League in 1910.

Things to do

Look at Source F. What message is the poster presenting about the evils of drink?

Effects of Prohibition: illegal alcohol, speakeasies and bootlegging

The ban on alcohol was not popular. Most people saw nothing wrong with having a drink and found ways to get round the law. Many people produced their own alcoholic drink – called moonshine – from home-made stills. The results were usually of poor quality and often caused illness and even death. Others, especially in the towns, looked to others to provide the alcohol they wanted. A whole new 'industry' was created. Secret bars called speakeasies were set up behind locked doors in cellars and back rooms. By 1930 there were nearly a quarter of a million speakeasies in America – over 30,000 in New York alone. The speakeasies sold alcohol smuggled by bootleggers from abroad – such as rum from the West Indies and whiskey from Canada.

Organised crime

It was not long before the vast profits to be made attracted groups of gangsters to the illegal alcohol trade. Rival gangs in cities fought to take over the other's 'territory' – and the rackets within it. Gangland murders increased. In Chicago, 227 gangsters were murdered in four years without anyone being convicted. In one day in 1929, the St Valentine's Day massacre, Al Capone's men machine-gunned seven members of the rival 'Bugs' Moran gang. The gangsters also operated protection rackets, prostitutes and drugs trafficking. They were helped by the inability of the authorities to do anything about it. Many police, judges and state officials were bribed to turn a blind eye to the gangs' activities. Organised crime also bought its way into legal business activities and into trade unions.

Reasons for the failure of Prohibition

Drinking illegal alcohol was too popular and too profitable. It could not be controlled without huge numbers of enforcement agents.

Yet in the face of organised crime the Prohibition Bureau employed about 4,000 agents to stop bootlegging and close speakeasies for the whole of America. While agents like Eliot Ness achieved some success, most were ineffective. Some were also guilty of taking bribes from the criminals who ran the trade – nearly 10 per cent of the agents were sacked for taking bribes. However, perhaps the most important reason why Prohibition failed was that, despite the strength of the temperance groups, the vast majority of the American people did not agree with Prohibition. They were prepared to break the law in order to consume alcohol.

Prohibition ended in December 1933 when President Roosevelt repealed the 18th Amendment. His feelings summed up those of most Americans: 'Let's all go out and have a drink.'

The Promised Land? – the USA in the 1920s

161

Case Study: Al Capone and Organised Crime

The most powerful of the Chicago gangs was led by Al Capone. His parents were Italian immigrants. Capone was brought up in New York but moved to Chicago as part of a gang run by 'Terrible Johnny' Torrio. In 1925 Torrio retired after being badly injured by the 'Bugs' Moran gang, and was replaced by Capone. In a short space of time Capone brought other gangs under his control. His gang of 700 men was like a private army, armed with sawn-off shotguns and sub-machine guns. Opponents and rivals were 'rubbed out' (killed). He used corruption to bribe the authorities in Chicago and had most of the leading police, judges and politicians in his pay.

Capone became a celebrity. His photograph appeared on the front cover of *Time*, America's leading weekly magazine. He mixed with businessmen, politicians and movie stars.

Capone was responsible for murders, extortion and corruption. Yet the only charge the authorities could make stick against him came in 1931 when he was sentenced to eleven years in prison for tax evasion.

This was Al Capone's attitude to Prohibition.

Source I

TIME
The Weekly Newsmagazine

ALPHONSE ("SCARFACE") CAPONE

Al Capone on the front cover of Time *magazine, 1930.*

Source J

I call myself a businessman. I make my money by supplying a popular demand. If I break the law, my customers are as guilty as I am.

Summary

The main features of Prohibition were:

- A ban on the making and selling of alcohol.
- Creation of speakeasies using bootleg or moonshine alcohol.
- Failure of the police and authorities to enforce the ban.
- Rise of gangs and organised crime to control the liquor trade.
- Control of the authorities by organised crime.

Things to do

1 Look at Sources G and H. How do they help us to explain why Prohibition failed?

2 Using the information provided in the case study do you think Al Capone was a criminal or a businessman? Give reasons for your answer.

Influences of the boom on American lifestyle

The economic prosperity of the 1920s brought a change in lifestyle for many American women. In 1920 they had been given the vote. More women entered work – in industry and the office – although this was usually because employers paid them lower wages than men. Greater independence brought other changes. Some 'flappers' made their dresses shorter and silk stockings and make-up were used. They had short 'bobbed' hair and smoked and drove cars. Only a small proportion of American women behaved like the flappers and most people condemned them. An Anti-Flirt League was even set up. But flappers were a sign of the times.

So too was jazz, a popular kind of black music usually performed by black jazzmen, such as Louis Armstrong and Duke Ellington. It became popular with all sections of the USA, especially the young. Radio gave Americans the chance to hear the new music. New dances like the Charleston and the Black Bottom came with the new music.

The cinema or 'movies' brought its own stars, with the likes of Charlie Chaplin, Mary Pickford and Clara Bow becoming household names. The most popular silent screen star was undoubtedly Rudolf Valentino. When he died in 1926 at the age of 31 crowds of fans queued for a mile to see his embalmed body. In 1927 the first 'talking film', The *Jazz Singer*, was released. The history of the cinema was about to change.

By then the film industry was based in Hollywood, a suburb of Los Angeles with plenty of locations in which to film. In the 1930s all the major film companies had studios there – it was the movie capital of the world.

Source K

In July 1920 a fashion-writer reported in the *New York Times* that 'the American woman ... had lifted her skirts far beyond any modest limitation', which was another way of saying that the hem was now all of nine inches above the ground. The flappers wore thin dresses, short-sleeved and occasionally [in the evening] sleeveless; and many of them were visibly using cosmetics.

An American writer describing flappers.

Things to do

Using Sources K and L, and the information provided in this section, explain the changes that took place in American society in the 1920s.

Dancing the Charleston in New York, 1926.

Source L

America in Depression

USA, 1929–33

In 1929 the economic prosperity, which many Americans thought would last indefinitely, suddenly ended. It gave way to depression. This brought unemployment and suffering to millions of Americans who found themselves reduced to a state of poverty – homeless and dependent on charity to survive.

3.1 Why did the USA fall into depression in 1929?

An unemployed worker during the Depression.

Source A

During the 1920s the American economy appeared to be strong and healthy but there were some serious weaknesses which would bring a change from prosperity to depression – these were the long-term causes of the Depression.

Overproduction

Mass-production methods meant that goods could be produced quickly and in large amounts. However, the market was becoming saturated. Once Americans had bought their cars, radios, vacuum cleaners and other consumer goods, the demand for these items fell. Factories were forced to produce fewer goods – and this meant cutting back on their work forces, which meant fewer people could afford to buy consumer goods!

Unequal distribution of wealth

The fall in demand was also a result of the unequal distribution of wealth. Many Americans no longer wished to buy new consumer goods, but there were millions more who could not afford to do so. A survey in 1928 showed that 60 per cent of American families earned less than $2,000 a year – the minimum needed to survive. So even during the boom years more than half of Americans lived 'below the poverty line'. Worst affected were farmers and farm workers, black workers, new immigrants and workers in the old industries. For such people the boom had never been a reality.

Things to do

1 Explain why America went into an economic depression after 1929. Use the information on pages 164–5 to answer the question.

2 Explain how the factors which produced prosperity could lead to depression.

Tariff policy

One way of selling surplus goods was to find new markets overseas. However, when the Americans put tariffs on foreign goods in the 1920s many foreign governments responded by doing the same to American goods. So American businessmen found it difficult to sell their manufactures abroad.

Soon a 'cycle of depression' set in. Reduced demand led to factories closing down and workers being made unemployed. So there was less money to spend on consumer goods which further reduced demand and led to more closures.

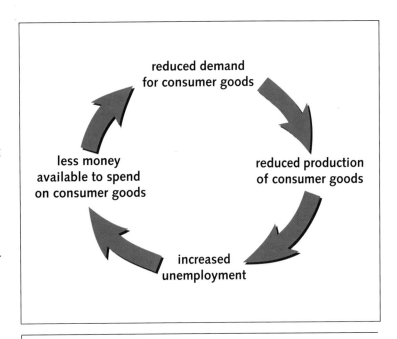

The cycle of depression.

Financial crisis: speculation

The confidence that had helped produce prosperity was now shaken. It led to the final reason for the Depression – the collapse of the financial markets.

During the 1920s more and more Americans were buying shares on the stock exchange in Wall Street. Share prices kept rising and there was confidence that they would keep doing so. People bought shares on credit expecting to sell them for a profit and settle their debts. This is called 'speculation'. However, during 1928, share prices did not rise as much as in previous years. Many companies were not selling as many goods, so their profits fell and people were less willing to buy their shares. Some, more experienced, investors began to sell their shares before values fell. When other smaller investors saw this they began to sell too.

The Wall Street Crash, 1929

Prices began to fall dramatically as investors tried to sell increasing numbers of shares. On Thursday 24 October – Black Thursday – nearly 13 million shares were sold. Prices dived as few buyers could be found. A group of bankers spent nearly $250,000,000 buying shares in the hope that this would encourage investors to buy rather than sell shares. It seemed to work and share prices stopped falling. However, on Monday, 28 October, there was renewed panic and over 9 million shares were sold at falling prices. Finally on Tuesday, 29 October, over 16 million shares were sold by panic-stricken investors for whatever price they could get. As a result prices tumbled – shareholders lost a total of $8,000 million on that day alone. Although this was the worst single day on the stock market, share prices continued to fall for the next few weeks until they 'bottomed out' (stopped falling) in mid-November. By then the damage was done.

Effects of the Wall Street Crash

The effects of the Wall Street Crash were as dramatic as the Crash itself. Confidence in America's economy was gone and many rich Americans lost all their money in the Crash. Companies had to cut back and dismiss some of their workforce. During the period of the Depression (1929-33) over 100,000 businesses shut down completely.

Banks too suffered in the Crash. Many had invested in shares and lost the money customers had placed with them. People lost confidence in the banks and withdrew their money. This caused a 'run on the banks', which began to run out of money. In 1929 alone nearly 700 banks collapsed. In an attempt to try and recover some of their money banks began to call in loans from companies and the ordinary people who had borrowed money from them. But they were being asked to repay money which they did not have and so more companies closed and some people had to sell their homes and possessions.

Summary

The causes of the Depression were:

- The production of more goods than were needed.
- Many Americans did not share in the economic prosperity of the 1920s.
- Failure to find markets abroad.
- Speculation in shares.
- Loss of confidence.
- Wall Street Crash.

Company	Share Prices	
	3 September	13 November
Anaconda Copper	131.5	70
General Electric	396	168
Radio	101	28
United States Steel	261	150
Woolworth	100	52
Electric Bond &Share	186	50

Share prices of some leading US companies in 1929.

Things to do

Look at the table of share prices and the information in this section. Imagine you are a share-holder. How would you explain to people who don't own shares what happened in the Wall Street Crash?

Unemployed workers in New York queuing for free bread in 1930

Source B

3.2 What were the effects of the Depression on the American people?

Unemployment

The financial crash affected nearly every American in some way as depression hit the USA. In 1929 the unemployment rate in America was just over 3 per cent of the workforce; by 1933 it was 25 per cent. In the industrial cities of the North, the rate was even higher as factories and businesses cut down on production or shut down completely. In Chicago, for example, nearly half the labour force was unemployed in 1933. For those in work wages were cut by 25 per cent. Some Americans took to the roads, travelling from place to place trying to find work wherever they could. They became tramps or 'hobos'. The exact number of hobos was not known but it was estimated to have been hundreds of thousands.

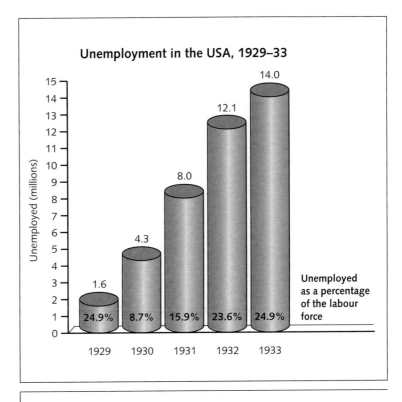

Unemployment in the USA, 1929–33

Unemployment in the USA, 1929-33.

Homelessness

The Depression made many Americans homeless. When people became unemployed, there was no dole to help them. They had to sell their possessions to pay back loans or credit taken out during the good years. If they had mortgage payments they could not meet, their homes were re-possessed. If they fell behind with their rents, they were evicted. In 1932 alone a quarter of a million Americans lost their homes.

The homeless ended up on the streets, sleeping on park benches or in bus shelters. Some deliberately got themselves arrested so that they could spend the night in jail. Many moved to the edge of towns or to waste grounds in towns. There they built shelters from whatever they could find – corrugated iron, scrap metal, old wood. They called these collections of shelters 'Hoovervilles' as an insult to the President, Herbert Hoover.

Things to do

1 Look at the graph above, and Source C, and the information in this section. Describe how people in cities like New York suffered in the Depression.

America in Depression, 1929–33

A 'Hooverville' in the centre of New York.

Help from charities

The homeless needed help. It did not come from the state because the USA did not have a social security system, as in Britain, which would pay unemployment benefit to those who had lost their jobs. Some towns and cities decided to run their own public relief programmes which organised temporary homes, food, clothes and even jobs for the unemployed. Private charities run by bodies like the Salvation Army were also set up. In some cases, wealthy individuals gave help (even the gangster Al Capone provided food in Chicago). These charities set up soup kitchens, bread kitchens or cheap food centres to feed the hungry. 'Breadlines', long lines of men and women queuing for free bread and soup, became a common sight in most American towns.

America was in deep depression. One of the most popular songs of the time sums up the mood: 'Buddy, Can You Spare A Dime?'.

Governments in Action: USA 1919–41

Farmers

The Depression made life even more difficult for farmers. Unemployment in the towns meant that farmers sold less of their produce. Prices of farm produce fell so much that it was not profitable to even harvest the crop. Wheat was left to rot in the fields and farmers went bankrupt. In 1932 one farmer in every twenty was evicted for failure to make mortgage repayments.

Around 1930 another problem hit some farmers – the dust bowl. In the states of the South and Midwest, such as Kansas and Oklahoma, farmers had changed from cattle farming to growing crops during the First World War. This continued in the 1920s but the land was being farmed too much and was becoming infertile. Then in the years after 1930 there was drought. Strong winds and little rainfall turned the top soil to dust. The land became like a desert. Thousands of farmers were ruined. They were left with no choice but to abandon their farms and look for work elsewhere. Many drifted to California where the fruit farms seemed to offer new opportunities.

Source D

In the State of Washington I was told that forest fires were caused by bankrupt farmers trying to earn a few dollars as fire-fighters.

In Oregon I saw apples rotting in orchards. I saw sheep farmers feeding mutton to the buzzards.

An American journalist writing in 1932.

The Republican government and the Depression

Case Study: the Bonus Army

At the end of the First World War, soldiers had been promised a 'bonus', or pension, by the government which would be paid in 1945. By 1932 many of the veterans of the American army had been hit by the Depression and wanted the government to pay the bonuses now. In the summer of 1932 between 15,000 and 20,000 veterans reached Washington to protest to the government. There they set up a 'Hooverville' opposite the White House.

Congress voted against paying the bonuses. The 'Bonus Army' decided to stay in Washington and continue the protest. Hoover first used the police to contain the veterans. Then he called in the army. Armed troops, using tanks and tear gas, cleared the Bonus Army out of the camp and set fire to the tents and shelters. Two veterans were killed and nearly a thousand others were injured. The Bonus Army had been defeated but Hoover became even more unpopular.

Source E

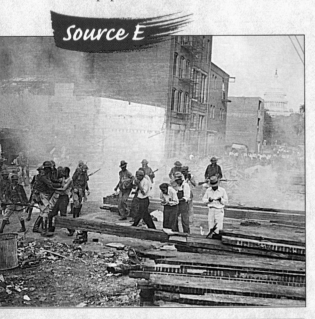

Fighting between the police and the Bonus Army, in 1932.

The Republican government of Herbert Hoover believed in 'rugged individualism' – that is, the government should not involve itself in people's lives, and should let people sort out their own problems. The government was convinced that the Depression would not last long and that America would return to the boom of the 1920s.

But Hoover's government did take some action to try to improve the situation. In 1930 taxes were cut to increase people's spending power. The government provided over $4,000 million for major building projects in the construction industry to provide new jobs. For example, in 1931 work began on building the Hoover Dam on the Colorado River. In 1932 an Emergency Relief Act gave $300 million to the states to help the unemployed. Also in 1932 the Reconstruction Finance Corporation provided loans of $1,500 million to businesses to help them recover from the Depression. However, these actions were not enough to halt the Depression. Resentment of the government sometimes turned to violence. In the cities the unemployed held marches and demonstrations, which often turned into riots.

Millions of Americans blamed Hoover for the Depression and all the problems that came with it. With bitterness they said: 'In Hoover we trusted, now we are busted'.

They also talked of such things as 'Hoover leather' (cardboard soles for shoes) and 'Hoover blankets' (newspaper that people slept in). They were looking for a more positive approach in dealing with the Depression. They found it in F. D. Roosevelt, who promised 'a New Deal for the American people'.

Things to do

1 (a) How did the Depression affect the people of America?
  (b) How successful was Hoover in dealing with it?

Recovery from Depression

USA, 1933–41

In 1932 the American people turned to F.D. Roosevelt to take the USA out of depression. The new president offered a different approach to solving the problems caused by the Depression. The New Deal introduced new measures to bring 'relief, recovery and reform'.

4.1 What measures did Roosevelt introduce to bring 'relief, recovery and reform' to the USA?

The 1932 Presidential election

By 1932 the American people felt badly let down by the Republican government of Herbert Hoover. In the 1928 Presidential election Hoover had promised that the economic prosperity of the 1920s would continue. The opposite had happened and the USA had been hit by depression. The policies of the government had done little to ease the suffering caused by the Depression. In the 1932 Presidential election campaign, Hoover offered only the hope that the Depression would soon end and that the USA had 'turned the corner' back towards prosperity.

Source A

F.D. Roosevelt.

Source B

A cartoon, dated 3 March 1933, showing President Roosevelt throwing out the policies of the previous government, which are seen as rubbish.

Governments in Action: USA 1919–41

F.D. Roosevelt, promised 'a New Deal for the American people'. He outlined policies which would provide jobs and relief for the poor and unemployed, action to help industry and agriculture and resolve the banking crisis.

The result of the 1932 Presidential election was never in doubt. Even so the scale of Roosevelt's victory surprised many Americans. He won 42 of the 48 states of the USA. It was the biggest victory in a Presidential election that anyone had ever won.

The New Deal

During the period between the election victory of November 1932 and taking office in March 1933 – the 'lame duck months' when the new government is not in place – Roosevelt worked out the New Deal in greater detail. To carry it out the government would put money into the economy to provide new jobs. This would give people money to spend and the demand for goods would increase. This in turn would lead to more employment. The 'cycle of prosperity' would be restored.

The Hundred Days

The New Deal required massive state involvement in the economy and the setting up of government controlled agencies. Roosevelt was given the authority to do this when Congress granted him 'emergency powers' – the sort of powers he would have if the USA had been at war. Roosevelt acted quickly during his first 'Hundred Days' in office and set up a number of agencies which became known as the 'alphabet agencies' because the people found it easier to remember them by their initials than by their full names. Roosevelt also realised the need to explain to the American people what he was doing. They needed to have trust and confidence in his measures and in the recovery of the economy. As he said when he was sworn in as President: 'The only thing we have to fear is fear itself.'

He used the radio to reach a large audience of millions of Americans and to talk directly to them. In his 'fireside chats', in which he sat in a chair by a fire in his office, he explained in simple terms why the USA had fallen into depression and what he proposed to do to end it. The broadcasts were hugely successful – especially the first one which dealt with the banking crisis.

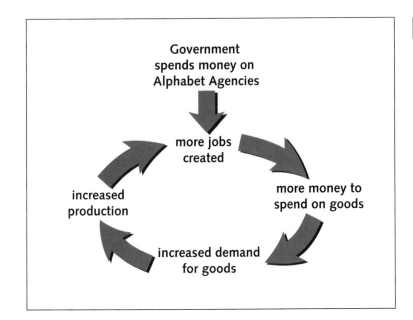

Government spends money on Alphabet Agencies

more jobs created

more money to spend on goods

increased demand for goods

increased production

The cycle of recovery.

Things to do

1 Why did Roosevelt win the 1932 Presidential election?

2 What was 'New' about the 'New Deal'?

3 What did Roosevelt mean when he said, 'The only thing we have to fear is fear itself'?

The banking crisis

During the Depression, people lost confidence in the banks. Many banks had closed as savers withdrew their money and businesses were unable to pay back bank loans. In March 1933 Roosevelt introduced an Emergency Banking Act. All banks were closed for four days. During that time government officials inspected the accounts of every bank. Only those banks that were properly managed were allowed to re-open – and these were supported by govern-ment loans. When the banks re-opened after the four-day 'holiday', savers kept their money in them and customers who had withdrawn their money even started to put it back into their accounts. The banking crisis was over.

Agriculture: the AAA

In May 1933 Roosevelt set up the Agricultural Adjustment Administration (AAA) to help farmers to increase their income. It was controversial because it paid farmers to produce less food, either by ploughing less land or by reducing their livestock.

This meant that food prices went up and farmers' income increased. Any loss of profit was made up by government subsidies. Government money was also used to help farmers who were having difficulty in meeting their mortgage payments. As a result of these measures farmers' income doubled in the period up to 1939. However, it failed to help farmworkers. Many of these were evicted as there was less work for them to do.

Source C

Roosevelt meeting a farmer in Georgia in 1932.

Dealing with unemployment: FERA, CWA, PWA, WPA

The key to the success of the New Deal was the creation of jobs to reduce the high level of unemployment which the USA experienced in the Depression. A number of agencies were set up to deal with this problem.

'Yes, you remembered me,' a cartoon of 1933.

As a start, the Federal Emergency Relief Administration (FERA) was created in 1933 to give quick relief to the hungry and homeless. $500 million was spent on providing soup kitchens and clothing, and setting up employment schemes.

The Civil Works Administration (CWA) aimed to provide as many jobs as possible in the short term – especially before winter arrived. During the winter of 1933-4 over four million jobs were created in areas such as building and improving roads, schools, airports and other public buildings. People were paid to sweep up leaves in local parks or even to frighten pigeons away from public buildings. Once the winter of 1933-4 was over, the CWA ended – and so did the four million jobs it created.

In the meantime, another agency was set up to provide work – the Public Works Administration (PWA). This aimed to organise long-term work schemes that would be of lasting value to Americans: building schools, hospitals, airports, dams, bridges, battleships. All were built under the direction of the PWA, which also directed improvements in sewage and drainage systems. Such schemes created jobs, but generally they were for skilled workers rather than for the millions who lacked a skill or trade.

To help meet this need, the Works Progress Administration (WPA) was set up in 1935. In some ways it was similar to the PWA. It helped to build roads, schools and other public buildings, but the schemes were on a small scale. It also gave work to writers, artists, photographers and actors. For example, unemployed writers were paid to write a series of guide books on American states and cities; 12,000 actors were paid to tour the country and perform plays. The WPA became the country's biggest employer – two million Americans were employed each year by it.

The three agencies, CWA, PWA and WPA, provided work for millions of Americans. The money they earned from this work could be used to buy food, clothing and other goods. This increased demand and in turn helped businesses to provide more jobs.

Recovery from Depression, 1933–41

Helping the young: CCC

Some of the agencies set up in the New Deal had more than one aim. For example the Civilian Conservation Corps (CCC) not only provided work but also helped agriculture and the environment. This agency gave work to single, unemployed young men between the ages of 18 and 25 for a limited period – usually six months. They lived in camps in the countryside, planted trees to stop soil erosion, cleared land, created forests and made reservoirs. In return they received food, clothing and shelter, and pocket money of one dollar a day. By 1938 over two million young people had served in the CCC. It was criticised by some Americans as being cheap labour but it was not compulsory and, through it, many young men learned skills which later allowed them to get a job.

Helping industry: NRA

Roosevelt tried to help both sides of industry, employers and workers, through the National Recovery Administration (NRA). Employers and businessmen were invited to follow codes fixing fair prices for the goods being sold, setting the minimum wages to be paid to workers, and laying down conditions of work including maximum hours of work. Child labour and cheap 'sweated' labour were forbidden. Businesses that signed the NRA code could advertise using the Blue Eagle with the motto 'We Do Our Part'. Americans were encouraged to buy goods with the Blue Eagle on them. The scheme was a success. By the end of 1933 two million employers, employing 22 million workers, had agreed to the codes.

Other measures of the New Deal

The New Deal introduced a number of measures which tried to help the American people in other ways. The Home Owners Loan Corporation (HOLC) helped people who were having difficulty meeting their mortgage repayments. The government, through the Corporation, lent money to people at low interest rates to prevent them from losing their homes.

The Social Security Act was introduced in 1935. It set up a national system of state pensions for people over 65, for widows and for the disabled. It also provided for an unemployment insurance scheme to be run by each state with financial support from the government. The National Labour Relations Act, or the Wagner Act, was also introduced in 1935. It gave American workers the right to join and form trade unions. It also stopped employers from dismissing workers who were members of a union.

Summary

The New Deal brought:

RELIEF – by helping the poor and homeless, the farmers and people in danger of losing their homes.

RECOVERY – by helping industry and providing jobs.

REFORM – by introducing measures to help people who were old, unemployed, disabled and in need.

Summary

The Alphabet Agencies:

AAA	Helped farmers by paying them to produce less food.
FERA	Provided relief for the hungry and homeless in 1933.
CWA	Created jobs on public work schemes, 1933-4.
PWA	Created jobs in public work schemes, including construction.
WPA	Created jobs in public work schemes, including community schemes.
NRA	Introduced codes of fair competition for industry and business.
CCC	Provided jobs for unemployed young men in the countryside.
TVA	Brought improvement to states in the Tennessee Valley.
HOLC	Helped people in difficulties with their mortgage repayments.

Governments in Action: USA 1919–41

Case Study: The Tennessee Valley Authority (TVA)

The TVA aimed to bring relief to the Tennessee Valley – what Roosevelt called 'the nation's number one economic problem'.

The Tennessee river caused massive problems across a large area of south-east America. In the spring it flooded, washing away good soil. In the summer it almost dried up, causing soil erosion and dust-bowl conditions. As a result the people of the Tennessee Valley lived in poverty. As the Tennessee river ran through seven different American states, it was also difficult to get common agreement on what actions to take to solve the problems. So Roosevelt set up the Tennessee Valley Authority (TVA) which developed a detailed scheme to improve the whole area. Trees were planted and forests created to improve the soil. Twenty-one dams were built to control the river and prevent flooding. Power stations were built at the dams to provide cheap electricity for homes and industry. The dams also created lakes and these were used for water transport which linked into the major river systems of the USA. The cheap source of power and good transport facilities attracted industries to the Tennessee Valley. The lakes also provided sporting and leisure facilities. As a result the Tennessee Valley recovered and became a prosperous area. Thousands of jobs were created, the land became fertile and the quality of life of the people who lived there greatly improved.

Things to do

Use the information in the case study to explain why Roosevelt thought that the TVA was his greatest achievement.

Source E

A dam built by the TVA.

4.2 How far was the New Deal successful in ending the Depression in the USA?

In 1936 Roosevelt's first term of office as President was coming to an end. He sought re-election for a second term and based his campaign on the promise to continue with the New Deal. Only two states out of the 48 voted against Roosevelt. He had received a clear vote of confidence for his policies from the American people.

Opposition to the New Deal

Despite his landslide victory, 16 million Americans had not voted for Roosevelt. Many of these were Republicans who continued to believe in the old ideas of self-reliance and 'rugged individualism'. They felt that Roosevelt was behaving like a dictator, forcing Americans to do what he wanted. Republicans also objected to the huge cost of the New Deal and felt that the people's money was being wasted on worthless jobs. Businessmen also did not like government interference in their affairs. Many opposed the codes of fair competition set up by the NRA. They objected to the support for trade unions and the attempts to increase wages. This was the government interfering in business, which was not its job.

But there were also other Americans who felt that he was not doing enough. For example, Huey Long, Senator for Louisiana, set up an alternative 'Share Our Wealth' movement. He promised to confiscate all fortunes over $3 million and share out the money so that every American family would have between $4,000 and $5,000. He also wanted free education for all Americans, a national minimum wage and old age pensions. His ideas were popular, especially in Louisiana. However, they did bring opposition for being too extreme. When he was assassinated in 1935 support for his movement collapsed.

Source F

In this 1933 cartoon Roosevelt said he was 'priming the pump' of the American economy. Priming a pump is getting it started.

Things to do

Study Source F. What criticism does it make of The New Deal?

Governments in Action: USA 1919–41

The Supreme Court

It is the responsibility of the Supreme Court to decide if any measure passed by the President and Congress is unconstitutional – that is, whether it goes against the American Constitution. If it feels that this is the case, the Supreme Court can block the measure and declare it illegal.

Roosevelt was unfortunate in that a majority of the judges on the Supreme Court were Republicans. They felt that the New Deal and the increased powers it gave the government was against the Constitution. As a result, a number of the alphabet agencies were declared illegal.

In 1935 the NRA and all the codes it had introduced had to be withdrawn because the Supreme Court ruled that they were unconstitutional. In 1936 the AAA was declared unconstitutional because the Supreme Court ruled that it was the responsibility of each state, not the federal government, to help agriculture. All the help that the AAA had given to farmers stopped. In another eleven cases the Supreme Court ruled against the alphabet agencies.

In this 1936 cartoon Roosevelt shows 'Uncle Sam' the achievements of the New Deal.

Roosevelt was furious at the actions of the Supreme Court. After his 1936 election victory he tried to add six judges to the Supreme Court so that there would be a Democrat majority. This threat to 'pack' the Court made Roosevelt unpopular throughout America, even among Democrats. He backed down – but so too did the Supreme Court. After this no more of Roosevelt's measures were rejected by the Court.

Was the New Deal a success?

The New Deal achieved much and helped millions of Americans who had suffered in the years of depression, but there were areas where it was less successful.

Black people generally benefited less from the New Deal than white people: in 1935 about a third of black people were dependent on relief payments. Many farmers and, especially farm labourers, continued to have a low standard of living. Those who lived in the areas affected by the dust bowl were even worse off.

Recovery from Depression, 1933–41

It is also true that the New Deal was not successful throughout the 1930s. In the first phase, from 1933 to 1936, it did bring recovery as the government pumped millions of dollars into creating jobs and reviving American industry. In 1933, 14 million Americans were unemployed; in 1938 it was 11 million. During 1937 Roosevelt reduced the amount of money the government was spending on the New Deal. He believed that enough had been done to bring recovery. However, production began to fall again as demand decreased. Share prices fell sharply on Wall Street. Businesses started to collapse once more. Unemployment in 1938 stood at 10½ million. Roosevelt was again forced to pump more money back into the economy and unemployment fell in 1939 – but only to 9½ million. It seemed as if the New Deal, with its massive amount of public spending, had achieved all it could.

The Second World War

What did help the American economy to recover was the Second World War. Although the USA did not enter the war until December 1941, its impact was felt from 1939. America sold goods to Britain and France which increased the demand for American manufactured goods and food produce. The level of unemployment fell. Finally, when the USA entered the war, its full resources – manpower, industry and agriculture – were absorbed in the fight against Japan and Germany. The economy was lifted out of depression.

Roosevelt and the New Deal had brought great changes to America. The federal (central) government became much more involved in people's lives than it had been in the 1920s. Most Americans now accepted that the federal government had a role to play in making sure that the weaker sections of society – the unemployed, the homeless, the old, the poor – were looked after. Roosevelt had helped to redefine the role of government in America.

Source H

The New Deal certainly did not get the country out of the Depression. As late as 1941 there were still six million unemployed and it was really not until the war that the army of the jobless finally disappeared.

An historian writing in 1963.

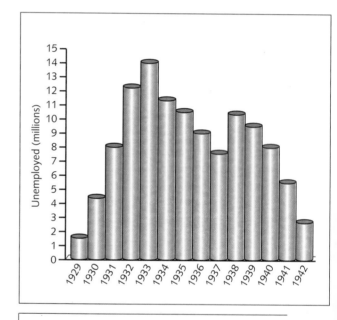

Unemployment in the USA, 1929-42.

Things to do

1 Was the New Deal a success? Explain your answer.

2 'Roosevelt was only trying to do his best for the country, so people were wrong to oppose his New Deal measures'. Explain whether you agree with this statement.

Exam-type Assessment
USA, 1919–41

This exercise is based on the sort of questions you could be asked on Paper 2 of your examination.

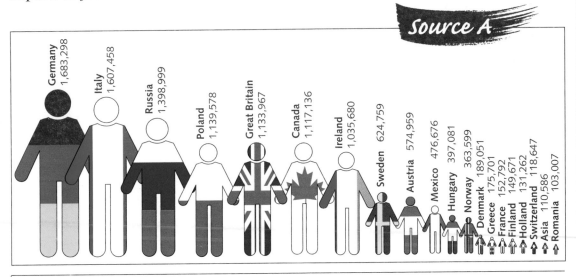

Germany 1,683,298
Italy 1,607,458
Russia 1,398,999
Poland 1,139,578
Great Britain 1,133,967
Canada 1,117,136
Ireland 1,035,680
Sweden 624,759
Austria 574,959
Mexico 476,676
Hungary 397,081
Norway 363,599
Denmark 189,051
Greece 175,701
France 152,792
Finland 149,671
Holland 131,262
Switzerland 118,647
Asia 110,586
Romania 103,007

A diagram of the number of foreign born people in the USA in 1920.

Model T Fords at a seaside resort near Boston in 1926.

Questions

1 **Study Source A.**
Use your knowledge to explain why the American government took steps to reduce the number of immigrants to the USA in the 1920s. *(5 marks)*

2 **Summary Essay.**
What actions did the American government take between 1919 and 1922 to move the country into isolation? *(15 marks)*

3 **Study Source B.**
Use your knowledge to explain why Henry Ford was such a successful businessman. *(6 marks)*

4 **Summary Essay.**
Explain how Prohibition and organised crime affected the lives of the American people in the 1920s. *(15 marks)*

The hunger queue for Christmas dinner in New York, 1931.

Source D

The visitor would be suprised to discover that, at first and even at second glance, New York City is much the same as it was in pre-depression days... Wandering about the city looking for disaster, the visitor will very likely find no more than he would have in New York in any other winter.

An extract from the magazine Fortune *in the winter of 1931.*

Source E

Dear Mr President, This is just to tell you everything is alright now. The man you sent found our house alright and we went down to the bank with him and the mortgage can go on for a while longer. You remember I wrote about losing the furniture too. Well, your man got it back for us. I never heard of a President like you, Mr Roosevelt. Mrs _____ and I are old folks, and don't amount to much, but we are joined with millions of others in praying for you every night. God bless you, Mr Roosevelt.

A letter written to President Roosevelt.

Questions

1   **Summary Essay.**
    Explain why the USA fell into depression in 1929.   *(15 marks)*

2   **Study Sources C and D.**
    Use your knowledge to decide which source gives a more accurate view
    of conditions in New York in the winter of 1931.   *(7 marks)*

3   **Study Source E.**
    What view of Roosevelt and the New Deal is given by the source?   *(4 marks)*

4   **Summary Essay.**
    What action did Roosevelt take in his New Deal to create jobs for the
    American people? How successful was he?   *(15 marks)*

Chapter 6

Governments in Action:
Britain, 1905–51

In 1900 Britain was a nation divided by class. Booth and Rowntree had shown that something needed to be done. Poverty was no longer seen as the fault of the poor. It was the fault of the society Britain had created. From 1906 the Liberal government attempted to tackle these problems with a wide range of social and economic reforms. By 1918 the beginnings of the welfare state had been established, the system of government reformed, women had gained the vote and the Labour Party was establishing itself as the opposition to the Conservatives. Industrial relations were poor in the first part of the century, culminating in a nine-day General Strike in 1926.

A world depression in the 1930s proved difficult to overcome despite the growth of new industries in the south of the country and government attempts to solve the problems facing towns such as Jarrow. It was only after the Second World War when nationalisation of key industries and further welfare reforms, such as the establishment of the National Health Service, took effect that further progress was made to overcome the economic and social problems which affected Britain in the 20th century.

This is a Paper 2 topic and you will be required to answer one structured question on it.

A changing society?

From 1905 the new Liberal government tried to tackle the social problems Charles Booth and Seebohm Rowntree had highlighted in their surveys at the beginning of the century. New laws were introduced to help children, workers, and the old. However, raising the money to pay for the new benefits led to a conflict between the Commons and the Lords which resulted in the Parliament Act and a restriction on the powers of the House of Lords.

1.1 How far was the welfare state established by 1914?

Life in Britain in 1900 was very different from life in Britain today. A very rich upper class or a 'well to do' middle class enjoyed a lifestyle which even people today would envy. Despite the number of enquiries which were held between 1890 and 1910 many of the governing classes still believed that most problems had been solved by providing workhouses for the very poor to live in and Public Health Acts to improve the health of the poor by ensuring cleaner water and better housing.

Source A

Living conditions for a London East End family at the beginning of the 20th century.

Pupils exercising at a school in 1908.

This was not the case. Many people needed help urgently. A Royal Commission in 1895 revealed that most working people were not earning enough for the basic necessities of life. The findings of the Commission were supported by surveys carried out by Charles Booth (in London) and Seebohm Rowntree (in York) which showed shocking poverty in England's cities.

In 1906 the Liberal government was elected and set about introducing a series of reforms which were the foundation of the modern welfare state.

Children's health

From the late nineteenth century education was compulsory. As children entered education in large numbers teachers complained that many of them were inadequately clothed and hungry. Voluntary charities had raised money to provide some clothing and meals but it was clearly not enough.

In 1906, the Education (Provision of Meals) Act enabled local education authorities to provide school meals for children. In Bradford food centres were set up to feed pupils with broth, pies, vegetables, puddings and, occasionally, meat and fish!

In some areas meals were even provided during the school holidays. But it was not until 1914 that the provision of school meals was made compulsory.

The Liberal government also introduced the School Medical Inspection Service (1907) which allowed doctors and nurses to visit schools regularly and inspect each child once a year.

The first school clinics, were opened in 1912, to treat childhood problems of the eyes, ears and teeth. These were the main way children's health was monitored and treated until after the Second World War.

Things to do

1   What evidence was there to suggest that many people were living in poverty at the beginning of the 20th century?

2   How reliable do you think Source A is in showing us what it was like to be poor?

3   How did the Liberal government try to help young people?

Britain 1905–19: A changing society?

Old age pensions

The Old Age Pensions Act (1908) was passed to provide pensions from the 6 January 1909 to people 70 years of age or over. Pensioners were entitled to 5 shillings (25 pence) each a week provided they had less than £21 income a year from any other source. This was about 60 per cent of all people over 70. Over 650,000 people applied for a pension in the first year, and by the start of the First World War in 1914 there were almost a million pensioners.

Until now old people with no support from relatives and too poor to support themselves were often forced to rely on the workhouse for accommodation and food. With the pension the fear of the workhouse almost disappeared. By 1912 the number of people over 70 years old in workhouses dropped by 5,590. At last many parents who had depended on their sons and daughters for food and shelter in their old age felt much less of a burden. As one pensioner exclaimed, 'Now we want to go on livin' for ever 'cus we give 'em the ten shillings a week.' Now all the government had to do was pay for the pensions. That was not to prove easy (see page 187).

(see page 187)

Source D

Friday was the beginning of a new era for the aged poor of this country, as the first payment of old age pensions was made. In Norwich there were old people waiting for the doors to open at 8 am, and by 9 am the first pensioners produced their coupon books without a word, answered one or two routine questions, made their signatures, pocketed their money and walked out.

A report in the Norwich Mercury, *9 January 1909.*

Pensioners queuing inside a post office for their pensions.

Source C

Things to do

1 Explain why 5 shillings a week pension was enough to make a difference to the lives of most pensioners.

2 a) Would you say the *Norwich Mercury* was in favour of pensions. Explain your answer.
b) Would all newspapers agree with this view? Explain your answer.

3 What problems would the government face if pensioners were to 'go on livin' forever?

Labour exchanges

To help the unemployed find work the President of the Board of Trade, Winston Churchill, pushed through the Labour Exchanges Act of 1909. The idea was to save unemployed people having to tramp from one factory to another in search of work. By 1913 there were 430 labour exchanges throughout the country. Today labour exchanges are called job centres.

National Insurance

Summary

1906 Workmen's Compensation Act. School meals could be provided for the needy.

1907 Medical inspection and some treatment for poor children.

1908 Old Age Pension Act provided pensions as a right.

1909 Labour exchanges start to be set up. Trades Board Act protects the low paid.

1911 National Insurance Act.

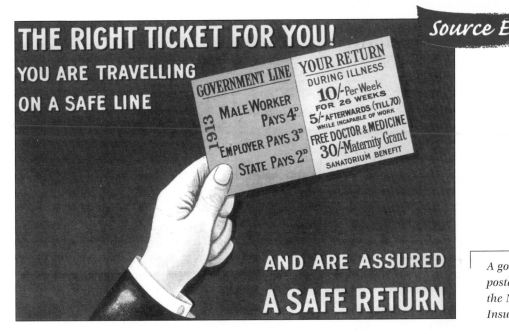

Source E

THE RIGHT TICKET FOR YOU!
YOU ARE TRAVELLING ON A SAFE LINE

GOVERNMENT LINE
1913
MALE WORKER PAYS 4ᴰ
EMPLOYER PAYS 3ᴰ
STATE PAYS 2ᴰ

YOUR RETURN
DURING ILLNESS
10/- Per Week
FOR 26 WEEKS
5/- AFTERWARDS (TILL 70) WHILE INCAPABLE OF WORK
FREE DOCTOR & MEDICINE
30/- Maternity Grant
SANATORIUM BENEFIT

AND ARE ASSURED
A SAFE RETURN

A government poster advertising the National Insurance Act.

The National Insurance Act of 1911 introduced an insurance scheme against ill-health and unemployment. Health insurance was only for manual and non-manual workers earning less than £160 a year. In this scheme the workman paid 4 pence into the scheme, the employer 3 pence and the state 2 pence, leading to the slogan '9d for 4d'. In return a worker was entitled to 'free' medical treatment and could claim 10 shillings (50 pence) a week for a maximum of 26 weeks if unable to work. After that a disability pension of 5 shillings (25 pence) could be awarded. The scheme itself was not available to women workers until 1920, but a male worker's wife was given a special payment of £1 and 10 shillings (£1.50) after the birth of a baby.

Unemployment insurance was introduced for men in industries such as building, engineering and shipbuilding, where short-term unemployment was common. A worker and his employer made contributions to the insurance fund and when unemployed a worker could claim 7 shillings (30 pence) a week for a limited period of 15 weeks. The scheme was extended to another eight million workers in 1920.

Things to do

How far had the welfare state been established by 1914?

1.2 How far was the system of government changed as a result of events between 1905 and 1919?

The Liberal reforms were expensive and so the Chancellor, Lloyd George, proposed a range of tax increases in the 1909 budget to pay for them. This included an increase in income tax from 5p to 7p in the pound for those earning over £3,000 a year (Remember that health insurance was later to be set up for people earning less than £160 per year!) and an extra 2 pence in every pound for those earning over £5,000. There was also an increase in death duties, a new land tax and increased duties on tobacco and alcohol. The proposals were very unpopular with many well-off people.

As the Liberals had most MPs in the House of Commons, the Finance Bill setting out the budget was easily passed. However their opponents, the Conservatives, had more members in the House of Lords. Many of the Lords were angry at the proposed land tax which would be paid on any profit made on land sold. In November 1909 the Lords rejected the Finance Bill. Members of the Lords who did not usually attend were summoned to London to make sure the Bill was defeated. These 'backwoodsmen', as the Liberal press called them, even had difficulty in persuading the policeman at the door of the Lords to let them in as he did not recognise them. The Prime Minister, Herbert Asquith, called a general election to see if his plans had the support of the country.

Mr Lloyd-George: What are you using this acre field for?

Owner: Agricultural purposes, I turn my pony in here!

Mr Lloyd-George: It can't be worth more than £50 for that purpose – couldn't you do something better with it?

Owner: There's no need for me to do anything – the builders over there are doing it all for me. They'll be wanting to build here soon. Why, I could get £500 tomorrow for this acre!

Mr Lloyd-George: Then, surely, it won't hurt you to pay tax of a halfpenny in the £ on an increased value which you had nothing to do with making!

A Liberal Party leaflet in 1909.

The general election: January 1910

The election which some described as the 'Peers against People' was hard fought. The result was that the Liberals and Conservatives won the same number of seats but the Liberals had the support of the Irish Nationalists and the Labour Party so they formed a new government.

They now set about getting the budget of the previous year passed. To make sure there would not be more obstructions they planned to reduce the power of the House of Lords through a new Parliament Bill. What was now known as the 'People's Budget' was eventually passed in April 1910, although the proposed land tax was dropped. The Lords and the Conservatives were more concerned about the proposed Parliament Bill. The opposition to it caused a contitutional crisis.

The consitutional crisis

The politicians now turned to the proposal to reduce the power of the Lords. The new king, George V, who had just succeeded to the throne and was almost immediately faced with this constitutional crisis, called for the parties to discuss the crisis at a conference in June. When talks broke down in November, the Liberal government called on the king to create 300 more Liberal peers for the House of Lords so that they would have more members than the Conservatives, making it possible to get the Parliament Bill passed. The king agreed, provided a general election was held to show that the people agreed.

In the second election of the year, in December, the result was almost identical to the first. Asquith knew that if the Lords rejected the Parliament Bill the King would create enough new peers for it to be passed. Eventually, in August 1911, the Lords passed the Bill by 131 votes to 114. As for the Conservatives, their leader, Balfour, resigned and the new leader, Bonar Law, continued the struggle against the Liberal government.

	1906	Jan 1910	Dec 1910	1918	1922
Liberal Party	377	275	272*	146*	117*
Labour Party	53	4	42*	59	142*
Conservative Party	157	273	272	338*	347*
Irish Nationalists	83	82	84*	–	–
Asquith Liberals	–	–	–	26	–

* Liberal Government
  (needing support from Labour and Irish Nationalists)
* Lloyd George Coalition Government
  (Liberals and Conservatives)
* Labour Government (depending on support from other parties to get budgets and bills through Parliament)

General election results, 1906-22.

THE PARLIAMENT BILL

- established that all money bills (budgets) passed by the Commons had to be passed by the Lords;
- limited the power of the Lords over other bills;
- said that MPs should be paid;
- established that general elections take place every five years rather than every seven.

Things to do

1 Explain how the Liberals hoped to raise money to pay for pensions and why there was opposition to their proposals.

2 How reliable do you think Source F is in explaining why the government wanted to introduce a land tax?

3 Explain how the Liberal government was able to get its budget through the House of Lords.

Britain 1905–19: A changing society?

Women's right to vote

The Parliament Act saw a change in the role of the House of Lords in passing laws, but there was a much more significant change in the way the country was governed during this period. Before the First World War women did not have a vote in general elections, could not be MPs or sit in the House of Lords. Many people, including Queen Victoria and the Prime Minister, Asquith, accepted this, but a campaign by suffragettes and the events of the First World War were to change that.

During the war the suffragettes suspended their campaign, changed their slogan to 'The Right to Serve' and committed themselves to the national effort to defeat Germany. Working on the land and in factories as well as serving in the armed forces, they proved their worth to the nation and in 1918 women aged 30 or over were given the right to vote. It was not until 1928 that women received the vote at the age of 21 on equal terms with men.

Women fire-fighters.

The Suffragettes

The suffragettes were women who fought for the right to vote in general elections. From 1903 the fight was led by the Women's Social and Political Union (WSPU), founded by Emmeline Pankhurst and her daughters. At first they used peaceful methods of drawing attention to their cause: marches, petitions and publishing their own newspaper.

In 1909 the WSPU decided peaceful methods were not working as well as they wanted and they turned to violent ways of making the public aware of their demands. Such action helped them gain publicity, but it also convinced some people that women were too 'unbalanced' to be given the vote.

Some of them went on hunger strike to highlight their case. Women who broke the law were arrested and some were imprisoned. To prevent them from dying the authorities force fed them, but this was considered too brutal. So the Cat and Mouse Act of 1913 was passed. It allowed the prisons to release women on hunger strike and arrest them again once they had recovered from their ordeal.

In 1913 the suffragette Emily Wilding Davison, in a highly dangerous attempt to win the suffragettes widespread publicity, tried to disrupt the Epsom Derby horse race by throwing herself at the King's horse. She was seriously injured and died four days later. Her funeral was a massive public affair, giving the suffragettes huge publicity.

Keir Hardie and the rise of the Labour Party

Keir Hardie was leader of the miners. In 1888 he stood as a Labour candidate for Mid-Lanark. He came last. He then formed the Scottish Labour Party and other parts of the country formed local Labour parties. Four years later he won the West Ham seat as an Independent Labour candidate. In 1893 local Labour parties formed the Independent Labour Party (ILP) and although Hardie lost his seat in the 1895 election the new party was born.

An important milestone in the history of the Party came in 1903 when it made a pact with the Liberal Party agreeing that only one candidate (Liberal or Labour) should stand against the Conservatives in a general election, except in the case of Scotland.

In the 1906 election 29 Labour MPs were elected. The Parliament Act of 1911 provided MPs with an annual salary of £400, which was a benefit to Labour MPs, who had few other sources of income. Further help came from the Trades Union Act of 1913, which allowed union funding for the Labour Party. It could now campaign at election time on a more equal footing with the main parties.

The election of 1918 saw an increase in Labour seats to 59, although the Party leader, Arthur Henderson, failed to be re-elected.

Events between 1918 and 1922 were to prove beneficial for the Labour Party. A number of problems for the government, including a slump in the post-war economy, helped to persuade people that it was time for a change. In 1922 the Labour Party gained 142 seats (25 more than the Liberals) and became the main opposition party to the Conservatives. An increase to 191 MPs in the elections of 1923 saw the formation of the first Labour government under Ramsay McDonald in January 1924.

Summary

1909 Liberals introduce 'People's Budget'.

1910 Liberals win two general elections.

1911 Parliament Act passed.

1913 Trade Union Act.

1918 Women aged 30 and over given the vote.

1928 Voting age is reduced to 21 for women.

Things to do

1 How did women try to get the vote?

2 Why were women eventually given the vote in 1918 and 1928?

3 What were the main events in the rise of the Labour Party?

Source H

DRINK & ENJOY LIPTON'S TEA
Largest Sale in the World.

Daily News
FINAL

No. 24522. LONDON, SATURDAY, OCTOBER 25, 1924. ONE PENNY.

RED PLOT AGAINST BRITAIN.

ALARM IN TORY CAMP.

Candidates Demand to Know What Baldwin Means.

RIDDLE OF FOOD PLEDGES.

SENSATIONAL EXPOSURE.

RUSSIAN INSTRUCTIONS SENT TO THE BRITISH COMMUNIST PARTY.

ARMED REVOLUTION.

ORDERS FOR TAMPERING WITH ARMY & NAVY.

EARTHQUAKE AT BIRMINGHAM.

City Surprised by a Sudden Jolt.

BUILDINGS TREMBLE VIOLENTLY.

CHINESE WARS TO END.

DRAMATIC NIGHT COUP IN PEKIN.

NEW REGIME.

TROOPS ENTER THE CITY SINGING A CAROL.

The front page of the Daily News, *25 October 1924.*

Britain 1905–19: A changing society?

Britain 1919–29

Post-war prosperity? A case study of the General Strike

In 1926 there was a General Strike in Britain. The causes of that strike can be traced back to before the First World War, although the immediate cause was a cut in miners' wages. The strike, which some people saw as a threat to the democratic system of government in Britain, lasted just nine days before the TUC told its members to go back to work.

2.1 Why was there a General Strike in 1926?

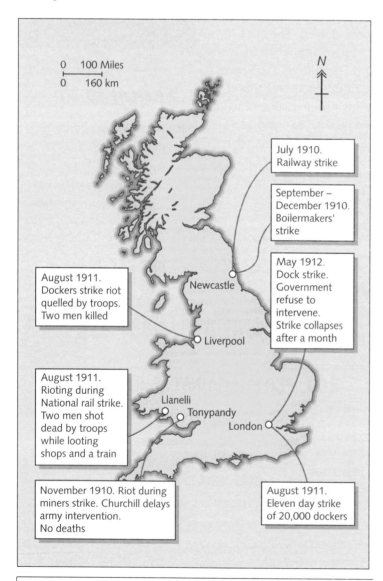

0 100 Miles
0 160 km

N

July 1910.
Railway strike

September – December 1910. Boilermakers' strike

May 1912. Dock strike. Government refuse to intervene. Strike collapses after a month

Newcastle

August 1911. Dockers strike riot quelled by troops. Two men killed

Liverpool

August 1911. Rioting during National rail strike. Two men shot dead by troops while looting shops and a train

Llanelli
Tonypandy
London

November 1910. Riot during miners strike. Churchill delays army intervention. No deaths

August 1911. Eleven day strike of 20,000 dockers

Industrial unrest in Britain, 1910–12.

Strikes, 1910–14

Although the Liberal government before the war was taking steps to improve living and working conditions in Britain, it still faced industrial unrest. Between 1910 and 1914 there were a series of official and unofficial strikes which challenged the government. In 1910 railwaymen, boiler-makers, miners and cotton workers all went on strike. In 1911, a dockers strike in Liverpool and a national rail strike were both ended by the government using troops. Four men died in street battles between strikers and soldiers. In February 1912, with over two million men unemployed, there was another miners' strike.

Some trade unions at this time believed that strike action was the most effective way of bringing about changes in society, in particular the trade unions taking over the running of industry. This was based on the idea of syndicalism, which was based on the idea that workers had the right to control the industries they worked in.

The British trade unions moved closer to realising this idea when they increased their power in 1913 through an alliance between miners, railwaymen, and transport workers – the Triple Alliance. This worried the government, but the outbreak of war in 1914 diverted people's attention from the issue.

Strikes, 1914-21

Although trade union leaders did agree in August 1914 to 'terminate all existing trade disputes' during the war, strikes in Glasgow, Clydeside, and South Wales showed that many workers were still unhappy about their wages and working conditions. Union membership also doubled during the war.

During the war, new industrial giants, such as Japan and the USA, began selling goods into traditional British markets and so fewer British goods were being bought overseas. Exports of British coal, which before the war had been 100,000,000 tons a year, fell as British prices were too high to compete with the cheaper coal produced by countries such as America, Germany and Poland.

Although after the war the economy picked up, there were still problems in the coal industry. During the war the government had taken over the running of the coal mines. The miners wanted this to continue. But the mine owners wanted the mines back. Although a government enquiry, the Sankey Commission, recommended that the mines be nationalised, the mine owners persuaded the government to return the mines to them in 1921. Unfortunately, the export price of coal fell at this time from £4 a ton to £1.75 a ton, and the mine owners were forced to try to cut wages and lengthen the working day. The miners opposed this.

The Triple Alliance had been renewed in February 1919 and so the miners called upon the transport workers and the railwaymen to support them in a strike against the cut in wages. However, on Friday 15 April 1921 they said they could not support the miners on strike. This day became known as Black Friday by the unions.

The miners were eventually forced to accept a cut in wages. In the following months there were pay disputes involving the railwaymen, dockers, building workers and others. Unemployment rose to over 2 million by June and union membership fell by over 2.5 million to about 5.5 million.

Things to do

1 Use the map on page 190 to explain the political problems which faced the government just before the First World War.

2 Explain how syndicalism and the Triple Alliance was a threat to the government between 1912 and 1926.

3 What effect did the First World War have on the coal-mining industry?

4 The article in Source A suggests that the Triple Alliance was a serious threat to the country. Do you agree?

Britain 1919–29: Post-war prosperity? A case study of the General Strike

Events leading to the General Strike

In 1925 falling prices forced the coal-mine owners to cut wages yet again and to increase the working day by one hour. The miners' leader, A.J.Cook, was furious. His reply, 'Not a penny off the pay! Not a minute on the day!' became the miners' slogan. This time it looked as if the Triple Alliance would hold together. The Prime Minister, Stanley Baldwin, thought so and on Friday 31 July 1925 he announced a government subsidy to keep wages at their current level and the setting up of a commission to be led by Sir Herbert Samuel to try and find a solution to the problem in the mines. Unions called this Red Friday and the disappointment of Black Friday seemed a thing of the past.

However, the subsidy was only for nine months. What would happen then? Some historians think that the government simply wanted time to build up stocks of coal and to plan what they would do if a general strike took place.

In the end the Samuel Commission failed to find a solution that could keep either side happy. It agreed with the owners' plan to cut wages but not to lengthen hours and also said that they should begin a programme of financial investment to modernise their mines.

Shortly after the Samuel Commission reported, Baldwin announced that the government subsidy would end on 30 April 1926. The owners then set wages lower than even Samuel had proposed. The miners refused to accept this and called on the other unions to support them by coming out on strike. The TUC (Trade Union Congress), the organisation which represents the unions, agreed to negotiate with the government on the miners' behalf and if necessary to call other trade unionists out on strike in support. The stage was set for the biggest industrial dispute of the 1920s.

Summary

1910 Series of strikes.

1913 Triple Alliance between miners, railwaymen and transport workers.

1919 Sankey Commission recommends mines stay under government control.

1921 Mines returned to mine owners. Black Friday.

1925 Red Friday.

1926 Samuel Commission fails to find solution.

Government withdraws subsidy.

Mine owners again reduce wages and increase working hours.

Things to do

1 The *Daily Herald* was a newspaper paid for by the trade unions. How reliable therefore is Source B?

2 Why was Red Friday seen as a victory for the miners?

3 Why were both sides unhappy with the conclusions of the Samuel Commission?

Source B

Yesterday was the heaviest defeat that has befallen the Labour Movement within the memory of man. It is no use trying to minimise it. It is no use trying to pretend it is other than it is. We on this paper have said throughout that if the organised workers would stand together they would win. They have not stood together, and they have been beaten.

An article in the Daily Herald, *commenting on Black Friday. The newspaper was paid for by the trade unions.*

Governments in Action: Britain 1905–51

2.2 Why did the General Strike fail after only nine days?

The strike begins

On the 30 April 1926 the employers made their final offer – a 13% cut in pay and a 'temporary' increase in the working day from 7 to 8 hours. It was rejected by the miners. Talks between the TUC and the government over how to resolve this situation broke down the following day when printers for the *Daily Mail* refused to print an article which described the proposed strike as 'a revolutionary movement intended to inflict suffering upon the great mass of innocent people'. The government called off the talks and the strike began at midnight on the 3 May 1926.

On the 4 May the people of many cities woke up to silence. Trains and buses were not running. (Later massive traffic jams replaced the silence as people tried to get to work by whatever means they could). Even the TUC was surprised. Union members had followed their leaders request and come out on strike. An estimated three million workers backed the miners.

Progress of the strike

At first the strike seemed successful and in the first few days the numbers on strike actually increased. The strikers were clearly well organised. They allowed essential supplies through and had no intention of bringing out on strike hospital workers or other key workers. There were even accounts that showed the good humour of both sides. In Plymouth and many other places there was a football match between strikers and police, and in Lincoln all the special constables were people already on strike!

However, the good humour was not evident everywhere, and some evidence suggests that it disappeared as the strike continued. In Glasgow and Doncaster strikers were arrested, tried and imprisoned. Fear of communism led to the arrest of two men in Wales for possessing communist literature.

Source C

London's Waterloo station is deserted during the General Strike of 1926.

Britain 1919–29: Post-war prosperity? A case study of the General Strike

In Hull, the mayor called out the navy after attacks on trams and serious rioting that seemed to threaten the city. In London, food stocks were moved from the docks to Hyde Park protected by armoured cars.

The volunteers played an important part in keeping essential services going during the strike. Students, stock brokers, and white collar workers could act out their boyhood dreams as train drivers, firemen and lorry drivers. On one day alone 6,000 men and women lined up outside the Foreign Office to sign up for the Organisation for the Maintenance of Supplies. Office workers even queued outside local police stations to be sworn in as special constables. If they were under 45 and with 'the required health, strength and vigour' they could join. Winston Churchill encouraged them to join to defeat 'the enemy'.

The attitude of both sides hardened as the strike went on and as it entered its second week violent clashes between the sides increased. Buses had their windows smashed, trams were turned over and trains were stopped when the tracks were blocked. There was even talk about the TUC bringing out their 'second line' of strikers, the electrical workers, which would have cut off electric light from the streets of major towns, but this did not materialise as the TUC took a different approach.

The TUC clearly felt that the situation could not continue. It had hoped to simply shock the government into surrender and had never intended to bring out on strike its second line, the electrical workers. It may have been afraid of not being able to handle the demands and threats of the communists. It may have simply not been able to handle the pressures that the strike had brought, or it may have thought that the Stanley Baldwin would still give the miners a fair deal despite his demands for unconditional surrender.

The end of the strike

Much to the surprise of the miners, the TUC did not extend the strike. Instead, on 12 May its leaders went to Downing Street and called off the strike! Why was this? No one is quite sure.

1926
Even greater British invention – television. John Logie Baird demonstrates his 'pictures by radio' in London. Meanwhile there is a 'General Strike' of miners, transport workers and many others. The government appoints 140,000 special policemen to sort the strikers out. The special police don't have enough truncheons to go round so they sent a lorry-load of chair legs. Ouch!

MAYBE I'D BETTER TAKE THE CHAIR OFF FIRST...

A humorous modern view of the conflict between police and strikers from a book designed to make history amusing for children.

Governments in Action: Britain 1905–51

Why the strike failed

1 Government prepared

Shortly after Red Friday the government established the OMS, the **Organisation for the Maintenance of Supplies**. It was to make sure that food supplies were distributed and electricity and gas supplies maintained. It even set up a government newspaper, *The British Gazette*, to give people the government's view of events! Lists of volueers to carry out vital jobs were drawn up and arrangements made to stockpile food just in case the strike dragged on for a long time.

2 Trade unions unprepared

Surprisingly, the trade union movement did not plan anything until five days before the strike started. By the time the talks collapsed the government was ready. When the TUC tried to re-open talks in the early hours of the 4 May 1926 the government ministers had gone home and the prime minister had already gone to bed.

3 Reaction of middle classes

An important factor in the defeat of the strikers was the reaction of many **middle-class** people. Protected by the army (and even the navy) they were gradually able to undermine the strike. For some people jobs such as driving a bus were 'good fun'.

It was important to maintain as normal a life as possible. As the secretary of the MCC (Marlyebone Cricket Club), the governing body of English cricket, said, 'As far as we can see, we have no intention to allow cricket to be interrupted.'

Britain 1919–29: Post-war prosperity? A case study of the General Strike

Source E

We set out from Oxford early in the evening in a vintage Bentley, but from Doncaster onwards groups of strikers tried unsuccessfully to interrupt our progress by occasionally throwing stones or attempting to puncture our tyres.

On the following day those of us who were to work on the docks received our orders, while others went to drive trams or work the cranes. We were under the supervision of a Cambridge don, Mr Owen Morshead, now librarian of Windsor Castle.

Some of the old hands who drifted back to work were surprised by the speed with which we unloaded the ships, but we realised that it was a different story working for a few days as an adventure, compared to regular work over a period of years.

*This is **an account by an Oxford undergraduate on his experience as a volunteer working in the Liverpool docks during the General Strike.***

Source F

Women volunteer as postal workers during the General Strike.

4 Propaganda

The government's other weapon against the strike was the careful use of **propaganda**. *The British Gazette* was edited by Winston Churchill and took every opportunity to attack the strikers, who Churchill called 'the enemy'. On the first day it was published, 5 May, it suggested that the 'strike was not so complete as hoped by its promoters'. Not surprisingly the TUC published its own newspaper, *The British Worker*, and began with the headline 'Wonderful Response to the call'.

Source G

The British Gazette

Published by His Majesty's Stationery Office.

No. 1.   LONDON, WEDNESDAY, MAY 5, 1926.   ONE

FIRST DAY OF GREAT STRIKE

Not So Complete as Hoped by its Promoters

PREMIER'S AUDIENCE OF THE KING

Miners and the General Council Meet at House of Commons

FOOD SUPPLIES

No Hoarding: A Fair Share for Everybody

MILK DISTRIBUTION

Control of Supplies in the Metropolis

HOLD-UP OF THE NATION

Government and the Challenge

NO FLINCHING

The Constitution or a Soviet

COMMUNIST LEADER ARRESTED

Mr. Saklatvala, M.P., Charged at Bow Street

SEQUEL TO MAY DAY SPEECH

THE "BRITISH GAZE AND ITS OBJECT

Reply to Strike Makers' P Paralyse Public Opinion

REAL MEANING OF THE S

Conflict Between Trade Union and Parliament

The front page of The British Gazette, *a government newspaper, covering the strike.*

Although the TUC could print its version of events it had no way of challenging the BBC **radio broadcasts**, which were to reach the majority of homes in the country. The BBC chairman, Sir John Reith, decided to allow only broadcasts by the government and refused to allow Ramsay McDonald, the Labour leader, to speak. So it was difficult for the TUC to put its case to the public, and, significantly, to other trade unionists.

5 Division among trade unionists

Many members of the TUC had been unhappy at the idea of a general strike. They feared that some revolutionaries in the union movement actually wanted to overthrow the government. They therefore refused to allow essential workers in health, water and sewerage to come out on strike and were determined to make sure that all picketing was done peacefully. So the TUC was looking for a way out from the start. On the 10 May 1926 it asked the miners leaders to accept the Samuel Commission's recommendations. When the miners refused the TUC met the prime minister and called off the strike, although the miners continued.

Immediately after this strike many employers cut the wages of their own workers even though the prime minister recommended such actions. The miners felt betrayed by the TUC. They remained locked out until November 1926, when hunger and the onset of winter forced them to accept the owners' terms.

Things to do

1 Explain how the government prepared for a strike.

2 'Red Friday was only a plan by the government to buy time so they could think of ways to defeat the Triple Alliance.' Do you agree? Explain your answer.

3 Source D makes fun of the General Strike. Explain how and why the author does this.

4 **(a)** Write down five reasons why the strike ended after only nine days.

   (b) Which of the reasons do you think was the most important? Explain your answer.

Governments in Action: Britain 1905–51

196

THE BRITISH WORKER
OFFICIAL STRIKE NEWS BULLETIN
Published by The General Council of the Trades Union Congress

| No. 1. | WEDNESDAY EVENING, MAY 5, 1926. | PRICE ONE PENNY |

IN LONDON AND THE SOUTH

Splendid Loyalty of Transport Workers

EVERY DOCKER OUT

" London dock workers are absolutely splendid," said an official of the Transport and General Workers' Union.

" So far as they are concerned, it is a 100 per cent. strike. There is no trouble and everything is going smoothly."

POLICE HELP REFUSED

At Swindon the railwaymen are obeying Mr. Cramp's injunction to remain steady and to preserve order. The Great Western works are, of course, closed, and no trains are running.

It was stated at a mass meeting of the N.U.R. that Mr. Collett (the

The General Council suggests that in all districts where large numbers of workers are idle sports should be organised and entertainments arranged.

WONDERFUL RESPONSE TO THE CALL

General Council's Message : Stand Firm and Keep Order

The workers' response has exceeded all expectations. The first day of the great General Strike is over. They have manifested their determination and unity to the whole world. They have resolved that the attempt of the mineowners to starve three million men, women and children into submission shall not succeed.

All the essential industries and all the transport services have been brought to a standstill. The only exception is that the distribution of milk and food has been permitted to continue. The Trades Union General Council is not making war on the people. It is anxious that the ordinary members of the public shall not be penalised for the unpatriotic conduct of the mineowners and the Government.

Never have the workers responded with greater enthusiasm to the call of their leaders. The only difficulty that the General Council is experiencing, in fact, is in persuading those workers in the second line of defence to continue at work until the withdrawal of their labour may be needed.

WORKERS' QUIET DIGNITY

The conduct of the trade unionists, too, constitutes a credit to the whole movement. Despite the presence of armed police and the military, the workers have preserved a quiet orderliness and dignity, which the General Council urges them to maintain, even in the face of the temptation and provocation which the Govern-

SOUTH WALES IS SOLID !

Not a Wheel Turning in Allied Industries

'MEN ARE SPLENDID !'

Throughout South Wales the stoppage is complete, and everywhere the men are loyally observing the orders of the T.U.C. to refrain from any conduct likely to lead to disturbance.

So unanimous has been the response to the call of the leaders, that not a wheel is turning in the industries affiliated to the T.U.C.

MONMOUTHSHIRE

Complete standstill of industries in the eastern valleys. Absolute unanimity prevails among the rank and file of the affiliated unions, and not a single wheel is turning in the allied industries.

Monmouth Education Authority— which has a majority of Labour representatives—has arranged to feed the school-children where required.

ABERDARE VALLEY

All railway and bus services are at a standstill. The miners' attitude indicates that they are absolutely loyal to the advice of their leaders to refrain from anything in the nature of riotous behaviour.

The TUC had its own newspaper to give its side of the strike to the public.

Wages were cut, hours were extended and fewer men were employed. Union leaders were targeted for dismissal and many never worked again in the coal industry.

Impact of the strike on trade unions

In 1927 a new Trade Disputes Act was passed. This made any sort of general strike illegal. Workers could no longer come out on strike in sympathy with other workers, and it made it more difficult for trade unions to contribute money to the Labour Party. (This act was later repealed by a Labour Government in 1946.) Although trade union members had stood together and shown they could make a generally peaceful protest, the General Strike was a disaster for the unions. They had lost the strike and the leadership had shown that it feared that some of its members were revolutionaries. Now the government had banned any future general strikes. Not surprisingly, disillusioned workers left their unions in large numbers. Trade union membership dropped alarmingly in the years after the strike and it did not go up again for over seven years.

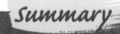 Summary

Reasons for the failure of the strike.

- Government preparation.
- Middle-class opposition.
- Opposition from political parties and the Churches.
- Division in the TUC.
- Government propaganda.

Things to do

1 How reliable is Source F to historians studying the General Strike?

2 Study Source E. How useful are accounts like this for an historian studying the General Strike?

3 Study Sources G and H. Do these sources prove that historians should not rely on newspapers when studying the General Strike?

Britain 1919–29: Post-war prosperity? A case study of the General Strike

Governments in Action: Britain 1905–51

unit 3 Britain, 1929–39

A decade of depression and recovery?

When in 1929 the Wall Street stock market in America crashed it sent economic shockwaves around the world. Britain suffered a depression which saw high unemployment and poverty in some areas. The government was forced to take unprecedented measures to try to solve the economic problems.

3.1 How far did Britain experience a depression in the 1930s?

The Wall Street Crash

The Wall Street Crash began on 24 October 1929. It brought the American economy to its knees. The Americans could no longer afford to lend European countries money to build up their industries or to buy goods. Consequently, economic depression soon hit Europe too and millions of workers lost their jobs.

Britain too followed the United States into economic depression, but in many ways the problems which brought economic depression in Britain had existed before the Wall Street Crash. Many British industries used out-of-date machinery and depended on the colonies for cheap raw material and export markets. As other countries began to develop their industries British industries such as coal mining, textiles, shipbuilding and iron and steel began to suffer.

The declining industries

You have already seen how the coal mining industry suffered in the 1920s. By the mid-1920s coal could be produced in America for 65p a tonne compared with £1.56 a tonne in Britain, and there was competition too from Poland and Germany. British mines could not compete with the superior technology being used in the mining industry of the USA and other countries.

Wall St. Crash

DEPRESSION IN THE USA

American companies go bust

Overseas loans recalled

Americans lose their jobs

Americans stop buying goods from abroad

British exports to America fall

Britons lose their jobs

World trade collapses

DEPRESSION IN BRITAIN

The American Depression hits Britain.

It was the same in the textile industry. Japan's workers were paid a fifth of their British counterparts and worked in modern efficient factories. So Japanese cotton was much cheaper than that produced in the outdated British factories. Matters were not helped when synthetic fibres, such as rayon, were

A slum scene in the North in the 1920s.

produced after the war and shorter skirts meant that less material was needed. Events in India also had a surprising effect. In Britain about 1,000 mills closed in the 1930s.

Shipbuilding also suffered. There was a post-war boom to replace the ships sunk in the First World War, but then a steady decline set in. As a result the iron and steel industry, which supplied ship-building with its raw materials, also suffered and like other industries faced competition from abroad. In the USA and Germany new efficient plants easily produced iron and steel more cheaply than their British rivals. In a world market Britain was finding it harder and harder to compete.

Summary

Reasons for the Depression in Britain.
- Wall Street Crash.
- Decline in old industries.
- Lack of investment in modern machinery.
- Competition from abroad.

Things to do

1 Explain how the following affected British industry after the First World War.

  (a) Out of date machinery.
  (b) Competition from abroad.
  (c) New synthetic fibres.

Poor north, rich south?

The decline in British industries tended to affect the traditional occupations such as shipbuilding, coal mining and textiles. Areas of the country where these industries were based therefore were hardest hit by the decline. This applied particularly to Northern Ireland, Wales, Scotland and the North of England (See Source D). In the South East and the Midlands cities such as Coventry thrived while towns in the north, such as Jarrow, were in the words of its MP, Ellen Wilkinson, 'murdered'.

Why set up in the south?

The greater employment in the south encouraged owners and directors of new companies to set up their businesses there to be close to new customers who had the money to buy the washing machines, radios and cars they built. An example was the Ford Motor Company, which decided to move from Trafford Park in Manchester to an area close to London. Over 2,000 Ford workers moved from the north to a new start in the south. Electricity provided the power to run the new washing machines and radios, as well to make them. Factories no longer needed to be close to coalfields as in the days of steam power. And raw materials no longer needed to be close by. Roads and railways could transport what was needed. It may have been that employers hoped for better industrial relations in the south after the northern industrial strikes of the 1920s.

Britain 1929–39: A decade of depression and recovery?

How did standards of living change?

It is not possible to talk in general terms of how the standard of living changed for British people in the 1930s. For many unemployed people life was extremely difficult and hunger and despair was common. But for many of those in work times were good. The high unemployment throughout Britain meant that prices were kept low, so those with a regular wage saw an increase in their standard of living.

Four million new houses were built in the 1930s. By 1939 27 per cent of houses were owner-occupied. An income of £200 a year was enough to own your own home, with mortgages easy to get and interest rates low. With the houses came the schools, churches and cinemas needed to support the communities. New chain-stores, such as Marks & Spencers and Woolworth's, were built. The quality of food improved as branded foods, breakfast cereals and canned foods became available. The cost of the car halved between 1924 and 1935 because of mass production. So did the price of a vacuum cleaner. Those in work could afford new modern houses with electricity, and they could even consider buying a family car. Cheaper loans helped encourage a housing boom.

New electrical products, the motor car, and the boom in consumer goods and branded foods continued to make daily life more comfortable. Entertainment expanded with the growth in radio, cinemas and daily newspapers.

Northern Ireland	26.2%
Wales	24.3%
North-East England	19.1%
Scotland	15.2%
Lancashire	12.9%
Yorkshire	9.2%
London	8.2%
South East	6.1%
Midlands	6.0%

Unemployment figures for 1937.

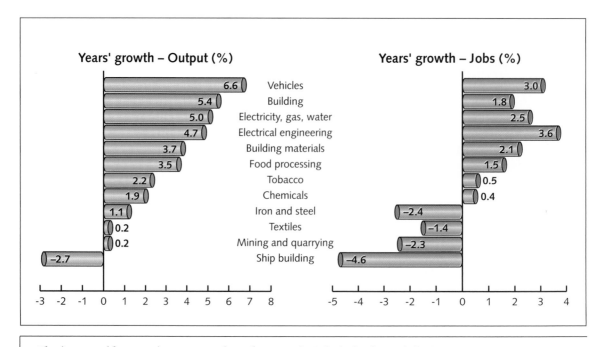

The increase/decrease in output and employment in Britain in the period 1920–38.

Despair for others

Source B

Whilst some workers, particularly in the south, prospered, others found it very difficult to maintain even a minimal standard of living. Areas which depended on shipbuilding or coal mining for employment were particularly badly hit with unemployment, poverty, malnutrition and ill-health common. In 1931 the national unemployment rate was 23 per cent, but this figure hid the real effects of the Depression. By the mid 1930s worst hit areas like Jarrow on Tyneside and Merthyr Tydfil in South Wales had over 60% unemployment, whilst Birmingham and Oxford had less than 6%.

In an area of high unemployment everyone in the community felt the impact. Local shopkeepers were hit hard. In some towns half the shops closed, with the shopkeepers themselves joining the masses of the unemployed. For others the search for jobs in the richer south meant leaving their home town. Many hoped that better times were just around the corner and they would not have to leave the communities they had grown up in. Charities tried to ease the pain but found it difficult to make a difference when so many people needed their help.

Things to do

1 Why were some areas of Britain hit harder than others by the Depression?

2 Why was it possible for some people to live in prosperity even though Britain was hard hit by the Depression?

3 The traffic jam in Source B must have occurred in the south of England. Do you agree?

This traffic jam in Britain shows how important motor transport had become in the lives of the people. Of course, for many others owing a car was little more than a dream.

Jarrow: a town 'murdered'

One town which was particularly hard hit by the Depression was Jarrow, a small town on the south bank of the River Tyne. In 1930 nearby Hebburn Colliery was closed and in 1931 one of Jarrow's major employers, the steel works, also shut down.

The government believed that the old industries needed reorganising. If some smaller factories and shipyards closed then the remaining fewer larger firms would be more competitive than many smaller ones. The National Shipbuilders' Security (NSS) was set up in 1930. It bought up shipyards and closed them down, hoping this would help other yards to stay in business.

For Jarrow this was disastrous. In 1934 the NSS closed Palmer's shipyard. By this time Jarrow was almost a one industry town, so the effect of closing the shipyard was devastating.

The Jarrow Crusade

The people of Jarrow decided to fight back. Public meetings were held. One desperate speaker even suggested going down to London with a bomb in his pocket to blow up the Houses of Parliament. The town council decided to draw up a petition demanding the right to work. They organised a march to London to present the petition to the government. Two hundred men were carefully selected by the council medical officer of health for the long journey to London. The men planned to walk between 15 and 25 miles a day carrying their petition from town to town.

Hunger marches were not new at the time of the Jarrow Crusade. They had taken place before, but were usually disorganised and frequently failed to win sympathy or support. Many people simply saw the marchers as beggars. What made the Jarrow march so different was that it was approved by the Jarrow town council and it was highly organised. The town council also allowed its headed notepaper to be used in making requests for food and shelter for the marchers as they marched south to London. The marchers were led on their journey by Miss Ellen Wilkinson, the town's Labour MP.

The Jarrow men captured the imagination of the country. They were accommodated each night along the route by sympathetic householders. The press gave them mouth organs so they could play music to march to and a rich lady in a fur coat handed out free cigarettes.

Governments in Action: Britain 1905–51

Source C

I have seen nothing like it since the war. There is no escape anywhere from the prevailing misery. One out of every two shops appears to be closed. Wherever we went there were men hanging about, not scores of them but hundreds and thousands of them.

The writer J.B. Priestley describing the scene in the town of Jarrow in 1933.

Year	Unemployment
1927	2987
1928	3233
1929	3245
1930	3643
1931	6603
1932	6793
1933	7178
1934	6462
1935	6053
1936	4065

Unemployment in Jarrow, 1927-36. The total workforce in the town was 9,700.

People in the more prosperous south began to understand the plight of those living in the old industrial towns and cities. Even the police in London praised the marchers for being well organised and disciplined. The government refused, however, to let them present their petition. This was left to their MP, Ellen Wilkinson, who was listened to sympathetically.

But the marchers failed to get the work needed for the town. Nevertheless, they returned home as heroes. But when they arrived they discovered that their benefit had been stopped as they were not available for work while on their march. Some men did find work in a small trading estate that had been recently established. Others found work on the Team Valley Trading Estate in nearby Gateshead. But most had to wait for the upturn in the economy, which began with the rearmament programme for the Second World War. But still many had to wait for the war itself to find work.

Jarrow men on their march to London, October 1936.

1936 First BBC television broadcasts – if you can afford the £110 for a set. The unemployed can't. Two hundred unemployed men march from Jarrow in north-east England to London with a petition asking the government to create jobs. After weeks of marching they reach London… and Prime Minister Baldwin refuses to meet them. They go home to houses without the new television sets – or even a loo.

At the time the first television broadcasts were made, and a television set cost £110, the Jarrow men were marching to London to protest at having no jobs.

A modern view of the contrast between the life of an unemployed Jarrow worker and the improvements taking place in society. It was written in a humourous book on history for school children.

Britain 1929–39: A decade of depression and recovery?

Source F

Amongst the marchers was Robert Winship. He was 42 and worked in Hebburn Colliery from the age of 13 until it closed in 1930. He did not have another job until the war started in 1939. The year the colliery closed his wife was taken to a mental hospital and eventually died there in 1935. He had to bring up two daughters, Jean born in 1922 and Peggy born in 1925. His income was 95p a week. On one occasion he broke three ribs in a fall and was taken to hospital. He was there for fourteen days during which his dole was stopped as he was not available for work. The authorities insisted that he was brought home as soon as possible because it was costing £3 a week to keep his children in care. So he was brought home on a stretcher to fend for himself and his daughters as best he could.

An account of the life of one of the Jarrow marchers.

Source G

The policy of marches is, in my view, a revolutionary policy. It involves substituting organised mob rule for the proper constitutional way of doing things.

A letter from the Bishop of Durham to The Times *in October 1936.*

Things to do

1 Why did the town of Jarrow decide to send a march to London?

2 What does Priestley (Source C) find particularly sad about Jarrow?

3 What could a historian studying the effects of the Depression learn from the chart on page 202?

4 Source E is just a piece of fun and has no value to a historian studying the Depression in the 1930s. Do you agree?

5 Do you agree that Source F shows that the government in the 1930s were very hard-hearted?

6 Are you surprised by what Source G says? Explain your answer.

7 Was the Jarrow March really just a waste of time? Explain your answer.

3.2 How effective was the government in dealing with economic problems?

For those out of work there was a least unemployment benefit (dole money) which they could be given. Unemployment insurance had been established for some workers in 1911 and by 1920 it had been extended to include anyone earning less than £250 a year, with the exception of domestic servants, farm workers and civil servants. It was expected to pay for itself through the contributions received from those in work and their employers. But when unemployment rose dramatically, this did not happen. Originally, anyone on the dole for 15 weeks was not entitled to any further help as it was expected that

Unemployed Welsh miners marching to London in 1932 to protest about the lack of job opportunities.

an unemployed person would have found a new job before then and so further benefit would be unnecessary. This was not the case in the inter-war years. So in November 1922 the government had to extend benefit to all those unemployed for an unlimited period.

However, the slump after 1929 meant that more money was being paid out in benefits to the unemployed than was coming in from those still in work. So the government was under pressure to make changes to the scheme even before unemployment reached its highest in the 1930s.

Government spending cuts

The Labour government, elected in 1929, faced great difficulties in 1931 as exports had fallen by a half and 3 million people were out of work. The government was spending £2 million a day more than it had available and was having to look to the USA and France for loans. It could only get the loans if it cut its spending. The May Committee, composed of businessmen and trade unionists and headed by Sir George May,

reported to the Labour cabinet with its sugges-tions to end the crisis. The prime minister asked for spending cuts but the government could not agree on them. MacDonald then formed an all-party National Government, at first seen as a temporary measure, to implement the cuts.

The government then began the unpleasant task of reducing public spending. Judges saw their pay cut by 10 per cent, and teachers by 15 per cent. The biggest saving however came from a 10 per cent cut in unemployment benefit.

The new National Government also decided to introduce a means test to make sure that payments were fair. Under the test a person's or family's sources of income were taken into account in deciding how much benefit they should be paid. Many claimed that the means test was more about the government trying to save money than providing a decent level of benefit.

Britain 1929–39: a decade of depression and recovery?

The means test

The means test was carried out by officials from the local authorities' Public Assistance Committees which had been formed in 1930 to take over from the Poor Law. The unemployed claiming benefit had to reveal what everyone in their house, including grown up children and lodgers, had in savings and earnings. The test even looked at the value of things in the home that could be sold to raise cash. A family might have the father out of work and children in work. Under the means test the children were expected to feed and clothe their parents and even their younger brothers and sisters. This was very degrading for those who had to go through it.

The government was, however, able to introduce several measures which had a significant impact on the British economy. It is true, however, that, as in other countries, the economy did not really pick up until the demand for war goods brought about by the rearmament programme in 1937.

Import Duties Act, 1932

The government also tried to protect British industry by making the cost of foreign goods more expensive in Britain. They did this by taxing all imports by between 10 per cent and 20 per cent. They hoped this would encourage British industry to produce and sell more goods. The idea was that if more British goods were bought more would have to be produced, and so more people would be employed to produce them. This would mean that unemployment would fall.

Governments in Action: Britain 1905–51

Things to do

1 Why did the dole cause problems for the National Government?

2 What solutions were suggested? Why were they unpopular?

3 Why was the means test so unpopular?

4 Read Source I. How do you think this miner felt about being means tested?

Source I

It was in June 1927 that I first began to draw unemployment benefit at the rate of £1.9s.0d a week. At that time my eldest boy, who was then fifteen, had not started work as he could not find a job until at last the manager of one colliery told him he would give him a start because he was ashamed to keep turning him away. Then my second son came out of school and found he could not get work, but he went to the training centre and there eventually got work. His wage was 15s too, so that we had £2.10s.0d allowing for rent.

My unemployment benefit came to an end in March 1932, when I was disallowed because I had not qualified for the necessary contributory period of thirty weeks. After this I was given a food ticket for 23 shillings a week, which continued until January 1933, when it was stopped because of the means test. Before the stoppage our income was over the minimum limit of £2.17s.6d. So now we have to depend on the boys and they have to keep all six of us, including my wife and the two children who are still going to school.

The thoughts of a miner on being means tested.

However, the effect of the import tax on foreign goods was not as great as hoped. Nevertheless, British cars and electrical goods did sell well. But this tended to benefit the south of the country rather than the areas of high unemployment, such as in the north of England, Scotland and Wales, those areas where traditional industries were in decline.

Special Areas Act, 1934

The government realised that economic problems varied across the country. It attempted to address this problem by introducing an Act which appointed two commissioners with a budget of £2 million to try and attract some of the new industries to the old industrial areas. It had limited success. Some industrial estates were established, such as the Team Valley Industrial Estate in Gateshead, which is still a major source of employment today. But many companies still did not want to move to the north. Small industrial estates alone could not replace the coal mining or shipbuilding industries which had made the region what it was.

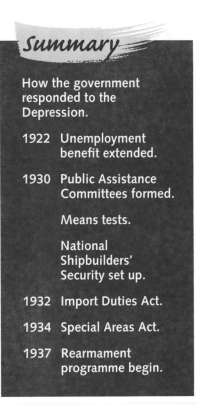

Summary

How the government responded to the Depression.

1922   Unemployment benefit extended.

1930   Public Assistance Committees formed.

       Means tests.

       National Shipbuilders' Security set up.

1932   Import Duties Act.

1934   Special Areas Act.

1937   Rearmament programme begin.

Source J

The Team Valley Trading Estate in Gateshead.

Britain 1929–39: a decade of depression and recovery?

A Changed Society?

Britain, 1944–51

When the Second World War ended, Britain was in debt, poverty was common and there were shortages of food and housing. The new Labour government of 1945 took greater responsibility for the care of its people and took control of key industries in its attempt to set up a new and improved society.

4.1 How far had the welfare state been fully established by 1951?

The Beveridge Report, 1942

This report was the result of the work of a committee set up during the war to suggest ways in which life in Britain could be improved after the war. It proposed that the state should support its citizens 'from the cradle to the grave', that is, from their birth until death. Beveridge identified five giant problems which had to be overcome to make progress and create a better society.

The first of the giants was *want*, which was the lack of the basic needs of life, especially food. It was proposed this could be defeated by a new system of national insurance. The second giant was *ignorance*, the lack of a proper education for everyone, which would be defeated by the building of new and better schools. The prevention of *disease*, or unnecessary illnesses, would be achieved by setting up a new health service for the whole nation. *Squalor*, or living in poverty, was to be remedied by a massive programme of house building. *Idleness*, or unemployment, was to be solved by the government helping industry create more jobs for everyone.

Conservatives	213
Labour	393
Liberals	12
Other parties	22

Result of the 1945 general election.

The general election, July 1945

During the war Britain had a coalition government led by Churchill. In July 1945, a general election was held. The Labour Party, led by Attlee, won a landslide victory. This was the first time they had ever won with a clear majority to govern on their own. The Conservative leader, Winston Churchill, himself was very popular, but his party were still seen by many people as the party of appeasement and the unemployment of the 1930s. The electorate also seemed to have decided that that the Labour Party was more likely to implement the Beveridge Report and develop the welfare state.

The attack on want

To improve the standard of living a family allowance was set up in 1945 and the first payments made in August 1946. A family received 5 shillings (25p) a week for each child after the first until each child reached the age of 16 or was employed full time. There was no means test, so all families received the benefit.

The Labour government's next step in the fight against want was the National Insurance Act of 1946. Employers, workers and the government all paid into the scheme which provided benefits to workers who were out of work through sickness, unemployment or pregnancy.

TACKLING THE FIRST GIANT

Source A

" WANT is only one of the five giants on the road of reconstruction " — T h e Beveridge Report.

This 1942 cartoon shows Beveridge setting out to defeat the problems of British society.

If someone was sick, there was no limit to how long they could claim sickness benefit for, but if they were unemployed they could only claim unemployment benefit for six months.

A further Act, the National Insurance (Industrial Injuries) Act of 1946, gave benefits to workers who were injured or disabled while at work and set up tribunals to decide the amount of compensation to be paid. The National Assistance Act of 1948 set up the National Assistance Board to provide for those in exceptional need, including those not covered by the National Insurance Act. The Board's purpose was to prevent extreme poverty and provide everyone with a minimum income. It was expected that only a few would need to apply for National Assistance, but demand was greater than expected.

The attack on disease

Aneurin Bevan, the Minister for Health, was responsible for improving the nation's health. Under the **National Health Service Act** of 1946 everyone received free medical, dental, hospital and eye treatment, and there was no charge for spectacles, false teeth and medicines. Most hospitals came under the control of the government as part of the National Health Service (NHS). Local councils provided midwives, home nurses, health visitors and ambulances. All this was paid for by taxation and National Insurance contributions. Doctors were paid under the National Health Service, which encouraged GPs (general practitioners) to practise in poorer areas without fear of not getting paid because people could not afford to.

Source B

The men and women of this country who have endured great hardships in war are asking what kind of life awaits them in peace. They need good homes, sufficient food, clothing and the amenities of life, employment and leisure, and social provision for accident, sickness and old age. For their children they desire an educational system that will give them the chance to develop all their faculties.

An excerpt from a radio election speech by Clement Attlee in 1945.

A Changed Society? – Britain 1944-51

But there were anxieties among medical professionals about how the changes would affect them. Doctors and dentists were afraid of losing their independence and some of their income if they joined the scheme. The BMA (British Medical Association) organised a campaign against the new act and many doctors threatened to refuse to work in the new service. Most of their worries however were resolved. The new scheme came into being on 5 July 1948, the same day as the National Insurance and National Assistance schemes. In the NHS's first year, over 95 per cent of the population registered with it, as did the same percentage of doctors.

The NHS greatly improved the health of the nation, with a fall in deaths from diseases such as tuberculosis and diphtheria. Infant deaths also fell. At first people rushed to have eye and dental treatment, many having neglected their eyes and teeth for years because of the cost. In the first year, 8½ million people received dental treatment and 5¼ million pairs of spectacles were provided. This made the NHS very expensive to run – it cost £400 million in its first year. In 1951 the government decided to offset some of this cost by making patients pay towards the cost of dental treatment, prescriptions and spectacles. Aneurin Bevan, Minister of Health when the NHS was set up, resigned from the government in protest at the introduction of charges for what had been set up as a service free at the point of use.

Things to do

1 Explain the meaning of Source A.

2 How did Attlee's speech in Source B fit the Beveridge Report?

3 How did the Labour government try to get rid of (a) want; (b) disease? Were they successful?

4 What evidence is there of waste in the National Health Service in Source C? Why do you think this happened?

5 Is Source D in favour or opposed to the National Health Service? Explain your answer.

Governments in Action: Britain 1905–51

Source C

When the National Health Service came in it was much easier to see a doctor, and it was free!. My teeth had been bad since I had a baby and I was now able to have false teeth at no cost. They were sore at first but soon bedded in and became comfortable. Some of my friends got teeth because they were free but never used them. My mum got free spectacles and we all noticed how much better she could see.

An 83-year-old woman remembers the start of the National Health Service.

Source D

A Daily Mirror cartoon from May 1946.

4.2 Which features of British society were changed as a result of the work of the Labour government of 1945-51?

The attack on ignorance

The **Education Act** of 1944, sometimes called the Butler Act after the Education Minister who introduced it, introduced 'free secondary education for all'. It set up three types of secondary school: grammar, technical and modern. The old 'elementary schools' which took children from the age of 5 to 14 were to be phased out. Now when they were 11 children would take a test called the '11-plus', the results of which decided which type of secondary school the child was suited for. The secondary grammar schools provided an academic education and were the normal route to university and careers in the professions. The secondary technical schools were meant to have a bias towards vocational education while the secondary modern schools had an emphasis on practical subjects.

These schools were supposed to be equal, but this is not how it turned out. Very few technical schools were set up, so most children either went to a grammar or secondary modern school. Grammar schools were seen as the way to better-paid jobs. They won a reputation for high achievement and there was intense competition for places in them. The 11-plus became a very important test and many parents complained that the age of 11 was too young to divide children in this way.

The Education Act also recommended the raising of the school leaving age to 15 and this was introduced in 1947. The demand for courses increased so much after the war that local colleges provided full-time and part-time courses. There was an increase too in university education with a new university established at Keele in 1950. More grants were provided for those whose parents could not support their children through their university course.

Source E

Mum and dad woke me up shouting: 'You've passed! You've passed!' I knew what they meant and I was very excited. I would be going to the grammar school. My joy turned to tears when I got to school. My best friend was going to the local secondary modern school. She felt she had failed. I was sad because we would be going to different schools.

A 60-year-old woman remembers her feelings on the day she received her '11-plus' results.

Source F

Children in the playground of a school in a new town in 1954.

A Changed Society? – Britain 1944-51

The attack on squalor

During the Second World War, many houses had been destroyed by bombs and there had been no building to replace them. As a consequence there was a housing shortage which had to be dealt with after the war. Families were housed in temporary accommodation such as 'pre-fabs'. The Labour government began to build a series of estates of council houses which were built to rent. Over one and a quarter million council houses were built in the period 1945 to 1951.

Another wartime report had recommended the building of new towns. Instead of allowing large cities such as London to continue developing, new towns should be set up about 30 miles away and separated from the city by an area of 'Green Belt' countryside which could not be built on. The Labour Government accepted this idea and the New Towns Act of 1946 provided government money to set up new towns close to London and other major cities. Twelve towns were planned in all, eight around London, two in Scotland, one in Wales and one in County Durham. They were intended to provide extra dwellings and also get rid of the overcrowding in the cities.

The population of the new towns was about 50,000 and they were carefully planned in districts, each with their own amenities, within walking distance of the houses. Soon further new towns were built and people moved from overcrowded cities to places such as Stevenage, Hemel Hempstead and Welwyn Garden City in the south, Peterlee in the north-east and East Kilbride in Scotland. Industry was attracted to the area with loans and grants. Mistakes were made as there were far too few garages and parking spaces in the new towns. There were also difficulties in building community spirit as so few of the residents had known each other before moving to the new towns. But they were successful enough to be repeated by later governments in the 1960s and 1970s.

Source G

An aerial photograph of Harlow, one of the new towns.

Source H

An open cast mine at Templenewsham, Leeds in 1944.

The attack on idleness

Beveridge had argued that there should always be more jobs available than workers. The Labour government managed to achieve virtually full employment by 1950. There were serious problems during the extremely cold winter of 1946-47 when frost and snow increased the need for fuel and interrupted transport. As a result over a million workers had to be laid off for a time because of coal shortages which forced the factories to close down.

Industry recovered quickly after the war helped by Marshall Aid, the demand for more houses and repairs to wartime damage. The 'austerity' measures of the Chancellor of the Exchequer, Stafford Cripps, also helped. Imports were restricted and exports encouraged. Trade unions accepted a wage freeze in 1948 and the devaluation of the pound in 1949 gave British goods a temporary advantage abroad. There were a million fewer unemployed in 1948 than there had been in 1938.

Nationalisation of key industries

Nationalisation, that is the ownership of industry by the state, was not new in 1945. During the wars the government had taken over important factories in order to ensure that industry and transport met the special needs of war. The Labour government believed that nationalisation would help the workers. If industry was taken from private ownership and placed under state control then the workers' interests would come before profit. Government money would be spent modernising industry and improving working conditions.

The nationalisation of the Bank of England, cable and wireless and air transport in 1946 followed by electricity and gas in 1947 caused little opposition. Transport, the coal industry and iron and steel were more of a problem. The aim of the Transport Commission 1947 was to run the railways and road transport services and set up a system of transport which would benefit the whole population.

A Changed Society? – Britain 1944–51

Long-distance hauliers were taken over to form British Road Services, but this only lasted until 1953 when they were de-nationalised by the Conservative government. The nationalisation of railways did not solve the problems overnight. Trains were still dirty and slow but now the government was blamed instead of the private owners.

The **National Coal Board** took control of the coal mines on 1 January 1947. The severe winter of 1947 led to a shortage of fuel and many placed the blame on nationalisation. The problem with both the transport and coal was that the government was unwilling or unable to put enough money into their modernisation. Both had been neglected for a long time by their owners. The pits needed increased mechanisation, which was very costly. Nevertheless, coal production did increase under the Labour government but there was always a shortage.

The iron and steel industry was different as it was profitable and efficient. The government wanted to nationalise it because it was so vital to the economy of Britain. Opposition from the Conservatives and the House of Lords meant that the Iron and Steel Bill was delayed in parliament, but finally passed in 1950, after the Labour Party had won the general election in that year. The nationalised iron and steel industry began in 1951 only to be returned to private ownership in 1953 after Labour's defeat in the 1951 election by the Conservatives.

Things to do

1 How did the Labour government attack 'ignorance'?

2 What were the weaknesses of the '11-plus'? Use the text and Source E to answer.

3 What were the advantages and disadvantages of 'New Towns'?

4 Why was there full employment in Britain in 1951?

5 Look back at Source B on page 209. How far had Attlee carried out his promises in the years 1945-51?

6 Explain the meaning of nationalisation. Was Labour's policy of nationalisation a success between 1945 and 1951?

7 How did (a) the setting up of the Welfare State; (b) the nationalisation of key industries; contribute to Labour's defeat in the 1951 Election?

Summary

1942	Beveridge Report.
1944	'Butler' Education Act.
1945	General Election.
1946	National Insurance Act.
	National Health Service.
	Industrial Injuries Act.
	New Towns Act.
	Beginning of nationalisation.
1947	Transport and coal nationalisation.
1948	National Assistance Act.
	Children's Act.
1951	Iron and Steel nationalisation.

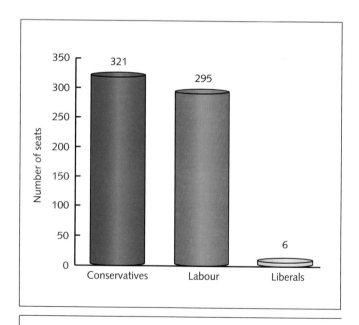

Result of the 1951 general election.

Exam-type Assessment
Britain, 1905–51

This exercise is based on the sort of questions you could be asked in
Paper 2 of your exam.

Source A

Between 1886 and 1903 Charles Booth made a
survey of the lives of the poor in London. He judged
any family living on £1 per week to be 'poor' and
those who had less as 'very poor'. He calculated that
8 per cent of people in London were very poor and
another 22 per cent were poor. Seebohm Rowntree
made a survey in York with similar results. He
concluded: 'We are faced with the startling
probability that from 25 and 30 per cent of the town
populations of the UK are living in poverty.' Booth
and Rowntree described a miserable way of life,
with bad housing, poor diet and frequent illness.
They also agreed on the causes of poverty, blaming
low wages, unemployment, old age, sickness and
bereavement.

A description of Britain at the beginning of the 20th Century
in a modern school textbook.

Source B

A general strike is not an
industrial dispute. It is a
revolutionary movement
intended to inflict
suffering upon the great
mass of innocent people
and put constraint upon
the government. It is a
movement which can
only succeed by
destroying the
government and
subverting the rights and
liberties of the people.

From an article written for the
Daily Mail. The paper's print
workers refused to print it.

1   **Study Source A.**
     What does this source tell us about conditions in Britain at the beginning of the
     20th century?   (*4 marks*)

2   **Summary Essay.**
     Many people were living in poverty at the beginning of the 20th Century.
     What did the Liberal Government do to overcome these problems? How far
     do you think they were successful?   (*15 marks*)

3   Why did the General Strike take place in May 1926?   (*15 marks*)

4   **Study Source B.**
     Do you agree that the General Strike was 'not an industrial dispute'?   (*6 marks*)

Part of a town on Tyneside in the 1930s.

The Hoover factory in West London in the 1930s.

Questions

1 What can we learn about the Depression from Sources C and D? (*8 marks*)

2 How far do Sources C and D explain why historians tell us that there was a 'rich south and a poor north' during the 1930s? (*10 marks*)

3 Which of the sources do you think is more useful for an historian studying the Depression? Carefully explain your answer. (*10 marks*)

Coursework or Examination Paper?

Candidates may complete two coursework assignments or sit a third examination paper. The following chapters on Vietnam and the Arab-Israeli conflict are both coursework and Paper 3 options.

Chapter 7

Vietnam Post-1939

In the early part of the 20th century Vietnam was a French colony. However, the Second World War saw Japanese rule in Vietnam and the growth of terrorism as the Vietminh struggled against foreign domination. When the French finally left Vietnam in 1954 after the defeat at Dien Bien Phu, it became divided into two countries. The USA gave support to South Vietnam to counter the threat of communist North Vietnam. Soon the Americans found themselves fighting a war to support the South Vietnamese government against Vietcong guerrillas trying to overthrow it. The war saw the use of chemical weapons, huge quantities of bombs and atrocities on both sides. But the effective use of guerrilla tactics by the Vietcong were very difficult for the Americans to counter. Many Americans were horrified by the war and called for America to leave Vietnam. President Nixon adopted a policy of Vietnamisation and pulled American troops out. Today North Vietnam and South Vietnam are united as one communist country.

Chapter 8

The Arab-Israeli Conflict

Arabs and Jews have lived in Palestine for hundreds of years. By the beginning of the 20th Century however, both claimed Palestine as their homeland. After the First World War both groups thought that Britain had promised Palestine to them. But it was Britain that gained control of the area after the war ended. The British found the area too difficult to control and in 1947 handed it over to the United Nations. The war of 1948 saw Israel come into existence. Wars in 1956, 1967 and 1973 resulted in victories for the Israelis and many Arab groups turned to terrorism. The Arab refugees resented the formation of Israel and demanded that they be given land for themselves. Attempts at bringing peace to the area in the 1970s and 1990s have brought a solution closer, but it has yet to be achieved.

Origins of conflict, 1939–65

From the late-nineteenth century Vietnam was a French possession.
After the Second World War, the French withdrew and a struggle developed
between the Communist North Vietnam and democratic South Vietnam.

4.1 How did the Second World War make conflict in Vietnam more likely?

Vietnam today

Vietnam today is known as Cong Hoa Xa Hoi Chu Nghia Viet Nam (Socialist Republic of Vietnam). Its capital is Hanoi. It has a population of 74 million with its largest city being Ho Chi Minh City. Just over half the people are Buddhists though there are many Catholics. Its main occupations are farming and fishing with 11 per cent of the population involved in industry.

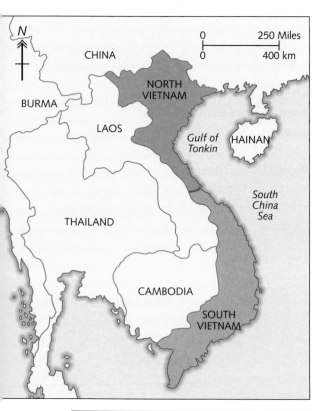

Indo-China.

Early history 1471-1945

The kingdom of Dai Viet was established in 1471 after the Chinese were driven out of the country. In 1802 the north and the south were united under the leadership of Nguyen Anh. He had been helped by the French and in return France hoped to receive trading and missionary privileges. However, in the 1830s some Catholic missionaries and their Vietnamese converts were persecuted. They suffered branding of the left cheek with the word 'infidel' and some were executed. This shocked Europeans. In 1858 a naval expedition was sent to punish the Vietnamese for this. In the end some provinces were given over to the French. In the 1880s the French launched an attack on the north and by 1893 France controlled all of Vietnam, as well as Laos and Cambodia. It became known as the 'French Indochinese Union'.

French colonial rule

French colonial rule was barely resisted by the Vietnamese people, but their harsh rule led to growing anti-colonial feeling. Working conditions in the factories were poor. Peasant farmers struggled with high taxes and rents and the use of forced labour for public works projects did little to help. Few Vietnamese could rise to positions of importance in the colonial government. In 1885 the Vietnamese emperor, Han Nghi, began a revolt against the French and by the early 20th century nationalist parties were formed and demanded independence.

Surprisingly, thousands of Indochinese fought in the First World War. On their return to Vietnam they brought with them the democratic and communist ideas common in Europe. An uprising in 1930 led by the Nationalist Party of Vietnam was ruthlessly suppressed by the French authorities. In the same year the Indochinese Communist Party was formed.

The Second World War

In 1940, as France fell to the Germans and the pro-German Vichy government was established, the Japanese took over Vietnam, Cambodia and Laos. They allowed the French government to remain in power, but they had control of the country with free use of the roads, railways and airfields. The Japanese were only interested in Vietnam as a provider of rubber, coal and rice for its war effort. By forcing the Vietnamese people to grow food other than rice they created a famine that killed an estimated two million people.

The only resistance to this Japanese rule was the Vietminh. They were formed in 1941 by Ho Chi Minh. Throughout the war they attacked the French. Support grew in 1942 and 1943 and by late 1944 they were strong enough to attack two French outposts. In 1945 the Japanese finally overthrew the French government and concentrated on controlling the towns, leaving the country areas alone. This allowed the communists to rapidly build up their support in those areas. Soon afterwards the Japanese themselves were defeated and the war was over.

'Independence' 1945: the August Revolution

In March 1945 the Vietminh summoned the people to fight the Japanese. After the dropping of atomic bombs on Hiroshima and Nagasaki the Vietnamese planned an uprising. On 2 September 1945 they entered the northern city of Hanoi and Ho Chi Minh declared independence. The Vietminh moved into villages and conducted summary trials and executions of anyone who had sided with the French or the Japanese. Few minded as they saw the Vietminh as liberators.

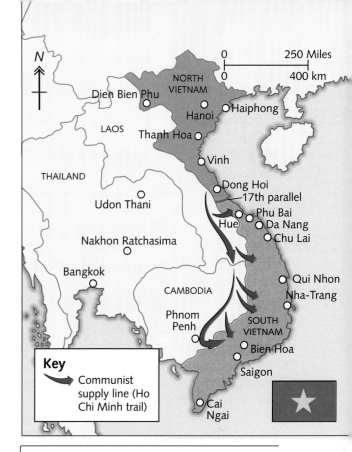

Vietnam, showing the location of the Ho Chi Minh trail.

Source A

Compatriots!

Everyone, arm yourself with clubs, spears, knives, expel the Japanese brigands and recover control of your rice paddies and homes.

Our blood boils
Our stomachs are empty
Our belongings are plundered
Our hearths are destroyed

It is the Japanese who are responsible for all these disasters. There is only one way for us to save our lives; it is to prepare with all our compatriots to chase out the Japanese birds of prey.

Everyone, rise against the Japanese fascists, the seizers of lands.

Long live Vietnam independence!

Vietnam: Origins of Conflict, 1939-65

The Vietminh summons to fight the Japanese, March 1945.

Ho Chi Minh

Born in 1890 as Nguyen That Tan, the son of a district magistrate who had been dismissed for involvement in the nationalist movement, Ho Chi Minh left Vietnam in 1911 to live in the United States, Great Britain and France. In 1920 he was one of the founding members of the French Communist Party. He later spent time in the USSR, learning communist and revolutionary theory. In 1930 he brought the communist groups of Vietnam together as the Indo-Chinese Communist Party.

When war broke out in 1939 he realised that the time was right to begin the communist revolution. Using the name Ho Chi Minh ('Bringer of light') he organised the Revolutionary League for the Independence of Vietnam (Vietminh). During the war years the Vietminh was supported by the OSS, the American Office for Strategic Services, which provided weapons and supplies in return for Vietminh attacks on the Japanese and the rescue of American airmen. Ho Chi Minh hoped that when the war ended the Allies would support independence for Vietnam. He was disappointed when French troops forced the communists out of Saigon using weapons supplied by the British.

Ho Chi Minh negotiated with the French in 1946. This allowed 25,000 French troops to return to Vietnam for five years. Gradual withdrawal would take place and eventually Vietnam would be a state within the French Union. This was not independence, but it would mean that the Chinese, who were occupying the north of the country, would be forced to leave. Ho Chi Minh knew from history that Chinese troops in Vietnam were a threat, and possibly a greater threat than the French.

Ho Chi Minh.

Things to do

1 Explain how French rule of Indo-China began in the 19th century.

2 What mistakes did the French make in their attempts to rule Indochina?

3 Did the Japanese make problems in Vietnam more likely?

Summary

The French misrule of Vietnam caused nationalist groups to grow against any foreign interference. Revolutions in Russia and China made revolution more likely. Ho Chi Minh was taught his revolutionary techniques by those that had already succeeded. These methods, including guerrilla warfare, were already tried and tested. The guerrilla war between 1941 and 1945 was simply a forerunner for the long Vietnam War that followed in the 1960s.

1.2 Why did the French leave Vietnam in 1954 and the United States become involved?

Indochinese War, 1946-54

Ho Chi Minh hoped that the power of the French would soon diminish in South East Asia. In October 1946, despite recognising the Democratic Republic of Vietnam (North Vietnam), France forced the Communists out of the south of the country and took over the northern city of Haiphong.

In the war that followed, the French controlled the major cities and the Vietminh the countryside. The Vietminh used guerrilla tactics and avoided the kind of all-out open battle that the French would win. The Communists were supported by the Chinese and the Soviet Union and the French by the USA. As the war dragged on the cost to the French rose from 27 million francs in 1946 to a massive 435 million francs in 1952. By 1953 74,000 French troops had been killed and 190,000 were still fighting to break the stalemate. It was at this point that the French attempted a bold move to end the war.

Dien Bien Phu, 1954

The French had a new commander in Indochina, General Henri Navarre. He tried to draw the Vietminh into an open war where he believed the superior firepower of the French would lead to an important victory. In late 1953 French paratroopers took control of Dien Bien Phu and built a fortified garrison.

The Vietminh leader, General Vo Nguyen Giap, grasped the opportunity to attack the French garrison. Using 50,000 peasants to carry 200 pieces of artillery and 25,000 shells, as well as food for the 40,000 Vietminh soldiers, he surrounded the French base. The siege lasted several months. Giap destroyed the airfield nearby and the French were totally cut off.

Source C

A photograph of French paratroopers and supplies landing at Dien Bien Phu, 1954.

Over 3,000 French soldiers were killed in battle and a further 8,000 died in captivity. For the French it was a devastating defeat. They had lost 90,000 men in nine years of fighting. The Vietminh lost an estimated 200,000 men, but significantly this small nation in South East Asia had defeated a major European country.

Things to do

Why was the Battle of Dien Bien Phu so important?

Vietnam: Origins of Conflict, 1939-65

The Geneva Conference

A peace conference was convened quickly. North Vietnam was represented by the Vietminh, the South by Bao Dai's and Cambodia, Laos, USA, Great Britain, China, USSR and France were also present.

Vietnam was divided into two countries. North Vietnam and South Vietnam were divided along the 17th parallel and Laos and Cambodia became independent states. A cease-fire was to be declared and the French troops were to withdraw. Two years later a national election was to be held to create one country. (These elections never took place.)

Summary

How the US became more involved in Vietnam:

April 1961
Treaty of Amity and economic relations.

December 1961
President John F Kennedy pledges support for the South.

December 1961
400 uniformed army personnel arrive.

December 1962
11,200 US troops in South Vietnam.

Source D

Diem's anti-communist government

The USA and the Saigon government did not agree with the Geneva accords. As soon as the French left Vietnam the US began supporting the South Vietnamese government with economic aid and military advisers. Uncertain that fair elections could take place in the Communist North the South Vietnamese government refused to hold national elections. The new president of the South, Ngo Dinh Diem, was anti-Communist. He attempted to root out all members of the Vietminh, wrongly assuming they were all Communist. Many were, but others had simply wanted an end to French rule. Many people turned against the Diem government. As an anti-Communist Diem kept the support of the USA.

Increased US involvement

US economic and military aid to Vietnam in the 1950s amounted to more than $1,591 million. As the 1960s began the North Vietnamese declared their intention to 'liberate South Vietnam from the ruling yoke of the US imperialist and their henchmen'. Guerrilla attacks by the newly formed Vietcong were having an effect and the south even tried to claim that it was the North Vietnamese army that was attacking them. As things got worse the US increased its involvement.

Even with this support Diem's government made more mistakes. It tried to separate the villagers from the Vietcong by creating 'strategic hamlets', or fortified villages, that the Vietcong could not get into.

A Buddhist sets fire to himself to protest at the persecution of Buddhists by the South Vietnamese government.

However, most villagers did not want to leave the lands they had farmed for centuries or leave the graves of their ancestors unattended. A Buddhist protest over the flying of flags on Buddha's birthday ended with the South Vietnamese Civil Guard opening fire. Protests followed, including the suicide of the Buddhist monk Quang Duc, who burnt himself to death in public. The Diem government took little notice of this but lost further support. Even the US grew impatient and did nothing to prevent a military coup in November 1963.

On 22 November 1963 another incident dramatically changed the level of US involvement. President Kennedy was assassinated in Dallas, Texas. He had always kept the level of US military support low. His successor, President Lyndon B Johnson, wanted to create a 'great society' in the United States. Instead he found himself facing a 'bitch of a war' on the other side of the world. When US ships on intelligence gathering missions were attacked twice in the Gulf of Tonkin in 1964, the US Congress passed the Gulf of Tonkin Resolution which gave the President a 'blank cheque' to fight a war in South East Asia as he saw fit. Surprisingly, in the 1964 election Johnson was elected as the peace candidate. He hoped that he would still get the opportunity to create his 'great society'.

However, in February 1965 an attack on an American base in Pleiku in which 9 Americans were killed and 67 were wounded led to the US getting more involved. A bombing campaign began in March 1965 with the onset of Operation Rolling Thunder, and in the same month the first US soldiers arrived to defend the Da Nang airbase and its perimeter. The US was now committed to a war which was to involve them for the next eight years.

The domino theory.

The Domino Theory

The Domino theory played an important part in American thinking about the affairs of Vietnam. The great fear was that by ignoring events in Vietnam it might fall to communism and then be followed by other countries in South East Asia. There was even a fear that Japan could fall after the 'dominoes' of Laos, Cambodia, Thailand, Malaya, and Indonesia.

Things to do

1   Explain the part played by religion in events in Vietnam before 1965.

2   Study the list of reasons for American involvement in Vietnam. Explain why each was a reason. Are any missing?

  (a) It was anti-communist.

  (b) The domino theory.

  (c) America had been involved in Vietnam since the Second World War.

  (d) The USSR and China supported the North Vietnamese.

  (e) President Kennedy was assassinated.

Vietnam: Origins of Conflict, 1939-65

Changing Nature of Warfare

A military experience, 1965–73

The communists in Vietnam fought a guerrilla war that US troops were not trained for, although the US military believed its superior weaponary would bring victory. Despite massive investment in men and supplies American hopes proved to be misplaced.

2.1 Why did the communists use guerrilla tactics in the Vietnam War?

Background

Vietnam was no stranger to fighting a war using guerrilla tactics. They were first used in 1859 against the French soon after the fall of Saigon. In 1862 the French complained about rebel bands appearing from nowhere, destroying everything and disappearing without trace. The tactic was used again against the Japanese and the French in the 1940s, against the corrupt government of Diem in the 1950s and against the might of the United States in the 1960s and early 1970s. Clearly it was effective, so what was it?

In many ways the theory set out in Source A worked. It was especially effective when a small nation faced another which had massive military superiority. That was the case with Vietnam.

Source B

The following are the eight reminders on how to treat the people, the code of conduct strictly adhered to and enforced by the Vietminh.

1 Be polite.
2 Be fair.
3 Return anything borrowed.
4 Pay for anything damaged.
5 Do not bully.
6 Do not damage crops.
7 Do not flirt with women.
8 Do not ill-treat prisoners.

Vietminh Code of Conduct.

Source A

Guerrilla warfare operates as follows:

1 The revolutionaries build up support and strength and begin to attack the enemy in small groups and then disappear.

2 The revolutionary groups now have control of the countryside where they are careful not to annoy the local people on whom they depend for food and shelter. The guerrillas tend to control the countryside and the government controls the towns and cities.

3 The revolutionary leaders feel that they are strong enough to attack the towns and even the cities because they outnumber the government troops which might be worn down by the war and defecting to the communist side.

The theory of guerrilla warfare.

Imbalance of troops

Guerrilla tactics are used by one side when it is greatly outnumbered by the other side or is inferior to them in weapons or technology. As Source C shows, the Americans had large numbers of troops. They also had the best and most powerful weapons in the world and an economy strong enough to support the cost of using them.

Year	Number of troops
1962	9, 000
1963	15, 000
1964	16, 000
1965	60, 000
1966	268, 000
1967	449, 000
1968	535, 000
1969	415, 000

US troops in South Vietnam.

'As fish are of the sea'

In China Mao Zedong had gained power by winning a guerrilla war against government forces. He believed that all guerrillas should be of the people in the same way 'as fish are of the sea'. In a sense the first tactic used by the guerrillas was to make sure that they did not alienate the people. Without their support guerrilla tactics would be difficult to use.

Source C

Years of fighting the French had made General Giap a brilliant guerrilla fighter. His Vietcong guerrillas had won control of the countryside. They ruled the civilian population by terror. They murdered anyone who they suspected of opposing them.

An extract from a modern British school textbook.

Source D

North Vietnamese soldiers equipped for war.

Things to do

1 Explain why guerrilla tactics might be the best method of warfare to use in a country like Vietnam.

2 Sources B and C give different views as to the methods used by the Vietcong to persuade the local peasants to support them during the guerrilla war. Explain why you think they are different.

3 Source D is intended to show well-equipped and determined NVA soldiers. Would it have the same effect on an American audience?

Changing Nature of Warfare: A military experience

Guerrilla tactics 1965-73: infiltration of the countryside

The Vietcong (VC) were recruited from men and women who lived in or had come from South Vietnam.

Once the Vietcong had been recruited they were trained in the sorts of tactics that the US troops trained in conventional warfare would find difficult to combat. They needed to make sure that the local people accepted their presence. They made an effort to get to know local people. They treated them with respect and tried to make sure that they were not a burden on the local economy. Many worked by day in the fields and the villages to pay their way. They spread revolutionary ideas and persuaded more people to join them. If they found that these tactics didn't work then they could turn to torture and terrorism. In particular they targeted local officials loyal to the South Vietnamese government. Policemen, teachers and tax collectors were kidnapped and murdered as was anyone suspected of spying for the government or the United States. Local peasants were usually left alone.

It was essential that local people's support was maintained. The US troops also tried to gain local support (see Unit 3), but their failure to do so was an important reason for their defeat.

Ambush, tricks and traps

Once the Vietcong established themselves in the villages of South Vietnam they began their campaign of guerrilla warfare. Major face-to-face confrontations were avoided. They stood little chance against the superior weaponry of the US forces or the Army of the Republic of Vietnam (ARVN).

For the Americans the enemy seemed to be all around them. A civilian working for the US during the day might be a guerrilla at night and attack the camp with mortars or plant bombs or set booby traps.

Source E

1966	1,800
1967	3,900
1968	5,400
1969	6,100
1970	6,000
1971	3,400

Estimated numbers of civilians killed by the Vietcong.

This Vietcong poster shows the communist forces using guerrilla tactics of ambushing US troops under cover of the jungle.

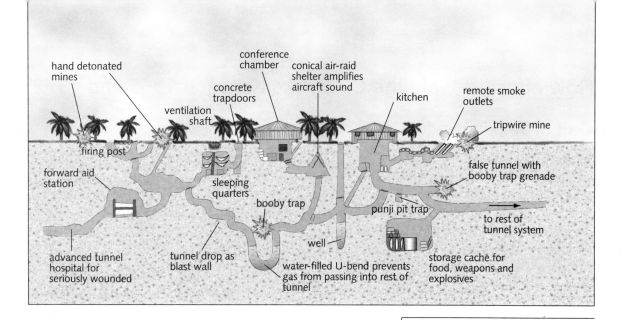

The Vietcong network of tunnels

The Vietcong built a network of tunnels through which they moved and lived undetected. Over 250 kilometers (150 miles) of tunnels are said to have been built under South Vietnam. A single network could be 30 kilometres long (20 miles). The Americans believed the Vietcong were forced to build these tunnels because of the devastation of American bombing. However, the diagram shows that the tunnels were much more than underground shelters. Some of them housed sleeping quarters, hospitals, storage for weapons and even lecture theatres.

Most tunnels were also well booby-trapped, making them potentially very dangerous for those US soldiers who had to check them out when they were discovered. Some of the tunnel networks actually passed under US bases, showing how effective they were in guerrilla war.

Historians have tended to see the tunnels as a sign of the Vietcong's determination rather than as a sign of weakness.

Ho Chi Minh Trail

The development of thousands of different routes around the countryside was also essential to the Vietcong for moving equipment, weapons, food and men about the country. The most famous of these routes was the Ho Chi Minh Trail running from North Vietnam to the South. It is said that 40,000 people worked constantly at keeping the trail open. In parts it was said to be 50 miles wide. It was often attacked by US and ARVN bombing and jets, which made life on the trail hazardous. Nevertheless, it was vital for moving the supplies and fighters needed by the VC for the war in the south.

This was the sort of tunnel system used by the communist fighters in Vietnam.

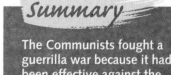

Things to do

1   Study Source E.
    (a) How effective do you think this poster would have been? **(b)** What might the Americans feel towards it?

2   Does the diagram above suggest that the Vietcong were forced underground by the bombing?

3   'Guerrilla tactics could win the war for the Vietcong.' Do you agree with this statement?

Summary

The Communists fought a guerrilla war because it had been effective against the French, the Japanese and the Americans. It did not save lives, as the casualty figures show. But it almost made it impossible for the ARVN and its American allies to win the war.

Changing Nature of Warfare: A military experience

2.2 How effective were the US tactics between 1965 and 1972?

Gulf of Tonkin incident

When the US destroyer *Maddox* was attacked in the Gulf of Tonkin by three North Vietnamese patrol boats the captain simply called in air support and returned fire. One enemy patrol boat was sunk and the other two were badly damaged. The *Maddox* was virtually untouched. The superior technology available to the US was clearly evident. The Americans may well have thought that this technological superiority would always be significant, and may even have been enough to guarantee victory. When two days later on 4 August 1964 a second attack took place, the US entered a war they must have expected to win. They responded with a bombing raid on the patrol boat bases and were able to claim that they destroyed 25 vessels at a cost of only 2 US airplanes.

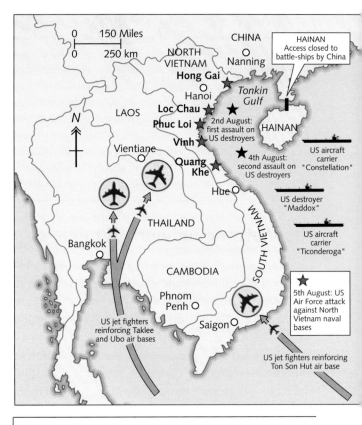

This map shows the action that took place at the time of the Gulf of Tonkin incident, August 1964.

Operation Rolling Thunder

On 5 February 1965 nine American 'advisers' were killed and 76 wounded in a Vietcong attack on the Pleiku bases. The US responded with Operation Rolling Thunder. This was an operation using the latest in weapon technology. Targets were carefully selected and 'surgically' bombed. Bridges, roads, railways lines, army barracks and supply depots were destroyed.

The Americans avoided bombing the major cities of Hanoi and Haiphong as they did not want to do any more damage to their relationship with the USSR. They hoped the bombings would show the North Vietnamese what power the US had at its disposal.

As the war intensified the idea of 'surgical' bombing was replaced in 1966 by a policy of 'saturation' bombing, using B52 bombers. The US actually dropped more bombs on North Vietnam than were dropped on Germany and Japan together during the entire Second World War. It should have succeeded. Instead it made the North Vietnamese even more determined to win the war and shoot down as many US aircraft as possible.

Source F

The world must never forget that aggression unchallenged is aggression unleashed. We of the United States have not forgotten. That is why we have met aggression with action.

President Johnson speaking about the American action against North Vietnam after the attack on the destroyer Maddox *in the Gulf of Tonkin.*

Vietnam, Post-1939

Attacks by North Vietnamese anti-aircraft guns, surface-to-air missiles, and highly skilled MIG 17 and MIG 21PF air-to-air missile-armed aircraft inflicted serious damage on the US airforce. In the three years between 1965 and 1968 more than 14,000 US aircraft were shot down. US technology was now being matched by what the Chinese and Russians were supplying to the North Vietnamese.

US tactics

The effectiveness of Vietcong guerrilla tactics persuaded the US military to find a way of combining the power of their high technology equipment with some form of guerrilla fighting. They began using helicopters in search and destroy missions, the speed of which gave the VC very little warning of attack. The helicopters were also able to land close enough to Vietcong-controlled villages to give the troops they were carrying the chance to attack any Vietcong fighters before they had a chance to organise themselves. Once a village was secured it was searched. If there were signs of a VC presence, the whole village would be destroyed.

American soldiers who had seen their compatriots killed or wounded very often harboured an intense hatred of the Vietnamese, particularly as they could not distinguish between friend and foe. In some cases they wreaked a sort of revenge by destroying a village, and in some cases slaughtering the inhabitants. They also interrogated and tortured villagers in the belief that they were Vietcong or knew where the Vietcong were.

Source G

An American soldier manhandling a South Vietnamese villager.

Changing Nature of Warfare: A military experience

The Tet Offensive, 1968

In 1968 the war on land intensified. By this time the Americans had 500,000 troops in Vietnam. The commander of the US army in Vietnam, General Westmoreland, believed the war was being won. The US seemed in control of the countryside and the ARVN seemed in control of the cities. Blanket bombing of North Vietnam was also expected to produce results.

Just as the Tet New Year festival was being celebrated the war took a dramatic turn. The North Vietnamese Army and VC launched attacks through-out South Vietnam. More than 100 cities or military sites were attacked. In Saigon a Vietcong suicide squad of 19 attacked the US embassy. Dressed as South Vietnamese soldiers they blew a hole in the wall of the embassy and occupied it for six hours. US troops recaptured it room by room, killing every Vietcong. Cholon, the Chinese suburb of Saigon, was taken over by the Vietcong. A bitter battle broke out at the Saigon race track as the VC defended the first-aid station they had established there before the attack.

With 4,500 fighters inside Saigon the Vietcong hoped to hold out for the 48 hours needed until reinforcements arrived. They also hoped the South Vietnamese people would support them and overthrow the South Vietnamese government and force the US out of Vietnam. The ARVN and US troops, however, fought back and ended the offensive.

But the world saw it as a victory for the North. No one suspected they would attack the southern capital, so they won considerable admiration for being so audacious. However, the reality was that they were beaten back by ARVN and US troops. Key positions were recaptured. Thousands of Vietcong were killed (the Communists lost at least 100,000 fighters) and the guerrilla war was weakened. With the VC badly weakened the North had to think about fighting a conventional war again.

The Tet Offensive: media damage

Many in the US military saw the Tet Offensive as a victory for them. They knew the VC was now severely weakened. It is said that it took the Communists four years to recover. However, the media had a different view. The images of fighting in Saigon, the fall of Hue and even its recapture at the end of February, failed to convince the American public that the war was going their way. The politicians were not convinced either. When General Westmoreland requested another 200,000 troops to finish off the war Congress refused. The American public were starting to believe the war was impossible to win. In the rest of the world there was a feeling that the war had to be brought to an end. By now the war had so damaged the standing of President Johnson that he decided not to seek re-election. This left the way open for Richard Nixon to be elected as President. He promised the American people he would end the war. The search for peace was now seen as the only way out of the war.

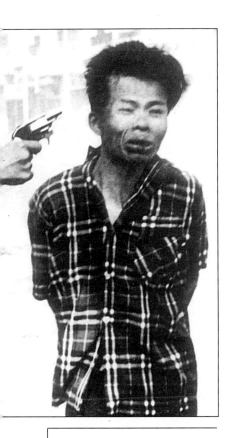

A Vietcong guerrilla suspect is executed in the streets of Saigon by South Vietnam's General Loan in 1968.

Bombing of the North, 1970-72

Talks to end the war began in Paris in March 1968. At the same time the US decided to maintain the pressure on the North Vietnamese government by increasing the bombing of the Ho Chi Minh Trail and Communist strongholds in South Vietnam. As more and more US troops were withdrawn from Vietnam the US continued to increase the bombing to prevent the North from gaining too much from the negotiations. In April 1972 Operation Linebacker launched 227 raids against the enemy. But the ability of the North to launch an offensive soon afterwards indicated that these raids were not as effective as was hoped.

Communist offensive, 1975

The last US combat troops left Vietnam in March 1973. US military aid for South Vietnam was dwindling and support for the North grew among the Vietnamese. In August 1974 President Nixon was forced to resign as President and was replaced by Gerald Ford. The question was whether the new president would support the South. In January 1975, the North Vietnamese decided to find out. They launched a new offensive. One of the conditions of the cease-fire agreement was that the US could give air support to the South if it was attacked. The Communists, however, pushed further and further south and on 30 April 1975 the North Vietnamese army captured Saigon.

Source I

In all honesty, we didn't achieve our main objective, which was to spur uprising throughout the South. Still, we inflicted heavy casualties on the Americans and their puppets and that was a big gain for us. As for making an impact in the United States, it had not been our intention – but it turned out to be a fortunate result.

North Vietnamese General, Tran Do, speaking about what they hoped to achieve in the fight to conquer South Vietnam.

Things to do

1   Study Source I.
    Using the information in this unit explain how far you agree with the statement of General Tran Do.

2   What was the importance of the Tet Offensive?

Summary

1964	Gulf of Tonkin incident.
1965	Operation Rolling Thunder.
1968	The Tet Offensive.
1970 –1972	Increased US bombing of North Vietnam.
1975	The fall of South Vietnam.

Changing Nature of Warfare: A military experience

Changing Nature of Warfare

A civilian experience, 1965 onwards

The use of Agent Orange and napalm were effective in the war but were so damaging to the image of the US at home and abroad that the overall effect on the course of the war was negative. The My Lai massacre also brought home to the American public the horrors committed by US soldiers in their name. These led to pressures within America and throughout the world to end the war.

3.1 How did the experience of war lead to the growth of the peace movement in America?

The experience of Vietnam

Source A

A Vietnamese family struggle across a swollen river to escape American bombing.

American troops had a varied experience of the Vietnam War. Only 10 per cent of them actually were front-line combat troops. About 75 per cent never saw action as they worked as headquarters and logistics staff and were based in the cities. However, many experienced mortar and rocket attacks or being shot at by enemy snipers, and would have been aware of the risks. The average age of US recruits was 19 and the tour of duty was 'only' one year. For many survival was the key. They never understood why they were fighting the war, or the culture of the country they were fighting in, or its people. The nature of the war, with the Vietcong using guerrilla tactics made it difficult to distinguish between friend and foe, and therefore made the experience much harder to bear.

Agent Orange and napalm

With the Vietcong using the jungles as cover for their guerrilla warfare, the US military decided to destroy the jungles. Bombing and bulldozing were too expensive and took too long. So they used powerful chemical weapons. Agent Orange and napalm were the most common ones used. Agent Orange was first used as part of Operation Ranch Hand in 1962. In nine to ten years about 86 million litres were dropped on 20 per cent of South Vietnam. Vast areas of the country's vegetation disappeared. Massive trees were destroyed and the air, rivers and soil were polluted. While this was effective in destroying the natural cover of the country it did little to change the way the war was being fought.

The jellied petroleum known as napalm was first used during Operation Rolling Thunder in 1965. Napalm sticks to the skin and burns through to the bone. It was used to attack large areas of the North and to attack enemy positions in the South. It was also used against enemy positions ahead of advancing American or South Vietnamese troops. However, its use made little difference to the way the war was fought.

Blanket bombing

America dropped more bombs on Vietnam than was dropped in the whole of Europe during the Second World War.

American airmen managed to distance themselves from their actions, but not all. Many ground troops had first-hand experience of the bombing.

Images of South Vietnamese children fleeing along a road with their skin burning and peeling from the napalm of a misdirected bomb stay in the mind. What about the soldiers who saw it close up? For those at home the television images were confirmed by letters from the battlefield and by stories from returning soldiers. For many Americans this was enough to convince them that the US had to withdraw from the war.

Vietnamese napalm victims.

Things to do

1 Why might it be difficult for us to understand the effect war can have on people?

2 Study Source A. How do images like this help us to understand the civilian experience of war?

3 'The United States' reaction to guerrilla warfare was barbaric.' How far do you agree with this statement?

4 Study Source B. Why do you think this famous image of warfare symbolised the war in Vietnam?

Changing Nature of Warfare: A civilian experience

Case Study: My Lai Massacre, 16 March 1968

The massacre of men, women and children at the village of My Lai in March 1968 was one of the most horrific incidents of the war. Maybe its significance has been exaggerated given it was not the only atrocity committed during the war. Certainly it was not the first, and not the last. These kind of events are always part of war. But it was significant in that Americans at home saw the dead bodies of men, women and children on their television screens and knew they had been killed by young Americans at war. This helped change the way many Americans saw the war and increased the pressure on the government to withdraw.

What happened at My Lai?

Just after dawn on 16 March nine US helicopter gunships landed close to the village of My Lai. Three US platoons disembarked from the helicopters and began a search and destroy mission. One platoon was led by Lieutenant William Calley. He ordered his men to kill the villagers who were suspected of supporting or being Vietcong guerrillas.

The following year a US marine, Paul Meadlo, gave his account of what happened in a television interview. Americans were horrified. A public enquiry was demanded.

At the enquiry there was no doubt there had been a massacre. This was confirmed by those who took part and by officials, though how many were killed varies from 175 to 500 people. Even so, only one American was held responsible enough to be punished for what happened. Lieutenant Calley was sentenced to life imprisonment, but was released in 1974 having served only three years. Everyone else 'got clean away with it'.

How do we judge My Lai?

Maybe it's impossible to say what the significance of My Lai is. Perhaps it's enough to remember what happened and learn from it.

It may be better simply to let those involved tell their story and to try and understand the views of those affected by those two hours in March 1968.

Source D

Most of the soldiers had never been away from home before they went into service. And they end up in Vietnam, going there many of them because they thought they were going to do something courageous on behalf of their country, something which they thought was in the American ideal.

But it didn't mean slaughtering whole villages of women and children. One of my friends, when he told me about it, said: 'You know, it was a Nazi kind of thing. We didn't go there to be Nazis. At least none of the people I knew went there to be Nazis.'

The feelings of a soldier on the killing of villagers at My Lai.

Source C

The most inexcusable act of American arms during this century.

What an American historian had to say about the massacre at My Lai.

The bodies of My Lai villagers killed by US soldiers.

Got up at 05.30 and we left at 07.15. We had nine choppers. We started to move slowly through the village, shooting everything in sight, children, men, women, and animals. Their legs were shot off and they were still moving. They were just hanging there. I didn't fire a single round yet and didn't kill anybody, not even a chicken. I couldn't.'

One US soldier's account of the My Lai massacre.

Source G

Lieutenant Calley came over and said, 'You know what to do with them [a group of Vietnamese men, women and children] don't you?' And I said 'Yes'. And he left and came back about ten minutes later, and said, 'How come you ain't killed them yet?' And I told him that I didn't think he wanted us to kill them, that he just wanted us to guard them. He said, 'No, I want them dead.' So he started shooting them. And he told me to start shooting.

A soldier's account of the shooting of the villagers.

Source H

The few Vietcong who had stayed near the hamlet were safely hidden. Nguyen Ngo, a former deputy commander of a Vietcong guerrilla platoon operating in the My Lai area, ran to his hiding place 300 metres away when the GIs came in shooting, but he could see that 'they shot everything in sight'. His mother and sister hid in ditches and survived because bodies fell on top of them.

From an historian's account of the massacre.

Things to do

1 Study the account and sources on these pages.
   (a) How far do they explain why the My Lai massacre occurred?
   (b) There were many examples of horrific death in the Vietnam War. Why do you think the My Lai massacre caused such an outcry?

Changing Nature of Warfare: A civilian experience

The protest movement, 1968-73

The anti-war movement in America began almost as soon as the war itself. In 1965 the draft (conscription) of young men into the armed forces rose from 3,000 a month to 33,000. In the same year more and more young people opposed the draft and did whatever they could to avoid it. Some got married, others fled to Europe and Canada, some claimed medical illness or disability, and some went back to college. Young middle-class men were more likely to avoid the draft than poorer ones. Poor black and white Americans did most of the fighting in Vietnam. The anti-war movement was growing, even so many Americans fully supported the war. Anti-war demonstrators in New York were pelted with rotten eggs and shouts of 'communist' and 'cowards' by supporters of the war.

In May 1968, 562 US soldiers died in one week of the war alone. About 15,000 died in 1968. This sparked off further protest. In October 1967 a poll revealed that 30 per cent of Americans wanted the US to withdraw from the war, twice as many as the last poll two years before had shown.

In November 1968 two Americans burnt themselves to death as Vietnamese Buddhists had done in 1963. Norman Morrison set himself on fire outside the Pentagon and Roger Laporte outside the United Nations building. At the end of the month 35,000 anti-war demonstrators gathered outside the White House to listen to speeches from Dr Spock (an expert on child rearing) and from Coretta King (the wife of the black civil rights leader, Martin Luther King).

Student protests

Many students opted out of American mainstream society in the 1960s. Some joined hippie communities, preaching peace and love, not war. Students protested in a number of ways:

- Teach-ins on why the US should leave Vietnam.
- Sit-ins to disrupt the draft offices.
- Blocking railway lines with human barricades to prevent the movement of supplies and troops.
- Burning their draft papers.
- Huge public demonstrations.
- Campus demonstrations.

Source I

American anti-war demonstrators.

Things to do

1 Study Sources I and K. What can a historian studying attitudes in the USA to the Vietnam War learn from these sources?

2 Study Source J. 'All Americans were against the war.' How far do you agree with this statement?

War veterans

The Vietnam Veterans against the War was formed in 1967 by former US soldiers who had fought in the war. Disabled veterans made speeches at demonstrations. Many made the symbolic gesture of throwing away their military medals.

Source J

During the campaign, Nixon had promised to end the war in Vietnam and so began to withdraw American troops slowly but steadily while continuing strong military campaigns and pursuing a negotiated peace settlement. Although most Americans seemed to support the President's policy of gradual withdrawal, increasing numbers of Americans came to favour an immediate end to the war. These dissenters made their views known in 'peace' demonstrations that were often of massive proportions. Settlement finally came in January 1973, and two months later the last American combat soldier left Vietnam. Fighting between the Vietnamese, however, continued. American participation in the war had cost the country more than 57,000 servicemen killed, more than 300,000 wounded, and more than $135,000 million.

An historian's overview of the last stages of the Vietnam War.

Violence

The protest movement gathered pace and sought to influence the presidential election of 1968. More than 10,000 demonstrators protested outside the Chicago Democratic Convention. Violence broke out between police and demonstrators with the police using heavy-handed tactics that cast a shadow over the Democratic convention candidate for the election, Hubert Humphrey. The Republican candidate Richard Nixon pronounced he would withdraw from Vietnam. He was elected, but it took him until 1973 to withdraw, four years later!

The media

The media's focus on My Lai in 1969 had an impact on the protest movement, helping it to spread out of the universities and to the rest of the country. It also spread to other parts of the world, with anti-war demonstrations being held in places such as London.

It sounds terrible to say we ought to kill kids, but many of our boys being killed over their are just kids too.
Cleveland woman

The company must have been hit hard before the action.
GI Serviceman in Vietnam

Your paper is rotten and anti American.
Cleveland woman to local newspaper

No American would ever kill 100 people like that.
Former Serviceman

I don't believe it actually happened. The story was planted by Vietcong sympathizers and people inside the country who are trying to get us out of Vietnam sooner.
Los Angeles salesman

Reactions in America to news of the My Lai massacre.

Changing Nature of Warfare: A civilian experience

Bloodshed at Kent State University

Source K

In May 1970 a peaceful anti-war demonstration was held by 1,500 to 3,000 students at Kent State University in Ohio. But this was against state law and the state governor sent in the National Guard to put down the demonstration. At about midday the guard fired tear gas canisters at the demonstrators and when the students tossed them back along with stones and rocks, the guardsmen opened fire. Four students were shot dead and nine wounded. It became clear from the evidence that the dead students had not been part of the demonstration. They were only 19 and 20 years old.

One of the four Kent State University students shot dead by National Guardsmen, May 1970.

Anti-war protests went on. How important they were in bringing the war to an end is hard to judge. One view is that they had no effect, claiming that the war would have ended when it did anyway. Also the American people in general were almost equally divided over the war.

3.2 Why did the Vietnam War have consequences for civilians long after the fighting had stopped?

The effects of chemical warfare

The use of napalm and Agent Orange by the US in the Vietnam War has been discussed in section 3.1. The use of these chemicals, however, was not confined to the war zone. The American botanist Arthur Galston was already worried about the effect these chemicals were having on the Vietnamese environment as early as 1967. Three years later their use was linked to outbreaks of cancer and within a year Agent Orange was banned.

By 1977 Australian Vietnam veterans were claiming to be suffering illnesses caused by exposure to Agent Orange. (Remember that over 46,000 Australians served in Vietnam and 501 were killed and 3,131 wounded.) In 1985 a report claimed there was no link between the chemical and cancers and deformities in soldiers' children and grandchildren. But by 1993 the link was proven and a multi-million dollar fund was set up to compensate veterans and their families. What happens in the future in cases of grandchildren and great grandchildren deformed by these chemicals still has to be decided.

Vietnam: an environmental disaster

The war destroyed 5.4 million acres of Vietnam's forests. The land was polluted with chemicals and the wreckage of war. Landscapes were transformed into moonscapes. Unexploded land mines and bombs are still claiming Vietnamese lives.

Farmland is still poisoned by chemicals. Vietnam was once a major producer of rice. It had enough to feed its own people and to export to other countries. But so much of the soil became contaminated by poisonous chemicals that it was impossible to grow rice on it. Not being able to grow as much rice as usual meant the country could not feed its people as it once had. Many people went short of food and Vietnam was forced to import what it needed to prevent starvation. So, for the Vietnamese people the effects of the war go on. But for them there is no vast pool of money to help.

Source L

Boat people fleeing from South Vietnam in 1979, after the communist takeover.

The boat people and economic problems

In 1975 the South was reunited with the North as the new Socialist Republic of Vietnam. Post-war economic and social problems were severe. The communist government tried to control every aspect of the economy. Farmers and industrialists were expected to accept the change to collective farms and nationalised industries. But these ways of running the economy were unpopular. Poor harvests because of polluted soil and the American embargo on Western help to Vietnam made matters worse. Also many skilled and professional South Vietnamese had fled the country at the end of the war.

Matters got worse when the country was drawn into wars with Cambodia, in 1978, and even China, in 1979. The hardships were too much for many. Thousands began leaving. Many managed to get out overland, but most escaped by boat. They became known as 'the **boat people**'. They almost used anything that floated. As many as possible crammed into the vessels and sailed for Hong Kong, Malaysia and Thailand. Malaysia did not have the resources to accommodate them and forced them to turn back. Many boats were attacked by pirates and others simply sank. At least 50,000 refugees drowned. About a million actually made it to the West, some settling in Britain, but most making it to the United States.

The problems of Vietnam continued. By 1986 inflation was about 700 per cent. More reforms were made to resolve some of the problems, but more bad harvests made things worse. The Russians stopped providing aid in 1991. But the Americans relaxed their embargo in 1993 when they allowed the International Monetary Fund (IMF) and World Bank to start investing in Vietnam. The US lifted their trade embargo in 1993 and in 1995 full diplomatic relations were re-established, more than 20 years after the war ended.

Psychological effects on the US troops

Early in the 20th century the psychological effects of war were still not recognised. Soldiers suffering shell shock in the First World War could have been 'shot at dawn' for cowardice. However, by the end of the war and certainly by the Second World War, the psychological impact of the horrors of war on soldiers fighting it were appreciated. Vietnam was no different.

Heroes or failures?

American soldiers returning from the Vietnam War may have expected a hero's return. But the American public had long lost its taste for a war that had been increasingly difficult to justify. Atrocities such as My Lai only served to confirm the growing distaste for the war. And the indignity of failing to defeat a peasant people and being forced to withdraw was too hard for many to bear or want to be reminded of.

Many Vietnam veterans found it hard to get jobs, with employers reluctant to employ them. With little hope of earning a living legitimately, some turned to crime. With the failure of the war and the problems of adjusting to civilian life many developed a sense of worthlessness. Holding down a job became hard, marriages broke down and divorces soared.

'Don't bet on it man'

Vietnam veterans experienced recurring nightmares of what they had done or what they had seen. One veteran passing a blind beggar holding a sign that read, 'My days are darker than your night', is said to have muttered 'Don't bet on it man.'

Books, films and music

The need for Americans to come to terms with the Vietnam War was played out in public in many ways. Veterans appeared on television to talk about their experiences. Some recounted their experiences by writing their memoirs. Musicians composed songs about the war. Hollywood was ready to film its versions of the war. *Apocalypse Now*, *Full Metal Jacket* and *Platoon* focused on what it was like to be a soldier in the war. Others, such as *Good Morning Vietnam*, represented life behind the lines. *Born on the 4th of July* and *The Deer Hunter* explored the psychological effects of war.

Vietnam, Post–1939

Things to do

1 Why do you think veterans of the Vietnam War threw away their medals?

2 What was the impact of events such as My Lai on American attitudes to the war?

3 Explain the story of the blind beggar and the Vietnam veteran.

4 What were the long term effects of the war on the people of Vietnam?

5 Study Source M. Explain how the photographer gets across the mood of many Americans after the end of the Vietnam War.

Summary

It is difficult to come to terms with much of what happened in Vietnam. For the American people, many with first hand experience of the war, it must still have a profound effect. They still have to live with the events of the My Lai massacre and the after effects of a war they must have thought was just. In many ways the civilian recovery in the USA and in Vietnam is still taking place.

Attitude to authority and government

Many Americans, disillusioned with the government's handling of the war, developed a more bitter view of government and various forms of authority, such as local police and local authorities. Some who had lost children and husbands in the war were aware that no member of the US Congress had lost a son in the war. Even President Clinton has been criticised for apparently avoiding the draft by going to college at the time.

Loss of status as a superpower?

There are some who believed that the United States lost its sense of role as a world 'policeman'. The inability to defeat such a small nation as North Vietnam made the Americans wary of conflicts that might turn into long drawn-out affairs. The US also had to suffer the indignity of being accused of war crimes by Vietnam (in its use of bombs, napalm and chemical weapons). Only with the more recent success of the Gulf War has the USA looked like it has resumed its role as the world's most powerful nation and policeman.

Though the war has been over since the mid-1970s, it continues to preoccupy the Americans and the Vietnamese. It continues to affect the thoughts and feelings of the people, their culture and their political and economic life.

Source M

A Vietnam veteran at America's memorial to its war dead in Washington.

Summary

From the Presidential elections of 1968 to the fall of Saigon in 1975 it was clear that the Americans wanted out of Vietnam. For the troops themselves it was a matter or survival. For the American government it was a matter of not losing face with the rest of the world. For the Vietnamese people it was a matter of facing an uncertain future and consequences (Unit 3) which might take until the 21st century to resolve.

Chnaging Nature of Warfare: A civilian experience

Finding Peace in Vietnam

The role of the peacemakers

Kissinger, Nixon and Le Duc Tho played a part in bringing an end to the conflict in Vietnam in the early 1970s. However, the peace of 1973 was short-lived and the fall of South Vietnam to the Communist North was almost inevitable. It was difficult to keep peace once the Americans withdrew from South East Asia.

4.1 How important were the roles of Nixon and Kissinger in bringing peace to Vietnam?

The Presidential election, 1968

Many things seemed to go wrong for the Americans in 1968. The Tet Offensive (see Unit 2) aroused further doubts about the war. The civil rights leader, Martin Luther King, and the Democratic front-runner for the upcoming Presidential election, Robert Kennedy, were both assassinated. Demonstrations against the war continued. Inflation was higher than it had been since the Second World War and more people were on welfare. President Johnson reacted to growing opposition to the war by entering into negotiations with the North Vietnamese and looking to reduce America's military presence in Vietnam.

Johnson also decided not to fight the Presidential election that year. It was won by the Republican candidate, Richard Nixon, whose Democratic opponent was Vice-President Hubert Humphrey. The election was won by Nixon on his promise to end the war in Vietnam. Humphrey only talked about de-escalating (reducing) America's involvement in the war. This strategy probably cost him the election, as Nixon won by only 1 per cent of the vote!

US President Lyndon B Johnson.

Its central thesis is that the United States will participate in the defence and development of the allies and friends, but that America cannot and will not conceive all the plans, design all the programmes, execute all the decisions and undertake all the defence of the free nations of the world. We will help where it makes a real difference and is considered in our interest.

An extract from President Nixon's doctrine on America's foreign policy for the future.

The role of President Nixon

Nixon did not want to be the first US President to lose a war. The Paris peace talks, which had started in March 1968, were going nowhere. He had to find another way of reaching peace without damaging the United States, international reputation. He devised the Nixon Doctrine, which set out the conditions for future US involvement in foreign affairs and his views on the Vietnam conflict.

Vietnamisation

Nixon's doctrine led to the Vietnamisation of the Vietnam War. US troops would gradually withdraw from the conflict, and the South Vietnamese army (ARVN) would be equipped and trained by the US to fight the war on its own. In May 1969 the first consignments of the massive build up of weapons for the ARVN began; on 7 July the first US troops started to go home.

Nixon knew that Vietnamisation would not end the war. It would reduce US losses, but he still had to negotiate a peace settlement with the North Vietnamese. At the Paris peace talks Nixon failed to convince the North Vietnamese to withdraw their troops from the South to match the American withdrawal.

With the peace negotiations in stalemate, the US escalated its bombing campaign against the enemy in the South and North. In 1970 US bombings extended to Cambodia in an attempt to destroy the North Vietnamese and Vietcong supply lines and sanctuaries in that country. The bombings went on into 1971 and 1972. In 1972 the Communists launched a successful Easter Offensive, but by September the well-equipped ARVN, backed up by American firepower, forced them back. The North Vietnamese government now realised it would not win a quick victory.

An account of how the South Vietnamese army depended on US support.

'If this boy of yours **is** real, how come we gotta wind him up all the time?'

A cartoon commenting on Nixon's Vietnamisation policy of 1969.

Peace talks, 1972

At the beginning of 1972 Nixon proposed an eight-point plan for peace. In February and May he visited China and the USSR to improve America's relationship with each country. These diplomatic moves and the ongoing bombing of the North started to pay off. Secret talks were held between the US Secretary of State, Henry Kissinger, and the North Vietnamese peace talks representative, Le Duc Tho. As a result the North Vietnamese accepted what they had never done before, South Vietnam's right to exist. The talks dragged on through November and into December. Nixon became impatient. To apply more pressure on the North Vietnamese to reach agreement, he ordered a massive bombing of Hanoi and Haiphong for Christmas. This lasted 11 days, during which 200,000 bombs were dropped on the North.

The bombing campaign demonstrated to the North that the US would not abandon the South at any cost. This forced the North Vietnamese back to the negotiating table and a cease-fire agreement was reached on 23 January 1973. American troops would be withdrawn and US bases dismantled. Soldiers from the ARVN, the North Vietnamese Army (NVA) and the Vietcong would remain in the positions they held at that moment. Nixon claimed peace with honour. Actually it was little more than withdrawal from a conflict that was likely to flare-up again.

Kissinger and Le Duc Tho

Kissinger and Le Duc Tho drew up a nine-point plan for peace in October 1972. It was opposed by the South Vietnamese. Further talks were held in December but these were postponed when the US Christmas bombing of the North began. The talks resumed after the bombings and the two men talked for six days before emerging with a solution. On 23 January 1973 Nixon announced agreement between the sides and this was signed on 27 January.

Later that year Kissinger and Le Duc Tho were awarded the Nobel Peace Prize. For some historians the achievements of Le Duc Tho are seen as the more significant. He got the Americans out of Vietnam with a cease-fire which gave the North Vietnamese army time to rebuild its strength and prepare for the final onslaught against the South.

Kissinger may have got the best deal he could. The US had come to realise it could not win the war with ground troops and there was no way the politicians could pour in reinforcements without massive casualties, and political disaster at home. Both sides may have got as much as they could from the peace process.

Source E

A British cartoon commenting on Nixon's policy of Vietnamisation in 1969.

4.2 Why was peace difficult to maintain in Vietnam between 1973-75?

Cease-fire, 1973

Nixon claimed that the cease-fire agreement would end the war and restore a lasting peace in Vietnam. By the end of March 1973 every American fighting soldier had left the country. Fighting between North and South eased up during the rest of the year.

In America, Nixon was deep in the scandal of Watergate, which was to cost him his job. His predicament made it impossible for him to win Congressional approval for military aid to South Vietnam

Source F

An American prisoner of war is welcomed home.

Watergate, 1974

The Watergate scandal dominated American politics in 1974. The President was linked to a break-in at the offices of the Democratic Party in the Watergate building in Washington. The burglars planted bugging devices so Republican party officials could listen in to the Democrats' election campaign plans. By July the government was paralysed by the threat to impeach the President and remove him from office. Given his position there was no chance he could persuade Congress to pass more military aid for South Vietnam when fighting flared up again. In August Nixon became the first American President to resign from office.

Growing conflict, 1974

In 1974 the fighting between the North and South resumed. Several major battles were fought. There was no more US help for the South Vietnamese when in August the US Congress passed laws to prevent US bombing in any part of Indo-China. In October it limited US financial support for the South to $700 million, which was only about half of what Gerald Ford, the new President, requested. American support for the South was dwindling. In December the North Vietnamese began their offensive. By the end of the month they had captured several important cities.

Things to do

1 Explain why President Johnson was succeeded by Nixon as President of the USA.

2 What does the Nixon Doctrine of Vietnamisation really mean?

3 Study Sources D and E on pages 243 and 244. What similarities are there between the two sources in the way they portray the policy of Vietnamisation?

Finding Peace in Vietnam, The role of the peacemakers

A family flee from the Communists advancing on Saigon, 3 April 1975.

Things to do

Study Sources G and H. What effect would these photgraphs have on the following groups of Americans:

(a) A Vietnam veteran;

(b) A US serviceman;

(c) An anti-war demonstrator;

(d) The American President.

Vietnam, Post-1939

The fall of Da Nang, March 1975

Da Nang was South Vietnam's second largest city. It was also a major military base for the South, with a sprawling network of air, sea and army bases full of American equipment.

At the beginning of March the ancient capital of Hue fell to the communists. Three weeks later they were on the edge of Da Nang ready to attack. They had advanced over 80 kilometres (50 miles) since taking Hue. Da Nang offered very little resistance to the communist assault. Civil and military officials fled and starving, demoralised South Vietnamese troops rampaged through the streets looting and drinking. There were reports of people so desperate to flee that they clung to the undercarriages of aircraft, only to fall to their deaths in the sea. Thousands trekked south to what they thought would be the safety of the coastal areas and Saigon. This mass exodus of people was later called the 'the Convoy of Tears.' The fall of Saigon was only a matter of time.

The fall of Saigon, April 1975

Saigon fell to the Communists on 30 April. Tanks led the victory procession through the city; one of them smashed through the gates of the presidential palace as if signifying the end of foreign rule. Convoys of trucks crammed with communist troops, many teenage boys and girls, were welcomed by thousands lining the streets. Those fearing reprisals were desperate to escape. One ARVN colonel marched up to a war memorial, saluted and shot himself.

People scrambled to get out of the city. Pilots loaded planes with relatives and flew them to Thailand. People panicked at Nha Trang airport as the last planes took off. Thousands squeezed into boats and set off across the South China Sea towards safety in countries such as South Korea, Japan and Taiwan. The NVA tried to force them to turn back by firing shots across their bows.

The fall of the US embassy

One of the abiding images of the evacuation of Saigon and the conclusion of America's involvement in Vietnam were the final scenes of people being airlifted by helicopters from the roof of the American embassy. These were the remaining American officials, servicemen and leading South Vietnamese citizens. They were helicoptered to US warships anchored in the South China Sea.

Almost immediately the North Vietnamese began the process of forcing a communist system on the people they had 'liberated'. Hundreds of thousands of Vietnamese were forced into 're-education centres'.

War against Cambodia, 1978, and China, 1979

In the years that followed the Vietnamese were involved in two other wars. In 1978 they invaded Cambodia (Kampuchea) and defeated the Khmer Rouge. This ended up as another guerrilla war, with the Khmer Rouge leader Pol Pot waging guerrilla war against the Vietnamese from the jungles of Kampuchea. In 1979 China invaded Vietnam with 80,000 troops. A fierce war was fought with the Chinese having to bring in a further 200,000 troops to avoid a humiliating defeat. They withdrew having destroyed a number of towns and valuable crops.

Lessons learnt?

The consequences of the Vietnam War for Vietnamese and Americans are dealt with in Unit 3. For the American government an important lesson was learnt. It could no longer assume that its superior power guaranteed that it could force its will on less powerful nations. Its role as world policeman had to be reconsidered. It was not until the Gulf War in 1990 that US power was once again tested. On this occasion its superior technology was highly effective against an inferior power. As for the US military, it would not be so easily drawn into another guerrilla war.

Source H

Vietnamese and Americans fleeing Saigon scramble on to a helicopter, 30 April 1975.

Finding Peace in Vietnam, the role of the peacemakers

The Arab-Israeli Conflict

Origins of conflict, 1900–48

In 1900 Palestine was under Turkish rule. There were about 50,000 Jews and 700,000 Arabs living there. When war broke out in 1914 many Arabs supported the British in the hope that they would gain their freedom. Arab and Jew both had strong claims to a homeland and were to spend the next 30 years fighting to gain control of Palestine.

1.1 Why did Arab and Jew feel they had a right to a homeland in Palestine?

Historic claims

The Jews

For both sides their claims to Palestine go back beyond the 20th century. For many Jews events in AD 73 represent a symbol of their claim. Jews living in Palestine fought against Roman rule. At Masada a small group of zealots held out against the mighty Roman army. After three years the Romans finally broke into the fortress only to find that the remaining Jews had committed suicide. Men had killed their wives, their children and finally themselves. Jews were expelled from Palestine and forbidden to return. Even after the Romans left few Jews returned as most preferred to stay in the new countries they had settled in. The symbolism of this archeological site is important. School children visit the site and soldiers swear loyalty there. Some Jews claim that Masada will not fall again.

Source A

Arab and Jewish protesters both demanding the right to Palestine/Israel as a homeland.

Even before Masada, the Bible added weight to the Jewish claim. Jews believe that God promised them Palestine. The story of Moses in the Bible is of him leading the Israelites to their promised land in Israel. Their temple of worship was built in Jerusalem and is still very important to Jews today.

Anti-Jewish feeling (anti-Semitism) in various parts of the world was another major factor in the Jewish desire for a homeland. Attacks on Jews had occurred in almost every country in which they settled. In 1881 Jews were blamed for the murder of the Emperor Alexander II of Russia and thousands of Jews were killed in what was known as pogroms. For many Jews the answer was the creation of a Jewish state. This idea was called Zionism.

The Arab-Israeli Conflict

The Arabs

Arab involvement in Palestine goes back well over a thousand years. It began with the start of Islam in 622. Although most of the story of the Muslim faith is set in Medina and Mecca, Muslims believe that Mohammed ascended into heaven from a rock on a hill in the city of Jerusalem. This made Jerusalem an important religious site for the Muslims too. The Mosque of the Dome of the Rock is as important a religious site to the Arabs as the Wailing Wall is to Jews. The Arabs captured the city in AD 638 and ruled it for most of the next 800 years until it became part of the Turkish empire.

In the same way as Jewish nationalism grew so did Arab nationalism. In 1905 the League of the Arab Fatherland was created. In August 1910 the Druze sect of Muslims massacred 100 Jewish settlers and in December 1910 Turkish troops had to quell an Arab uprising against their rule of Palestine. In 1914, an Arab Manifesto was written to encourage Arabs to continue the fight against the Turks and there were warnings of the increasing numbers of Jews emigrating to Palestine. By 1914 there were 40 Jewish settlements in Palestine and more Jews living in Jerusalem than Arabs.

In 1914, as war broke out in the rest of Europe, many Arabs saw their chance to rid themselves of 400 years of Turkish rule. Arabs, led by Sherif Hussein, were now willing to fight for the British in the hope of gaining their freedom at the end of the war. Britain was not going to miss this opportunity. The British officer T. E. Lawrence, famous as 'Lawrence of Arabia', was given the responsibility of persuading the Arabs to join forces with the British against the Turks. What would be their reward?

T. E. Lawrence in Arab headdress, which became a feature of his appearance.

Things to do

1 Why do you think stories like the fall of Masada are important to Jews living in Israel?

2 Explain why Jerusalem is an important religious centre for Muslims, Christians and Jews.

3 Source A was published by the Free Palestine Information Office in London. How useful is it in helping explain the Palestine problem?

Summary

Jews and Arabs

Events such as the siege of Masada have helped convince Jews that they must fight for Palestine. Some believe in creating a Jewish state. Arabs think they should have Palestine beacuse they ruled it for 800 years before the Turks took over. War broke out when the Arabs hoped to win back Palestine from the Turks.

Origins of conflict, 1900–48

Broken promises?: the McMahon Letter

In 1914 the Secretary of State for War, Lord Kitchener, wrote to Sherif Hussein of Mecca. He clearly stated that Britain would now support the Arabs instead of the Turks, who had joined the war on the side of Germany, and asked him to let all his followers know this. This was a clear message to the Arabs. During the war the British wrote a letter to Sherif Hussein. It contained the now famous phrase, 'Subject to modifications, Great Britain is prepared to recognise and support the independence of the Arabs in all regions.' Sherif Hussein was not totally convinced of British assurances but it was enough for an Arab revolt against their Turkish rulers to begin on 10 June 1916. Arabs fighting closely with Colonel T. E. Lawrence used terrorist techniques to destroy 17 Turkish locomotives and to bring civilian transport to a halt. In October Prince Feisal, the son of Sherif Hussein, captured Damascus, the capital of Syria. The collapse of the Turkish Empire was near. In December 1917 the Arab and British armies, led by General Allenby, entered Jerusalem. Allenby and Lawrence were considered to be great heroes by the Arabs.

Sykes-Picot Agreement, 1916

Arabs might not have been as pleased to see the end of Turkish rule if they had known about of the secret agreement between Sir Mark Sykes of the British government and Georges Picot of the French government. This agreement was made in October 1916 less than four months after the Arab revolt had begun. They were concerned about the future of sea routes through the Suez Canal and Red Sea which were so vital to British and French trade and oil supplies. They were also worried that the Russians might try to step in when the Turks were defeated. They therefore agreed to divide up the Middle East between themselves after the war. Jerusalem's religious importance was confirmed with international status. This agreement would be sure to offend the Arabs. It would have the same effect on Jews.

This map of the Middle East shows how the region was divided up according to the Sykes-Picot agreement of 1916.

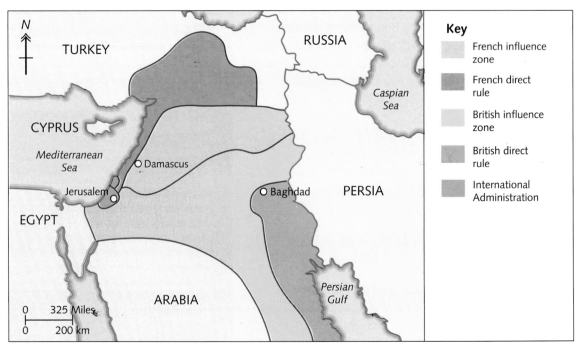

The Arab-Israeli Conflict

The Balfour Declaration, 1917

The last few months of 1917 went badly for the British government. The Russian government collapsed in November and the new Bolshevik government published the Sykes-Picot Agreement. The Arabs were angry that they could be blatantly betrayed by their British ally. This was made worse when the British Foreign Secretary, Arthur Balfour, stated that the British cabinet had agreed that they were sympathetic to setting up a national home for the Jewish people in Palestine.

The Arabs objected to the Balfour Declaration and protested. They said that a homeland for Jews could only be created at the expense of the Arabs living in Palestine. The British government made a further set of promises to the Arabs to set up a united Arab state but had no intention of keeping any new promise. On 11 August 1919 this was made clear in a note to the British government from Balfour which stated that giving Jews a homeland was more important than giving in to the 700,000 Arabs living there.

The Middle East peace settlement

The peace conference at Paris in 1919 decided that all countries that were part of the defeated empires should have the opportunity to be self-governing and independent nations. If a country lacked the experience to run its own affairs then one of the major powers (Britain, France, the USA) would help it. Any country governed under this system was called a mandate. In 1919 the Arabs thought they could run their own affairs but the major powers did not. The Middle East was divided up between Britain and France, with Palestine, Transjordan and Iraq becoming British mandates.

Britain appointed Sir Herbert Samuel, a Jew and a Zionist, as Governor of Palestine. He announced that 16,500 Jews would be allowed to settle in Palestine. Arabs protested fiercely about this and violence broke out, with 46 Jews being killed in 1921. The British mandate of Palestine had not got off to a good start.

Source C

His Majesty's government views with favour the establishment in Palestine of a national home for the Jewish people, and will use their best endeavours to facilitate the achievement of this object, it being clearly understood that nothing shall be done which may prejudice the civil and religious rights of existing non-Jewish communities in Palestine, or the rights and political status enjoyed by Jews in any other country.

The position of the British is made clear in this extract from the Balfour Declaration, 1917.

Summary

The Middle East in the war
During the First World War the situation became worse when Britain appeared to offer hope to both sides. They told Sherif Hussien that they supported Arab independence and they told the Jews that they would look with favour on a Jewish homeland. In the end Britain took over Palestine as a mandate.

Things to do

1 How could Britain be seen to be breaking promises to both Arab and Jewish people?

2 What reasons might the British government give for acting in this way?

3 Explain why Arabs and Jews would oppose the Balfour Declaration shown in Source C.

4 Why was Palestine not given the power to rule itself at the end of the First World War?

Origins of conflict, 1900–48

1.2 How successful was the British Mandate between 1922 and 1947?

The Arabs were so angry about the number of Jews allowed into Palestine that in May 1921 Arabs in Jaffa attacked Jewish immigrants. Within two days 46 Jews were dead and over 200 Jews and Arabs were wounded. The British reaction was to cut Jewish immigration to Palestine in the years 1922-29. Although Palestine was peaceful, 60 new Jewish settlements were created and the Jewish population increased by about 75,000. This was helped by the use of money sent by Jews from Europe and America to buy up Arab farms. Arab tenants were evicted and many of the new Jewish owners only employed Jews. Many Arabs now found themselves unemployed and landless.

The Mufti and the Haganah

Jewish immigration was one problem. Another cause of tension was the underground movements which were established in the 1920s. The senior judge in Jerusalem, Mohammed Amin al-Husseini, was the leader of an Arab group called the Mufti.

It assassinated Jewish settlers and any moderate Arabs who tried to live and work together with the Jewish settlers. In response the Jews created the Haganah, a secret defence force to protect the farmers.

In 1929 two events yet again brought the problems of Palestine to the surface. A Zionist speech suggested that Palestine and Transjordan (now known as Jordan) should become a Jewish state and a demonstration by Jewish extremists near the Mosque of the Dome led to riots throughout Palestine. 133 Jews died and 339 were wounded. Again Britain failed to tackle the problem and even allowed more Jews to settle in Palestine.

Nazi persecution of the Jews, 1933

The rise of Hitler to power in 1933 and the increased anti-Semitism of the Nazis led to a massive increase in immigration into Palestine. In 1933, 30,000 Jews fled from Europe, 42,000 in 1934 and 61,000 in 1935. The message was clear to Arabs. Britain, instead of preparing Palestine for independence, was planning to allow Jews to immigrate to Palestine in large enough numbers so that a homeland could be created. They decided to act.

Source D

Arab guerrillas who fought against the British in the 1930s.

The Arab Revolt of 1936

Arabs throughout Palestine went on strike. For six months the country was at a standstill. There were no buses or trains. Shops, offices, schools and factories were shut. Jewish homes and shops were attacked. In one month alone 21 Jews were killed. The British made a crucial mistake. They created a police force using Jewish volunteers. Well over a thousand of the volunteers were also members of the Haganah. Only now they were being given arms by the British and allowed to go wherever they pleased. The second mistake the British made was the creation of the Peel Commission.

The Peel Commission, 1936-37

The Peel Commission was set up in 1936 to try and settle Jewish and Arab differences, but it had little chance of success, even though the strike ended. The Commission proposed a solution which would give the Jews a homeland, but at the 'expense' of the Arabs, and left Britain with control of the area around the holy city of Jerusalem (see map).

The Arab Revolt, 1937-39

This led to the Arab revolt which lasted until the outbreak of the Second World War. It was a bitter guerrilla war involving attacks on homes, farms, synagogues, women and children. By 1938 Britain had over 20,000 troops in Palestine trying to keep order. Supported by the police force they countered the Arab tactics with guerrilla tactics of their own. By the end of 1938 the Arabs had lost at least 5,000 men. But Britain had decided that dividing Palestine up was not the solution to this problem. A conference in London failed to find another solution, but the British government announced that Jewish immigration would be limited to 5,000 a year until 1944 and after that no Jew would be allowed into Palestine without Arab agreement. Britain also declared that by 1949 there would be an independent state in Palestine with Arabs and Jews sharing control. But the Second World War broke out within four months and no further progress was made.

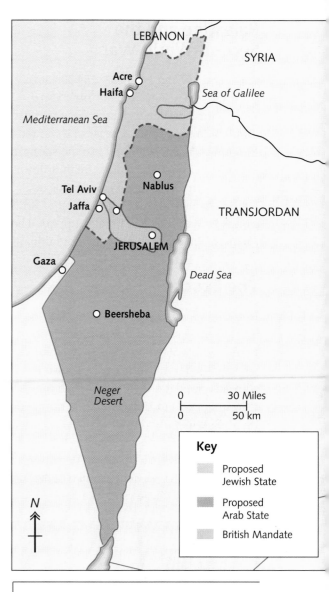

This map shows the main proposals of the Peel Commission's partition plan for Palestine.

Things to do

1 Why was increased Jewish immigration to Palestine seen as a threat to Arabs?

2 Study the map of the Peel partition plan on this page. Explain why Arabs would object to the Peel Commission's solution to the Palestine problem.

Origins of conflict, 1900–48

Palestine and the Second World War

Between 1939 and 1947 only 154,000 Jews were allowed to leave the horrors of Nazi Europe for Palestine. Britain reduced Jewish immigration to Palestine because it wanted to keep Arab support. But it lost the support of Jews all around the world. Treating Jews fleeing Germany arriving in Palestine as enemy aliens and shipping them off to British camps in Mauritius lost Britain support. The *Exodus* event made them even more unhappy.

The Exodus

In 1947 a group of Jews sailed the *Exodus*, an old paddle steamer from the south of France with 4,550 men, women and children who had fled from Germany. A British navy ship shadowed it until it approached the Palestinian port of Haifa, and then rammed the *Exodus* to try to prevent it docking. Britain returned the refugees to Germany where they were imprisoned in a Displaced Persons camp. An outraged US President Truman demanded a homeland for the Jews in Palestine.

Jewish terrorism, 1945-47

The Haganah had been well trained as fighters by the British army in the 1930s. Now they were fighting the British over a homeland for Jews. But some Jews criticised them for being too cautious. Two groups, the Irgun and the Stern Gang, broke away to begin a more violent campaign against the British. Most of the Stern gang, however, were arrested after assassinating the British minister Lord Moyne in November 1944. The British still refused to raise limits on Jewish immigration to Palestine. So the Irgun began a campaign of terror, culminating in the bombing of the King David Hotel on the 22 July 1946.

The King David Hotel bombing

The King David Hotel was an obvious target for terrorism. It was the British military headquarters in Jerusalem. The British surrounded it with barbed wire, machine gun posts and armed soldiers. At midday a lorry pulled up outside the entrance to the hotel kitchen. Irgun terrorists disguised as 'Arabs' unloaded milk churns packed with explosives. These exploded at 12.37 pm.

Source E

The refugee ship Exodus *docks at Haifa in Palestine with its European Jewish refugees.*

The explosion blasted through the building causing six storeys to collapse. A warning was sent, but only two minutes before the explosion. There was no time to evacuate the building. Menachem Begin, Irgun's leader, claimed they only intended to destroy records. The explosion did, but at the cost of 88 lives, including 15 Jews.

Other attacks were made on radio stations, power stations and bridges. Soldiers were shot on the streets and in their beds. British reprisals included long prison sentences, and two 16-year-old members of the Irgun were also sentenced to 18 lashes. Two days after this punishment four British soldiers, including Major Brett of the Parachute Regiment, were punished in the same way by the terrorists. In Britain there were anti-Semitic riots in Manchester, Liverpool, Glasgow and London. The British government had no solution. Ernest Bevin, the British Foreign Secretary, had little time for the Jewish cause, and with pressure coming from the US government to allow a further 100,000 Jews into Palestine, the government decided to end its mandate over Palestine. In April 1947 it handed the problem over to the United Nations.

The UN partition plan

In May 1947 the United Nations set up a UN Special Committee on Palestine (UNSCOP). The committee toured the Middle East and gathered evidence from Arabs and Jews. Finally, the UN proposed a partition plan with a Jewish state three times the size of the Palestinian one. On 14th May 1948 the new state of Israel was formed (see map on page 272). With the creation of the new State of Israel the Arabs would have no access to the sea at Jaffa. Arabs protested and violence broke out. Jews and Arabs were killed. Jews began conscripting 17-24 year olds into the Haganah and purchased 24,500 rifles, 5,000 machine guns, 54 million rounds of ammunition and 25 fighter aircraft for use in the civil war which followed.

IRGUN ZWAÏ LĔUMI BE-EREZ JISRAËL
ORGANISATION MILITAIRE NATIONALE JUIVE D'EREZ JISRAËL
JEWISH NATIONAL MILITARY ORGANISATION OF EREZ JISRAËL

An Irgun poster of 1946, declaring their fight for 'Homeland and Freedom'.

Things to do

1 Study Source D. Why can the Arabs in the photograph be described as freedom fighters and terrorists?

2 Why did the British government think it necessary to ram the *Exodus* (Source E)?

3 Study Source F. Why was this poster produced in 1946?

Summary

Palestine as a British mandate
The British found it very hard to control Palestine. More and more Jews wanted to come to live there, but the Arabs resisted this. Fighting between Arabs and Jews was common. Bith sides attracted the British who decided to leave Palestine. The UN took control of Palestine and divided it up, forming the new state of Israel on 14 May 1948.

Origins of conflict, 1900–48

Changing Nature of Warfare

A military experience, 1948–73

In 1948 the Arabs began their long military struggle against the Jews over Palestine. For Israelis it was a war of liberation, for the Arabs it was a catastrophe. For the next 25 years they suffered varying degrees of failure on the battlefield that led them to look for another way of securing an Arab Palestinian homeland. This unit explains why the Arab nations in the Middle East were unable to defeat an Israeli nation that was surrounded and outnumbered.

2.1 Why were the Arab nations unable to defeat the Israelis on the battlefield?

The 'War of Independence'

On 14 May 1948 the state of Israel was proclaimed according to the UN partition plan. On 15 May 1948 armies from Egypt, Lebanon, Transjordan, Iraq and Syria entered Palestine to help the Palestinian Arabs destroy the day-old state of Israel. The war that followed was not quite as simple as that.

The Arabs in outnumbering the Jews by 80 to 1 expected to win the war. They had tanks, planes and armoured vehicles to support them and even spread rumours of having an atomic bomb. The Jewish strategy was called Plan Dalet. This involved continuing a terror campaign they had begun a month before in Deir Yassin to drive Palestinian Arabs out of what was to become Israel.

Deir Yassin

On 10 April 1948, 132 members of the Stern and Irgun gangs had attacked the Arab village of Deir Yassin. Led by Menachem Begin, they fought a bitter battle, with the Jews gaining the upper hand, but the village did not surrender. Fighters from the gangs then moved from house to house killing anyone, including women and children. The Haganah commanders and the political leaders of the Zionist movement were embarrassed, but they did nothing to punish the Irgun or Stern gangs. The killings terrorised Arabs into leaving Palestine in their thousands. By the time Israel came into existence over 300,000 Arabs had left.

Source A

An uncontrolled panic swept through all Arab quarters, the Israelis brought up jeeps with loudspeakers which broadcast recorded 'horror sounds'. These included shrieks, wails and anguished moans of Arab women, the wail of sirens and the clang of fire alarm bells, interrupted by a voice calling out in Arabic 'save your souls, all ye faithful: the Jews are using poison gas and atomic weapons. Run for your lives in the name of Allah.'

An example of the terror tactics used by Israelis against Arabs in 1948.

Why did the Arabs fail to win the war?

At first the Arab armies had many more troops than the Israelis. The Israelis, however, were well equipped and had become highly trained and experienced after years fighting the British. The Israelis were also well led; the Arabs were not.

From July to October the Israelis focused on winning control of what was meant to be Arab territory under the UN partition plan. As the Jews made advances Arabs fled Palestine. By the end of 1948 Jews controlled 75 per cent of Palestine.

Out of an Arab population of 1.3 million less than half a million remained in the new state. The rest had fled to neighbouring Arab countries in the hope that one day they would return to the farms and villages that had once been their home.

When Iraq decided to withdraw from the north, Transjordan accepted a cease-fire arranged by the UN. But there would be no peace. Arabs did not accept the existence of Israel and the Jews did not accept Jerusalem as an internationally controlled city. They proclaimed it their capital.

For the Israelis they could at last look forward to a homeland they had desired since Zionism began in the 19th century. For thousands of Palestinians the future was one of life in refugee camps or in other countries, with only the dream of returning to their homeland.

Source B

If the Arabs were so attached to their land, why did they leave it during a crisis? The blame must be attributed to Arab leaders who, expecting a quick victory by their five combined armies over Israel, encouraged Arabs to leave Palestine, promising them that on their return they would be able to claim the property of the Jews as well. Arab propaganda led them to fear what would happen to them if they stayed, and threatened that they would also be considered traitors to the Arab cause.

An Israeli view of the Arab flight from Palestine during the war of 1948.

Source C

Arab soldiers who fought in the 1948 war against Israel.

Things to do

1 Explain how Plan Dalet was expected to work.

2 Sources A and B give very different views of the flight of Palestinian Arabs from Israel in 1948. Explain why they are different.

3 The Israelis claimed that the Arabs were better armed than appears in Source C. Why do you think they said this after they had won their 'War of Independence'?

After the Israeli success in the War of Independence its relations with the Arab countries was extremely tense. In 1956 Israel went to war with Egypt in the Suez War. You can read about this on pages 273–4.

Six Day War, 1967

In 1966 the army took over the government of Syria and took an aggressive stance towards Israel. It allowed guerrillas to attack Israel from Syria and bolstered its troops in the Golan Heights. Tension rose in April 1967 when Syrian soldiers shot at an Israeli farmer ploughing Arab-owned land close to the border. Israelis retaliated by bombing Syrian guns and shooting down six Syrian fighters.

On 12 May the USSR claimed that Israeli troops were about to invade Syria. Jordan and Egypt offered to come to the aid of Syria and sent troops to the border areas. On 16 May Nasser, President of Egypt, ordered the UN troops in the Sinai to leave Egyptian territory. On 23 May 1967 Nasser closed the Gulf of Aqaba to Israeli ships and on the 24 May Syria threatened to 'throw you (Israelis) into the sea for good'. On the 28 and 29 May 1967 the Arabs joined forces and prepared to launch an attack. But the Israelis attacked first. They called this a pre-emptive strike in self-defence.

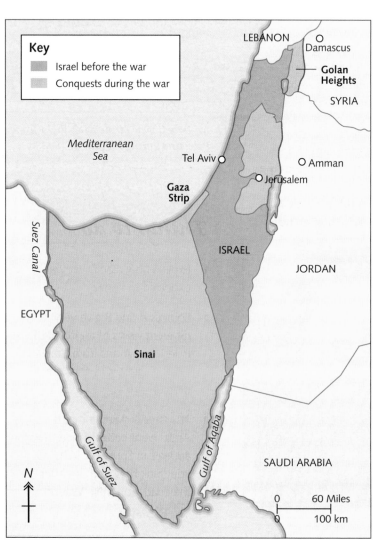

Israeli gains in the Six Day War, 1967.

Summary

The Six Day War, 1967

Day 1: 5 June 1967
Israeli troops attacked Syria, Egypt and Jordon at the same time. The airforce destroyed 300 enemy aircraft and the airfields of Syria.

Day 2: 6 June 1967
Israelis broke through the Egyptian defences and headed for the Suez Canal. Heavy fighting in Jerusalem

Day 3: 7 June 1967
Israeli troops took control of the Sinai and captured Jerusalem. Jordan accepted a cease-fire.

Day 4: 8 June 1967
Israelis gained complete control of the West Bank of the River Jordan. Egypt accepted cease-fire call.

Day 5: 9 June 1967
Israelis began attack on the Golan Heights.

Day 6: 10 June 1967
Golan Heights captured. Syria accepted cease-fire.

Source D

This cartoon shows Israel up against apparently overwhelming odds in the Six Day War.

Why did the Arabs fail to win the war?

Again the Arab forces outnumbered the Israelis in troops, tanks, and combat aircraft. On paper, at least, they could have won. What reasons have been suggested then for the massive Arab defeat?

The Israelis were defending their homeland and this was again important, but this time it was the element of surprise that was the key. Air supremacy in a desert war is crucial and Israel achieved this within 24 hours.

Some historians say that it had a lot to do with the attitude of the officers. It may have been simply that they had more to lose. The new state of Israel might have been wiped out had they lost this war.

Tactical errors by the Arab forces may also have played a part. When the Egyptians realised they lacked air support, plans were drawn up by the Chief of Staff, Fawzi, for an organised withdrawal. Before they could act their troops were already streaming out of the Sinai. Without an organised plan the retreat was a shambles. 2,000 troops had died on the battlefield; 10,000 died in the retreat.

Things to do

1   Study Source D. How useful is this source to historians studying the Six Day War?

Summary

Israel fights for survival

Following the foundation of Israel in 1948 the Israelis were forced to fight the War of Independence in 1948 and the Six Day War in 1967. Not only did they win these wars, but they gained land which made Israel larger.

Changing Nature of Warfare: A military experience

2.2 How far was the Yom Kippur War a turning point for the Arabs?

Background to the war, 1970–73

After the defeat of 1967 President Nasser of Egypt began a war of attrition against Israel. Every day his troops shelled Israeli soldiers occupying the Sinai and guerrilla-type attacks were launched against the Israeli army. Israel responded with reprisal attacks and bombing raids into the heart of Egypt. The USSR re-equipped the Egyptian army. The USA was now worried that its support of Israel might bring war between itself and the USSR closer. It wanted to avoid this and warned Israel's Prime Minister, Golda Meir, that US support was not always guaranteed. The Israelis called off a planned bombing of Egypt and agreed to a cease-fire.

President Nasser died during negotiations and the new president, Anwar Sadat, began overtures of peace with Israel. But the Israelis ignored him. This led him to believe that war was the only way to force Israel to negotiate for peace. By July 1972 his plans were well underway.

Sadat sent Soviet advisers home and began building up his relations with other Arab countries. The Egyptians led western journalists to believe that their army was unfit to fight, while holding regular military exercises along the Suez Canal so as not to alarm the Israelis who soon saw them as routine. By October 1973 Sadat was ready.

Source E

Israeli soldiers rest and take care of the wounded during the Yom Kippur War.

The coffins of Israeli soldiers killed in the Yom Kippur War.

Why did the Arabs nearly win the war?

The Arabs learned from Israel's surprise attack in 1967. They decided to produce a surprise themselves. They attacked on the 6 October 1973. This was Yom Kippur, the Day of Atonement, one of the holiest days in the Jewish calendar. At 2 o'clock in the afternoon 200 Egyptian and 100 Syrian planes took off to attack targets inside Israel. Five minutes later Egyptian troops crossed the Suez Canal. In the north 1,000 tanks crossed into the Golan Heights and forced the Israelis back to Galilee. General 'Gandhi' Ze'evi told the Prime Minister, Golda Meir, they had been 'caught with their trousers down'.

Israelis were at prayer in their synagogues. The warning sirens sounded, causing panic. Soldiers and reservists rushed to join their units. It was almost too late. The war looked lost. Egyptian troops had advanced 10 kilometres into Sinai. Syria seemed to be winning in the north. The fight back had to begin or the war would be lost.

Egyptians are putting in boats directly below us. They're crossing the canal now. Boats full of infantry. They've got anti-tank missiles. Some of our tanks are rushing at the Egyptians. Now we're under artillery fire, shells falling closer and closer. They're getting nearer. Armoured troop carriers crossing the canal now. Lots of Egyptians on our side now running forward with missiles. Six helicopters – must be Egyptian commandos – flying over us now. There's a T54 tank facing us now. It's shooting at us. More boats crossing – wave after wave of them. They're fanning out now. They've put up their flag. Now they are building a bridge. There's a huge convoy, lots of armour… tanks, missile trucks, lines of jeeps and masses of artillery. Where's our air force? We should be making mincemeat of them by now!

An Israeli soldier describing the scene as Egyptian forces launch their attack across the Suez Canal.

Changing Nature of Warfare: A military experience

Why did the Israelis 'win'?

At this point the Egyptians made a fatal error of judgement. Uncertain what to do next they decided to push further into Sinai. This played straight into the hands of the Israeli army and its vastly superior tank battalions. On 14 October the largest tank battle of the 20th century saw 250 Egyptian tanks destroyed at a cost of only 10 Israeli tanks. This led to the Israelis crossing the Suez Canal and encircling the Egyptian 3rd Army. Sadat was advised by the USSR to agree to a cease-fire. One error in tactics had led to the vastly superior Israeli tanks turning the war in the Israelis' favour.

General Gamasy of Egypt and General Yisrael Tal of Israel met with UN officials. At a private meeting which followed they negotiated a truce between the two sides.

Who won the war?

Israel claimed another victory over the Arabs as 22,000 Arabs had been killed against 2,800 Israelis. It had survived a surprise attack in the Sinai and in the Golan Heights and had by the end of the war captured more territory from Egypt and Syria. However, the picture is not that clear-cut. This was the first time Arab forces had inflicted major setbacks on the Israelis. Israeli prisoners were paraded in Cairo. Estimates suggest that 120 planes and about 650 tanks had also been destroyed. Also Arab nations seemed to have developed a much closer alliance.

Anwar Sadat was now the clear leader of Egypt and the Arab world. The Arab armies had shown that they could fight, and the Arab nations were now confident they could work together to begin a new type of war against the Israelis, the 'oil war'.

The 'oil' war

At the beginning of the War of Yom Kippur petrol in Britain was about 35 pence a gallon. With the war only two days old a routine meeting of the Organisation of Arab Petroleum Exporting Countries (OPEC) met and agreed to raise the price of oil by 70 per cent. As OPEC controlled 75 per cent of the world's oil and produced half of it, the rest of the world, and Israel's allies in particular, had to listen to the Arab view. When OPEC also announced that oil production would be cut by 5 per cent each month that the Israelis remained in territory taken in the 1967 war, the world began to worry.

A British cartoon commenting on the oil crisis. A horse trough is being set up on the hard shoulder of the motorway.

Reaction in Britain

In Britain the crisis of oil supplies and prices led to long queues at petrol stations with people trying to get as much petrol as they could before supplies ran out. The government considered introducing petrol rationing for the first time since the Suez crisis. There was concern about the future of the motor car and the car manufacturers began to look at the development of other power sources and smaller family cars.

Oil was not only used for running cars and heating homes. It affected every part of the economy. Unemployment rose from less than 250,000 in 1973 to 1.5 million in 1978. Before the war inflation had been running at about 8 per cent, by 1975 it had soared to 25 per cent; partly as a direct result of rocketing oil prices. A house that in 1976 cost £7,500 cost £30,000 ten years later.

Did the oil war work?

The Arabs had carried out their threat to raise oil prices and cut supplies. They also imposed a total ban on oil supplies to the USA and the Netherlands. This forced Western governments to pressure the Israelis into accepting a cease-fire in October 1973. The following year the USA, under pressure of the oil ban, sided with the Egyptians in negotiations with the Israelis over the removal of Israeli troops from the Sinai and the Suez Canal area.

Western governments responded by looking for alternative sources of oil and energy. Coal, gas, hydro-electricity and nuclear power were all used and as a result demand for oil actually dropped. The oil weapon was actually losing some of its effectiveness, especially as oil prices settled down and countries learned to adjust to higher prices. Some historians do not feel that the oil weapon was as effective as it might have been. Other methods had to be found. The next unit looks at one method that proved to be very effective.

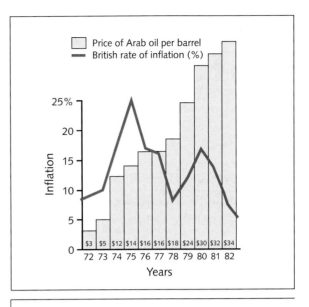

This graph shows how rising oil prices affected inflation in Britain.

The Yom Kippur War

For a time it looked like the Yom Kippur War would be a victory for the Arabs. In the end it was a further crushing defeat like those in 1948 and 1967. It was also a turning point. It was the last conventional war between Egypt and Israel. In addition, it showed that other tactics, such as the oil war, could also bring results.

Things to do

1 Explain why President Sadat thought a war was necessary against the Israelis.

2 Why did the Arabs feel confident of victory?

3 Study Sources E, F and G. Each of these sources illustrates the early successes of the Arabs and the horror Israel must have felt at the possibility of defeat. How valuable are each of the sources to an historian trying to show the Israeli fears?

4 Study Sources H and I. Do the sources prove that the oil war was a success or a failure?

Changing Nature of Warfare: A military experience

Changing Nature of Warfare

Terrorism, a war by other means, 1964 to present day

Since 1964 many Palestinian refugees have believed that another way to regain their 'homeland' was through terrorism. This method became increasingly important after the failures of Arab nations to secure a military victory against the Israelis in 1948 and in 1967. This unit looks at why the PLO was formed and how terrorism became the main weapon in the fight against the Israelis.

3.1 What tactics did Palestinians use?

During the War of Independence in 1948, 900,000 Palestinian Arabs fled Palestine/Israel. The Israelis claimed that no Palestinian Arab had been forced to leave, but refused to allow them to return once the war was over (see Unit 1.1.) Some of those who left went to study in Arab universities in Beirut, Baghdad or Cairo. Some found work in the emerging oil states of Kuwait and the United Arab Emirates. But for most, the Palestinian farmers, there was little they could do but live in the hastily erected refugee camps of the Gaza Strip and the West Bank.

The camps

The first camps were little more than tented villages without running water or proper sewerage. During the 1950s the UN replaced the tents with huts and provided running water. Facilities were still fairly basic. These refugee camps soon became training grounds for the *Fedayeen*, or 'Freedom Fighters'. Al-Fatah was one such group.

Source A

Palestinians queue for food in a refugee camp in Jordan.

The Arab-Israeli Conflict

Kfar Kassim

Many Palestinians were ready to fight for the return of their 'homeland'. They started attacking targets in Israel. In 1951, 137 Israelis were killed and in 1955 238 were killed. The Israelis took steps to stop the terrorism, such as the curfew of 5.00pm to 6.00am they imposed on the village of Kfar Kassim. But many of the village men were out of the village when the curfew was imposed, and knew nothing about it. When they returned to the village they were shot. 43 Arabs were killed and many more wounded. Even Israelis were horrified by what had happened. World sympathy for the Israelis declined.

Formation of the PLO, 1964

At a meeting of Arab leaders in 1964 to discuss the fear that Israel was planning to divert the water of two tributaries of the River Jordan to irrigate the Negev desert, the Palestine Liberation Organisation (PLO) was formed to represent the Palestinian refugees. The Palestine National Covenant set out the aims of the PLO in twelve articles:

- Article 1 talked of an Arab homeland,

- Article 2 stated that Palestine could not be divided up.

- Article 12 called for all Arabs to work for the liberation of Palestine.

- Surprisingly, Article 7 accepted the existence of Jews of Palestinian origin and their right to live peacefully and 'loyally' in Palestine. The PLO was controlled by the Palestinians Arabs themselves. One of the PLO's groups was al-Fatah. It was founded in 1958 and one of its members was an engineering student called Yasser Arafat, a Palestinian who later became its leader. Al-Fatah was committed to winning back Palestine by terrorism.

The Battle of Karameh, 1968

This event was crucial to the growing importance of al-Fatah and its leader. The Israelis attacked al-Fatah headquarters in the refugee town of Karameh to avenge al-Fatah killing 97 Israeli soldiers the year before. The guerrillas, with the help of the Jordanian army, were up against 1,500 Israeli troops with tanks and air support. Losses were high, with 200 Palestinians and 40 Jordanians killed. Israeli losses were small, with only 28 deaths. However, for the PLO this was a momentous day in their struggle against the Israelis. Al-Fatah was now seen as the force behind the PLO, and Arafat himself became the organisation's political leader.

Things to do

1. How did the refugee camps become breeding grounds for Palestinian terrorists?

2. Why was the PLO created in 1964?

3. What tactics were used by al-Fatah and the Israelis to terrorise one another?

4. Why did the PLO see the defeat at Karameh as a sort of victory?

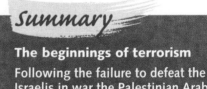

Summary

The beginnings of terrorism
Following the failure to defeat the Israelis in war the Palestinian Arabs turned to terrorism. The *fedayeen* were particularly strong in the refugee camps, where groups such as al-Fatah carried out attacks on targets in Israel.

Changing Nature of Warfare: Terrorism, a war by other means

Dawson's Field, September 1970

Relations between the PLO and King Hussein of Jordan became strained. PLO terrorists dominated certain towns in Jordan, which Hussein found intolerable. The issue came to a head in 1970 after a new extremist group, the Popular Front for the Liberation of Palestine (PFLP), pulled off a series of aircraft hijacks between 1968 and 1970. More than 50 hostages were killed in these attacks, which generated world-wide publicity for the Palestinian cause.

In September 1970 two hijacked planes were forced to land at Dawson's Field in Jordan. Passengers and crew were held hostage for four days. A third plane was flown to Egypt and blown up. When hijackers attempted to seize an Israeli flight to London, an Israeli security guard killed one terrorist and arrested a second. The captured terrorist was a young Arab woman called Leila Khaled. She was imprisoned in London.

The PFLP then seized another plane and forced the pilot to take it to Dawson's Field.

The PFLP demanded the release of seven terrorists held in prisons in Britain, Germany and Switzerland. These governments agreed but, not surprisingly, the Israelis did not. Then with the world watching on their television sets, the terrorists blew up the aircraft.

What did this achieve?

The publicity was exactly what the PFLP wanted. All the world had seen or heard about the hijack and blowing up of the planes. For the King of Jordan it was the last straw. He ordered his army to attack the *fedayeen* groups. Ten days of fighting followed before the PLO was forced to leave Jordan and seek refuge in Syria and the Lebanon. South Lebanon became the home for new terrorist attacks on Israel. A new terrorist group was also established, Black September.

Black September took revenge on Jordan in 1971 by killing the Jordanian Prime Minister. Its worst atrocity was to follow in 1972 with its attempt to disrupt the Munich Olympics.

Source B

Palestinians blew up at Dawson's Field this British Airways plane which they hijacked.

The Munich Olympics, 1972

The Olympic Games is a major media event, covered by television and thousands of journalists for a world-wide audience. The Munich Games of 1972 was an ideal opportunity for Black September to thrust the Palestinian cause back on to the world stage.

At dawn on the 5 September 1972 a group of Black September guerrillas broke into the Olympic village. They scaled the perimeter fence and slipped into the Israeli pavilion through an open door unnoticed by the 250 plain-clothes police who were there to deal with any trouble. As the Kalashnikov-armed Arabs entered the building they were challenged by Moshe Weinberg, the Israeli wrestling coach. He was killed instantly. Yosef Romano, a weightlifter, was mortally wounded as he held a door shut so that others in the room could escape. His action helped 17 athletes to escape, but 10 were captured and held hostage. One of them, Gad Tsabari, managed to escape. For the others the siege began.

Black September demanded the release of 200 Palestinians held in Israeli jails and their own safe passage out of Germany. They set a deadline of 9.00am. German police negotiated an extension to the deadline by offering free passage and a large sum of money. Meanwhile 12,000 police surrounded the Olympic village. The Germans did not want to give in to terrorism. The Arabs were told that they and their hostages would be flown to an Arab country. They were suspicious of this, but took the risk. Late that night they were taken by helicopter to the Furstenfeld military airport 40 kilometres (25 miles) away. A Boeing aircraft sat floodlit on the runway.

Source C

Members of the Israeli Olympic team attending a memorial service for those athletes who died in the terrorist attack at the Munich Olympics, in 1972.

Source D

We want them to know of the existence of a people whose country has been occupied for twenty-four years, and their honour trampled underfoot. There is no harm in the youth of the world understanding this tragedy for a few hours... Our land will be liberated by blood, and blood alone. The world only respects the strong.

These words are from a 'will' left by the Palestinians who took Israeli athletes hostage at the Munich Olympics.

Things to do

1   Study Sources B and C. How did images like these damage the cause of terrorism?

2   Study Source D. Why do you think Black September made this will?

Changing Nature of Warfare: Terrorism, a war by other means

What happened next?

Accounts of the failed rescue attempt by the German government vary. It is interesting to note what three different modern history books have said. (see Sources E, F and G.)

Source E

The police opened fire immediately. Unfortunately the surprise attack went horribly wrong, and when the shooting ended it was found that before five terrorists themselves had been killed they had managed to murder the remaining nine Israeli athletes.

Source F

When two terrorists left the helicopter to inspect the plane they were shot. Their comrades refused the call to surrender and killed their hostages as the military moved in. Five Arabs and eight hostages died. Three terrorists were taken to prison.

Source G

Just before midnight the guerrillas and their hostages began to walk across the tarmac to a waiting Boeing 727 aircraft. Suddenly all the airport lights were turned out and German police sharpshooters opened fire.

The rescue attempt failed tragically. In the gun battle all nine hostages were killed, as well as four Arabs and one policeman. Three Arabs were captured and one escaped to the nearby woods.

The aftermath

The world was stunned. Israelis withdrew from the Olympics complaining that security had been lax. There were those who thought the Games should be called off. The debate about a homeland for the Palestinian Arabs remained front page news.

The Israelis retaliated. Three days later the Israeli airforce attacked refugee camps in Syria and in Jordan. These bombings possibly killed as many as 500 people. Few were terrorists. The terrorist war went on, with both sides killing civilians in an attempt to win the terrorist war.

In February 1973 an Israeli jet shot down a passenger aircraft from Libya. 74 passengers were killed. Israelis claimed they had ordered it to land at a military airfield in the Sinai but the pilot refused. Within a month Black September had murdered three diplomats at the Saudi Arabian embassy.

Other terrorist attacks were carried out throughout 1973, with various terrorist splinter groups trying to grab the headlines. The Sons of the Occupied Lands, the Punishment Organisation, the Martyr Abu Mahmud Group and the Seventh Suicide Squad all committed atrocities in the name of freedom for Palestinian Arabs. By September 1973 Yasser Arafat decided to end these random attacks and to concentrate all future attacks against Israel only. Within six weeks war again broke out in the Middle East with Arabs making a surprise attack against Israel during the Yom Kippur religious holiday (see pages 260–1).

Terrorism, 1973-80

The war in 1973 again showed the Arabs unable to defeat the Israelis on the battlefield. The Arabs turned to alternative ways of hitting at Israel, such as the oil war (see Unit 2). However terrorism continued to be part of the strategy of the struggle in the Middle East.

Summary

Terrorist activities, 1974-78:

1974   May
Sixteen children killed in cross-fire between Israelis and Palestinian terrorists.

1975   December
OPEC ministers taken hostage at meeting in Vienna.

1976   July
Israeli commandos rescue over 100 hostages held by pro-Palestinian terrorists at Entebbe Airport.

1977   October
German anti-terrorist unit frees hostages of Lufthansa airliner at Mogadishu airport.

1978   January
PLO spokesman killed in London by extremist Palestinian terrorist.

1978   March
Buses in Israel hijacked by Palestinian terrorists.

Source H

The wreckage of a Libyan passenger plane shot down by Israeli fighter planes.

Changing Nature of Warfare: Terrorism, a war by other means

3.2 What tactics were the most effective in bringing the world's attention to the 'plight' of the Palestinians?

After the war in 1973 the United States worked hard to secure some sort of peace in the Middle East. It was at this point that the PLO decided to take a more moderate and peaceful approach. It set up offices in many countries and sent officials to talk to governments around the world about their cause. At the end of 1974 Yasser Arafat was invited to speak at the United Nations. Many countries now saw the formation of a Palestinian state as a way of getting peace in the Middle East. Arafat offered a sort of peace.

Source J

The burnt-out remains of an Israeli bus attacked by a Palestinian suicide squad, near Tel Aviv in 1975.

But peace was a long way off. The Israelis were furious that the leader of what they called a 'murder organisation' had been allowed to speak at the UN. They also believed that Palestinian Arabs would never settle for a smaller Palestine or the continued existence of Israel. Palestinians were divided. Extremists in the PLO did not accept the idea of a mini-state and continued to launch terrorist attacks on Israel.

Source I

Today I have come bearing an olive branch and a freedom fighter's gun. Do not let the olive branch fall from my hand.

Yasser Arafat making his speech to the United Nations in 1974.

Lebanon, 'Al-Fatahland'

In 1978 a PLO suicide squad based in South Lebanon attacked a bus near Tel Aviv, killing 37 passengers. Three days later the Israelis invaded Lebanon but failed to wipe out the PLO. In 1982 Palestinian terrorists tried to kill the Israeli Ambassador in London. This led to a further invasion of Lebanon. The Israelis advanced as far as the Lebanese capital, Beirut, and forced Yasser Arafat and the PLO to leave Lebanon. Arafat went to Tunisia, and his men became scattered around the Middle East.

Secret talks

In August 1987 secret talks took place between Moshe Amirav, an Israeli minister, and Faisal Husseini of the PLO, who was in prison at the time. After several meetings they jointly produced a memorandum which could have led to peace talks between the Israeli government and the PLO. Prime Minister Shamir was happy for the talks to take place as long as they remained secret. Once news of the talks leaked out Amirav was disgraced, Husseini was sent back to prison and Sari Nusseibeh, a Palestinian involved in the talks, was beaten up by four Palestinian youths as a 'punishment' from the PLO.

Intifada, 1987

In December 1987, after a Palestinian youth was shot dead by Israeli soldiers for throwing a rock at them, rioting broke out all over the Gaza Strip. This *intifada* (uprising) was different from others, which occurred regularly in the occupied territories. This time men, women and children were involved. They took to the streets to throw stones at the Israeli troops. The Israelis were reluctant to use lethal weapons against women and children throwing stones. So they followed a 'break their bones' policy. Even so, the sight of Israeli troops beating up civilian Palestinians was condemned throughout the world and damaged Israel's international standing.

On 16 April 1988 the Israeli secret police, the Mossad, and the army assassinated the PLO leader of the *intifada* Abu Jihad. Instead of leaving the *intifada* leaderless and weakened it only increased the ferocity of the *intifada*. As the violence continued in Gaza and the West Bank Israeli troops became increasingly disheartened. With morale among his troops so low Prime Minister Shamir realised that a political solution to the problem had to be found. Yasser Arafat came to the same conclusion. In November 1988 he announced that the PLO agreed with UN resolutions 242 and 338, that is the PLO accepted for the first time the existence of Israel.

Things to do

1   Explain why the Israelis were furious that Yasser Arafat was allowed to address the United Nations.

2   How was the Lebanon drawn into the Arab-Israeli conflict?

3   How was the *intifada* different from the sort of terrorism that Palestine/Israel had experienced over the previous 25 years?

Summary

After the Yom Kippur War there was a change in tactics by the PLO. Its leader, Yaser Arafat, decided to adopt a more moderate approach. However, some extremists rejected this and continued to attack Israel, which drove the PLO out of Lebanon. In 1987 an intifada started against the Israelis, though in November 1988 Yasser Arafat accepted for the first time the existence of the state of Israel.

Source K

Young Palestinians throwing stones at Israeli soldiers during the intifada.

Changing Nature of Warfare: Terrorism, a war by other means

Finding a Solution

The role of the rest of the world, 1947 to present day

By 1987 both sides of the dispute had reached the point where they realised a political solution was necessary. Attempts at bringing peace in the Middle East had proved unsuccessful until 1979 when the Camp David Agreement was signed. Even then peace was still fragile and it was only after the intervention of the Americans in 1991 that today's peace agreement was achieved.

4.1 Why did actions between 1947 and 1956 fail to bring a solution nearer?

As you read in Unit 1, under the new **UN partition plan** the Jewish state was to be bigger than the Arab state despite having only about 30 per cent of the population. The Arab state would be divided into three areas and have the poorer quality land and no sea port. Jerusalem would remain under international control.

The plan triggered violent protests by the Arabs. However, the United Nations voted in favour of partition in November 1947. The Arab delegation stormed out warning that 'The partition line will be nothing but a line of blood and fire.' The vote was followed by rioting in Palestine. Jews and Arabs were killed as both sides prepared for civil war against each other.

During the civil war, that went on until partition on 15 May 1948, atrocities were committed by both Arabs and Jews. Deir Yassin was one such incident (Unit 1.2).

An uneasy peace reigned in the Middle East during the next seven years.

The *fedayeen* became established and terrorist attacks on Jewish settlements began (Unit 2.1). Economic sanctions were imposed by Arab nations in an attempt to destroy Israel's fragile economy. The tension created was one of the causes of the Suez War of 1956. The involvement of Britain and France was also very significant.

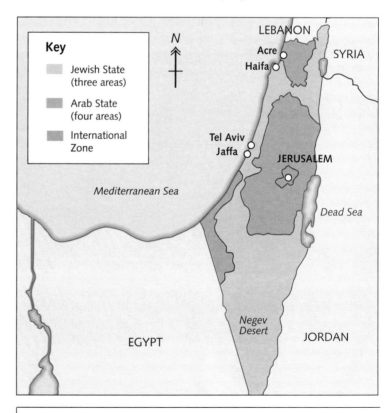

Key

- Jewish State (three areas)
- Arab State (four areas)
- International Zone

LEBANON
Acre
Haifa
SYRIA
Tel Aviv
Jaffa
JERUSALEM
Mediterranean Sea
Dead Sea
Negev Desert
EGYPT
JORDAN

The UN partition plan of Palestine, 1947.

The Arab-Israeli Conflict

President Nasser of Egypt

President Nasser wanted to avenge the defeat of Arabs in 1948, as well as raise his status amongst Arab nations. He did this in a number of ways:

- He persuaded the British to give up their military bases along the Suez Canal.

- He gave help to Arabs fighting against the French in Algeria.

- He formed an alliance between Egypt, Syria and Saudi Arabia with their armies under joint command.

- He persuaded King Hussein of Jordan to dismiss his British Chief of staff, General Glubb.

- He made an arms agreement with Czechoslovakia to get fighter planes, bombers, guns and tanks.

This last arrangement worried Britain and the USA as they believed that the agreement was backed up by the Soviets, who were using it to gain a foothold in the Middle East. They immediately cancelled the loans to Nasser which were needed to build the Aswan Dam. This was an important project to Nasser.

The withdrawal of the loans gave him the excuse to nationalise the Suez Canal. The tolls collected from shipping would help to pay for the dam. On 26 July 1956 the canal was nationalised. This angered the British and French who jointly owned the Suez Canal. So they held discussions with the Israelis about an attack on Egypt. Planning went on in secret throughout September and the final orders were given after a meeting in a private villa in Sevres on 22 October 1956. A week later the attack began.

The Suez War

On 29 October the Israelis attacked in Sinai as agreed with the British and the French governments. A day later France and Britain demanded that the Israelis and the Egyptians both withdraw 16 kilometres away from the canal. The Israelis agreed, as had been earlier planned, and the Egyptians refused, as had been expected. This gave the British the excuse they needed and on 31 October 1956 they bombed Egyptian airfields. The Israelis could now complete their take over of the Sinai. On 5 November 1956 British and French forces landed in Port Said and Port Fuad. The Egyptians responded by sinking ships to block the canal.

Source A

Ships sunk by the Egyptians to block the Suez Canal.

Why did Britain withdraw from the war so quickly ?

Britain agreed to withdraw within 24 hours of its invasion of Port Said after heavy pressure from the rest of the world. The United States went to the UN Security Council and demanded a cease-fire. Britain vetoed the proposal. A day later the General Assembly met. Britain had no veto here and as a result the Israeli invasion was condemned. British and French troops continued on towards Egypt. It was other pressures that were to force an end the war.

1 Arab nations stopped oil supplies to Britain and France.
2 The USA threatened to withdraw financial help to Israel.
3 The US refused to sell Britain any oil.
4 The US threatened to withdraw dollars banked in London.
5 The USSR said it was thinking about 'flattening' Israel.

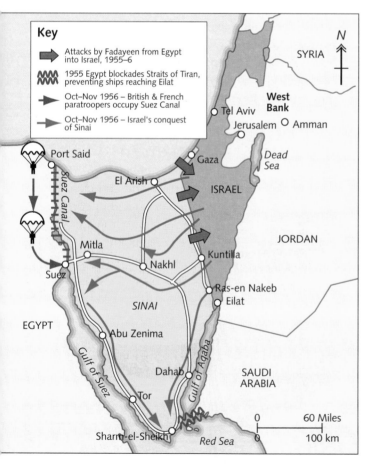

The Suez Crisis.

Had the rest of the world brought peace any nearer?

This war did little for the status of Britain. Many historians believe that it was the final act of Britain as a major world power. Clearly the USA and the USSR played a major part in ending this conflict. Britain could no longer act without the support of the USA.

The conflict brought a temporary peace to the Middle East. The United Nations Emergency Force (UNEF) guarded the border between Egypt and Israel for the next ten years. The Gulf of Aqaba and the Straits of Tiran which had been closed before the war were re-opened to Israeli ships.

The conflict may have made the next war inevitable. Britain had lost its influence in Jordan, Iraq and the Lebanon. Nasser became a leading Arab figure with the support of the USSR and used this position to plan a further war in 1967.

The UN had acted honourably, demanding the withdrawal of Israeli troops but had still needed the individual actions of the USA and the USSR to force the British and French to withdraw. For the first time oil had played its part. A solution may not have been any nearer, but at least the actions of Britain, France and Israel had not gone unchecked by the international community.

Summary

The Suez Crisis

President Nasser of Egypt had strengthened his country and made himself the leading Arab ruler by 1956. When Britain and America withdrew loans to help him build the Aswan Dam, he took over the Suez Canal. Britain and France got the Israelis to attack Egypt and then attacked themselves. They received strong criticism from the UNO and other world powers. Nasser became even more popular in the Arab world.

4.2 How far has peace been achieved in the Middle East?

Egypt and Israel make peace

The war of Yom Kippur had shown Arabs and Jews that peace would not emerge from armed conflict. In January 1977 the new American president, Jimmy Carter, began working towards a political settlement in the Middle East and in talks with President Assad of Syria stated that he wanted to see a homeland for the Palestinian Arabs. But with Menachem Begin, Prime Minister of Israel, proclaiming the need for further Jewish settlements, an Arab homeland in Palestine seemed a long way off.

In an attempt to break the deadlock President Sadat of Egypt declared he was willing to talk openly to the Israelis. This meant accepting the existence of Israel, something no Arab nation was willing to do in 1977. Begin was suspicious, but took a risk and invited Sadat to speak to the Israeli parliament, the Knesset. Sadat not only sought peace between Egypt and Israel, he was also looking for a solution to the Palestinian problem. The talks dragged on for a year and it proved very difficult to reach an agreement. At this point the Americans stepped in.

Source B

The Camp David agreement.

In September 1978 President Carter, Sadat and Begin met at Camp David, the US president's holiday retreat in Maryland, to discuss how they might reach some agreement for peace in the Middle East. Two frameworks were worked out.

In the first framework document Israel agreed to hand back the Sinai over a period of three years. In return the Egyptians would allow the Israelis use of the Suez Canal and the Straits of Tiran. One problem that still remained was what would happen to the Israeli settlers living in the Sinai? Sadat insisted that they should leave when the troops left. Begin agreed to put the issue to the Knesset

The second document was less than clear. It talked about the possible negotiations between Israel, Egypt, Syria, Jordan and the Palestinians over the occupied territories of the West Bank and Gaza Strip. In reality it simply listed the problems still to be faced. Nevertheless, in May 1979 the peace treaty was signed by Carter, Begin and Sadat.

The price to be paid

Egypt got the Sinai back, but the price was high. It lost the support of many Arab countries and the treaty was vague about the future of Gaza and the West Bank. Muslim extremists, furious at Sadat's dealings with the Israelis, assassinated him in October 1981. He paid the greatest price of all for peace. By April 1982 the Israelis had completed their withdrawal from Sinai but the planned elections in the West Bank, talks with the Jordanians and a settlement of some sort of the Palestinian problem never materialised. Peace between Egypt and Israel had been the only success.

> *The assassination of President Sadat in Cairo, 6 October 1981.*

Eleven years of peace or conflict?

Despite the Camp David Agreement there was still conflict in the Middle East. Israel was at war with the PLO in the Lebanon; terrorists tried to murder the Israeli Ambassador in London; innocent people were killed in the Chatila refugee camp in Lebanon; terrorists killed 240 US soldiers in the Lebanon and in 1987 riots broke out in the West Bank and Gaza (Unit 3). Then, in August 1990, the Gulf War broke out as UNO forces attacked Saddam Hussein of Iraq.

Yasser Arafat and the White House agreement

Days after the Gulf War ended in 1991 the United States took the opportunity to open talks again. The US Secretary of State, James Baker, travelled to and from the Middle East for eight months trying to persuade both sides to reach agreement. In October 1991 he persuaded Israelis and Arabs to hold a peace conference in Madrid. Although the conference did little to resolve the problem, it was a beginning.

But by the summer of 1992 the talks seemed to grind to a halt. Then the Israeli Prime Minister Rabin, agreed to talk directly to the PLO. But the murder of an Israeli border policeman and the subsequent expulsion to Lebanon of 415 members of 'Hamas', an extremist Muslim group, disrupted the talks yet again. However, secret talks were set up in Oslo in December 1992. These made progress, though the Israelis refused to discuss control of Jerusalem. They were, however, willing to discuss the future of Gaza and part of the West Bank. The discussions dragged on until in September 1993 an agreement was reached. Arrangements were made for the leader of the Palestinians, Yasser Arafat, and the Israeli Prime Minister, Rabin, to sign the agreement. What they signed was a Declaration of Principles.

There was another setback when a Jewish extremist murdered 29 Muslims at prayer in the tomb of the patriarchs in Hebron. Arabs and many Jews were outraged. Hamas retaliated, as expected, and launched bomb attacks on Israeli buses. Once again peace seemed beyond anyone's grasp.

Source C

An official photograph of the Camp David meeting showing Prime Minister Begin and Presidents Carter and Sadat.

Despite this, progress towards peace was made. On 4 May 1994 the Gaza-Jericho Agreement was signed. Two months later Arafat returned to Gaza. Early in 1995 further talks began for what would be called the Oslo II Agreement. Signed on 28 September 1995 this agreement led to the withdrawal of Israeli troops from six major West Bank cities. But tragedy was soon to mar these momentous events. On 4 November 1995 Prime Minister Yitzhak Rabin was assassinated by a right-wing Jewish zealot. He too had paid the highest price of all for talking to 'the enemy'.

How far has peace been achieved?

On 29 May 1996 Prime Minister Peres, who had succeeded Yitzhak Rabin, lost the general election in Israel. He was succeeded by Benjamin Netanyahu. Elected on a slogan of 'Peace with Security' few expected peace to progress under his leadership. However, President Clinton secured an agreement between the two sides. The Maryland Agreement involves Israeli troops withdrawing from a further 13.1 per cent of the West Bank, and in return the Palestinians agreeing to a security plan which will reduce the risk of terrorism in Israel. The future of this agreement is uncertain, with the life of the Israeli Prime Minister at risk from extremist assassins.

Source D

Netanyahu suspends negotiations on land-for-peace-deal

Hussein unites with Clinton to break deadlock
20 October 1998

JEWS SEEK REVENGE FOR GRENADE ATTACK

ISRAELI WARNS OF SHOWCASE HAMAS ATTACK
21 October 1998

CLINTON CLEARS PEACE HURDLE   **Netanyahu faces hardliners' backlash**
24 October 1998

Extra guard on Israeli leaders   *26 October 1998*

Campaign of hate targets Netanyahu   **Netanyahu's aides fear assassination**
28 October 1998   *29 October 1998*

Things to do

1   Explain **(a)** what the United Nations hoped to achieve by its partition plan? **(b)** why the UN partition plan would not be acceptable to the Arab people?

2   Why did Britain decide to challenge President Nasser of Egypt?

3   Why, in the light of the secret agreements between Britain, France and Israel, do you think Britain considered using force against Nasser?

4   Source C is an official photograph of the Camp David meeting. How useful is it to an historian studying the meeting?

5   Source B illustrates the assassination of President Sadat. Source D is a list of newspaper headlines from 1998. Why are leaders in this conflict at risk from assassination from their own people?

6   Find out what has happened in this conflict since 1998. How far could any of these events be predicted?

These 1998 newspaper headlines give some idea of the latest progress in the Arab Israeli conflict.

Finding a Solution: The role of the rest of the world

Chapter 7

Vietnam Post-1939

Chapter 8

The Arab-Israeli Conflict

Exam-type Assessment
Vietnam War

These exercises provide students with an opportunity to attempt questions which are similar to those set as part of Board approved coursework or in preparation for the Paper 3 alternative.

The Changing Nature of Warfare: a Civilian experience

1   Explain why the Vietnam war became so unpopular in the USA in the period 1968-73. *(12 marks)*

2   Do you think that any of the reasons you identified in Question 1 were more important than others in causing people to protest against US involvement? Explain your answer. *(8 marks)*

The Changing Nature of Warfare: a Military experience

Source A

Nothing was happening here. It was a very normal life. Then the helicopters came and all the troops surrounded us. They were firing their guns and people were dying. Oh, it was so horrible! I pushed my son into the paddy-field and lay on top of him. Corpses fell on top of us. I told him, "Don't cry and see if we can survive." I lifted my head and saw Americans pointing in all directions. Those people who were still alive were shot again and again. I hate the Americans; I shall never forgive them.

An account of the massacre at My Lai by Truong Thi He, a villager who, with his son, survived the attack.

Source B

The understanding, or the order that was given, was to kill everyone in that village. Someone asked if that meant women and children and the answer was that it meant everyone. Those people, the women, the kids, the old men, were Vietcong or they were sympathetic to the Vietcong. It was quite clear that no-one was to be spared in that village.

An account of the massacre by Kenneth Hodges of C Company, who carried out the attack on My Lai.

Study Sources A and B.

3   **(a)** What can a historian studying the My Lai incident learn from Source A? *(6 marks)*
    (b) How reliable is Source A about what happened at My Lai? Explain your answer. *(8 marks)*

4   'Source B has limited value to an historian because it was written by one of the US soldiers who was involved in the My Lai massacre.' Do you agree with this statement? Explain your answer. *(8 marks)*

Vietcong (VC)	47%
North Vietnamese Army (NVA)	24%
Civilians	22%
South Vietnamese Army (ARVN)	5%
United States Army (US)	2%

People killed as a result of the Tet Offensive, 1968.

What the hell is going on? I thought we were winning the war?

Walter Cronkite, an American News broadcaster, on hearing about the Tet Offensive.

5   Study Sources C and D

(a) Does Source C suggest that the Tet Offensive was a success or a failure for the Vietcong? Explain your answer.   *(10 marks)*

(b) Are you surprised by what Walter Cronkite says in Source D?   *(8 marks)*

I WANT OUT

A US poster protesting against the Vietnam war.

A Vietnam War veteran studying the list of dead at the
Vietnam War Memorial in Washington.

Source G

'How do you feel
about killing all of those
innocent people?' The
woman asked me. I
didn't know what to say.
The bartender got a little
uptight.

'Excuse me,' I called the
bartender over. 'Could
I buy these people a
drink?' I felt guilty. I did
kill. I tried to make up
for it somehow.

'We don't accept any
drinks from killers,'
the girl said to me.

*A former soldier describing
comments made to him in an
airport bar when he returned
from Vietnam.*

Source H

The USA was certainly weakened by the Vietnam
War. At home, it prevented President Johnson
building his 'Great Society'. But more importantly,
the USA became unwilling to involve itself in any
international conflict until the Gulf War in 1991.
When the Gulf War was over, Bush said: 'By God,
we've kicked the Vietnam syndrome once and for all.'

*An account from
a British school
textbook written
in 1998.*

6   **Study Sources E and F**
     How far do these two sources explain the effect the Vietnam War had on the
     American people?   (*12 marks*)

7   **Study Source G.**
     How reliable is this source about the feelings of the American people towards
     the Vietnam War?   (*10 marks*)

Exam-type Assessment
The Arab-Israeli Conflict

These exercises provide students with an opportunity to attempt questions which are similar to those set as part of Board approved coursework or in preparation for the Paper 3 alternative.

Terrorism: a war by other means.

1   Explain why many Palestinians turned to terrorism after the failure of Arab nations to win the Six Day War. *(20 marks)*

2   Which terrorist tactic do you think was the most effective in bringing the world's attention to the plight of the Palestinian refugees? Explain your answer. *(20 marks)*

The Changing Nature of Warfare: A military experience 1948–73

Source A

On 14 May 1948 the state of Israel was proclaimed. Less than 24 hours later the armies of Egypt, Jordan, Syria, Lebanon and Iraq invaded our country forcing Israel to defend its ancestral homeland.

From a book published by the Israeli government in the 1990s.

Source B

Palestine is our country
Our aim is to return
Death does not frighten us
Palestine is ours
We shall never forget her
Another homeland we shall never accept.

From a Palestinian oath written after many Palestinians fled from Israel. It was normally spoken by Palestinian children at the beginning of the school day.

3   **Read Sources A and B.**

   (a) Source A suggests that Israel had a right to Palestine as a homeland.
   Source B suggests that Palestine is the homeland of Arabs.
   Explain why they give different views about Palestine. *(8 marks)*

   (b) Use your own knowledge to explain how the United Nations tried to solve this problem. *(12 marks)*

A refugee camp in 1966.

A street scene in Tel Aviv in 1966.

4   **Study Sources C and D.**

Do these two sources provide historians with sufficient evidence to explain
why there was a war between Arab nations and Israel in 1967?
Explain your answer carefully.

(*12 marks*)

Source E

It was one o'clock in the afternoon and I was driving my jeep to meet my commander. Suddenly I saw planes. I was very surprised. The Israeli air force flying on Yom Kippur. And then I saw black things coming out of the planes. It was only when these reached the ground and blew up that I understood we were at war.

General Amram Mitzna recalls the outbreak of the War of Yom Kippur in 1973.

Source F

Although the Israelis were taken by surprise on Yom Kippur, the fact that it was a holiday helped them recover.

Most of the Israeli's 254,000 reserve soldiers were at home that day and were quickly contacted with orders telling them to report for duties.

Taken from a school textbook written in the 1900s.

Study Sources E and F.

5   Which of the two sources do you think is more reliable in explaining the effect of the surprise attack on Israel in 1973?   (*8 marks*)

6   Use your own knowledge to explain how the Israelis were able to win the War of Yom Kippur.   (*12 marks*)

Source G

My parents live in the camp over the road. They lost their home in 1948 and then had to get out again in 1967. Nobody can take that kind of life. Life is very hard in the tents. When it rains all the blankets get wet, and you have to huddle up together to keep warm. I want to join the fedayeen to liberate our country, and I think everybody ought to join the commandos, so as to change this terrible way of living.

A fourteen year old boy explaining in 1974 why he supported the fedayeen.

Study Source G.

7   How far does Source G explain why it has been difficult to reach a lasting peace in the Middle East?   (*12 marks*)

Index